ENTERPRISE AND INDIVIDUALS IN FIFTEENTH-CENTURY ENGLAND

Edited by
JENNIFER KERMODE

ALAN SUTTON

First published in the United Kingdom in 1991 by
Alan Sutton Publishing Limited · Phoenix Mill · Far Thrupp
Stroud · Gloucestershire

First published in the United States of America in 1991 by
Alan Sutton Publishing Inc · Wolfeboro Falls · NH 03896-0848

British Library Cataloguing in Publication Data

Enterprise and the individual in fifteenth century England.
    1. Economic conditions, history, 1399–1485
    I. Kermode, J. (Jennifer) 1945–
330.94104

ISBN 0–86299–908–1

Library of Congress Cataloging in Publication Data applied for

Typeset in 10/11 Goudy.
Typesetting and origination by
Alan Sutton Publishing Limited.
Printed in Great Britain by
    WBC Ltd., Bridgend

Acknowledgement

The editor gratefully acknowledges financial contributions towards the publication of this volume received from The Twenty-Seven Foundation and the University of Liverpool.

Contents

List of Tables

Abbreviations

AgHR	*Agricultural History Review*
EETS	Early English Text Society
EHR	*English Historical Review*
EcHR	*Economic History Review*
CCR	*Calendar of Close Rolls*
CPR	*Calandar of Patent Rolls*
PRO	Public Record Office
TRHS	*Transactions of the Royal Historical Society*

Introduction

Convening a conference is rather like choosing presents: you can try to guess what the recipients might want but in the end have to rely upon your own taste and what is available. The Fifteenth-Century Colloquium, held at Liverpool in September 1988, blatantly opted for the convenor's preferences on the grounds that, after all the organizational effort, she might as well enjoy papers on topics which she hoped to learn more about. Such indulgence was richly rewarded as the following papers amply demonstrate. Hopefully the wider audience here addressed will find stimulation and enjoyment as well as knowledge. An added bonus to the colloquium, for which the convenor can claim no credit, was the quality of the audience. This was an amicable, relaxed and chatty gathering of scholars, whose questions widened into lively discussions after each paper. The argument was sometimes fierce, but then if we value historical enterprise, our intellectual passions must inevitably be aroused on occasion. Few of us 'get it right' the first time and, as Chris Dyer remarks in his contribution, the debate generated by his own key-note paper helped to clarify some of his own perceptions and ideas.

Within the global effort to explain the decline of feudalism[1] and the onset of capitalism, the fifteenth century has emerged as a pivotal period of concentrated economic and social changes. Against a background of demographic crises and slow recovery, and the consequent fall in agricultural rents and production, people and institutions had to respond to changing circumstances. If *homo economicus*[2] can be spotted in the fifteenth century, what characteristics did he display? Most of the papers in this volume address that question from several different perspectives.

Documents are fundamental to the thinking of most historians and Chris Dyer is well aware of the tension between traditional historians 'burdened with information' and social scientists intent upon the creation and testing of hypotheses. His paper provides an accessible exploration of the conceptual models currently available: the Malthusian view of a drift into capitalism, Wallerstein's emphasis on the exogenous factors of overseas commerce; and the Brenner debate and its focus upon internal factors such as enclosure and the exploitation of peasants. Ultimately the validity of a hypothesis rests upon the evidence, and Chris Dyer produces just the individual to support his claims for the increasingly visible capitalist, a certain Roger Heritage (!), a Warwickshire leaseholder whose astute farming management during the late fifteenth century identifies him as an early agri-businessman.

Similar entrepreneurial developments and shifts in attitude towards land can be sought elsewhere. The estate records of religious institutions have been quarried by several generations of historians, and Andrew Butcher,[3] on familiar Kentish soil, examined the impact of the economic strategies deployed by Canterbury Priory upon its hinterland. The priory effectively manipulated the fifty-five manors under its control to its own best advantage, ensuring its needs were met by a regular supply of foodstuffs, clothing, and building materials. Its direct labour force was moved around priory properties as need arose. As a consequence, the priory avoided the fluctuations of the market-place to a considerable extent, but to the detriment of Canterbury itself. A large percentage of the priory leaseholders were in fact townsmen from Canterbury, Folkestone, New Romney and Sandwich, and while they took advantage of their landlord's flexible approach to rents, urban activities became 'largely display'. Like so many other fifteenth-century towns, Canterbury found itself caught up in a regional economic restructuring dictated by external priorities.

Enclosure has been claimed as a movement which produced still visible evidence of deliberate manipulation for personal profit. In his paper Alan Cameron considered[3] what the pre-conditions to enclosure were in several Nottinghamshire parishes. The Black Death and subsequent epidemics had left an ageing population, increasingly unable to cope with the arable economy. The region's geology meant that untenanted land returned rapidly to waterlogged grazing. Communities either drifted piecemeal into enclosure or chose to enclose as a survival policy. In the context of Nottinghamshire it is difficult to see any individual who was both the instigator of and beneficiary from enclosure.

One characteristic claimed for capitalism is the propensity to accumulate selfishly. Concern that property should be retained within the family and transmitted to succeeding generations, was reflected in the apparently growing trend to make wills in the late Middle Ages. Villeins as a rule were not numerous among will-makers and instead made deathbed dispositions, nuncupative rather than written wills and testaments. In lieu, the evidence from manorial court rolls can illuminate some peasants' reactions to changing opportunities and Richard Smith has chosen to look specifically at married women. In the early fifteenth century the depreciating value of land and rising costs of labour gave women a more important role in the shift towards a pastoral economy. Partnerships became more common as customary tenants were increasingly using different legal devices to give their wives secure title and the right to devise. Peasants accumulated substantial holdings, and, as Chris Dyer found, peasant estates of 80 acres and more were not unusual in Warwickshire. Remarriage became less common, as widows could enjoy better prospects as independent individuals; a tendency observed in some fifteenth-century towns.

Marriages, astute or foolish, and the absence of clear title to property, were just some of the pitfalls negotiated by the Pastons. Colin Richmond's reflections on the Pastons as landlords,[4] suggest that if we free ourselves from the need to measure the past against an optimistic model of progress, we will be better able to understand the Pastons' responses for what they were: random, *ad hoc*, and the actions of survivors. Progressive strategies of any sort, and particularly economic schemes, were notably lacking from the Pastons' lives, but why should we expect them? Furthermore, as this paper suggests, at the bottom among the cottage folk it probably didn't make much difference who the landlord was, even supposing it was clear at any given time. The incidence of 'hedge thieves' might vary as tenants were dragged by litigious landlords into their disputes, but rents still had to be paid, and someone's bailiff turned up to collect them in the end.

Whether or not rents were paid in coin or 'on tick' would bear further examination, given that in the early to mid-fifteenth century a scarcity of coins and precious metals loomed large in the minds of government and poets alike. Most historians agree that there was a bullion famine from *c.* 1390 until *c.* 1415 and again from the 1420s until the 1460s, but would argue about its causes and impact. 'Tight money' should have encouraged a greater reliance on credit but it may have been that as trade was contracting at the same time, under the impact of hostilities with the Hanse, so did the need for credit. This is a contentious area and although it is difficult to quantify fluctuations in credit transactions, its all-pervasiveness in English society is unquestioned.

Long-distance trade demanded greater flexibilty and security than cash transactions allowed, and had stimulated the development of a variety of financial networks and arrangements. Sales credit was still probably the most common form of credit used by English people, although more sophisticated instruments such as the bill of exchange were employed between major international trading centres. Alien merchants, trading English wool and cloth, had access to a wider range of financial networks, and together with their credit agreements, were regarded with suspicion. Governments on the whole welcomed their business but did introduce restrictive legislation to appease indigenous merchants. Wendy Childs uses the occasion of the government's effort to prosecute an unusually high number of aliens in 1459/60, to examine the role of credit in international trade. Suggestions as to the extent to which credit underpinned the economy remain speculative: as much as 50 per cent of English commerce may have been locked into a chain of credit and that was without the advantages of international credit-cards and high-technology banking! It is also of interest that, when it chose, the English government could use the process of law to replenish its coffers as well as to reinforce trade policy. Intrinsic to entrepreneurship was an ability to negotiate deals, to calculate exchange rates and prices in distant markets, and the temperament to venture your own (or someone else's) capital/credit in a range of enterprises. The risks were high and, in spite of formally written and witnessed commercial agreements, things often went wrong. The parties in dispute had recourse to several courts, both local and central, but many still preferred or indeed were directed to subject themselves to arbitration. The joy of the records thus generated is that often the personalities of the protagonists, and the detailed circumstances of their deals are opened to view. Carole Rawcliffe's deft study draws out the sort of risks and uncertainties which surrounded medieval trade, and the sharp practices individuals could deploy in their pursuit of profit. A modern reader is torn between admiration at the complexity of deals and amusement at the variety of unlikely situations graphically described.

Business quarrels could be symptomatic of deeper hostilities and rivalries between factions in craft guilds and companies and indeed within a town. As an acceptable procedure in all manner of disagreements, arbitration could sometimes ease political resentments as well as resolve commercial disputes, and court records thus reveal divisive tensions in many areas of urban life.

An obvious conclusion is that the expansion of trade and the efforts to free land from feudal constraints generated employment for anyone associated with the creation of written records. Not surprisingly, specialists appeared to serve the growing need for formal documents and the demands of litigants. Scriveners were not the creation of late medieval economic changes, but Nigel Ramsay argues that their numbers did increase during the fifteenth century and their professional identity became more distinct. They acted at times more like attorneys in local and central courts, advising on the substance of the law as well as preparing documents. In these ways they mediated between the public and the law, filling a role somewhat akin to that of early clerks of the peace.

The changes wrought by a more competitive market were not simply economic. It has been claimed that society was becoming less cohesive and more individualistic. Was this universal or do the surviving records only reveal the atypical assertive individuals and not the other folk? Community has become a convenient umbrella term to describe everyone living within a given locality: the people, the populace, townsfolk, villagers. It can also mean being organized in social unity, sharing something of a common identity. Historians confusingly use the word in both senses simultaneously and Miri Rubin considers definitions of the term and its misuse as well as suggesting what the cohesive elements in medieval society were. Transcending, religious rituals, such as Corpus Christi processions, can be set alongside the smaller, self-selecting association of fraternities. In these, she claims, it is possible to see individuals asserting their identity in groups which met their shifting needs in a period of change.

'Historical capitalism', Wallerstein claimed somewhat patronisingly, 'did breed a *homo economicus* but . . . he was almost inevitably a bit confused'.[5] The evidence of this collection of essays would suggest the opposite. Where individual institutions and people are visible, they display a confident grasp of complex financial, commercial, and legal affairs. The ability of even peasants to improve their position and to enlarge their opportunities within the constraints of feudal tenure, does not suggest confusion. The picture which emerges from these studies of the fifteenth century, is a mixture of careful enterprise, opportunist initiatives, and *ad hoc* survival.

Jennifer Kermode
University of Liverpool

Notes

1 Although some historians continue to doubt the existence of feudalism as anything more than a pedagogically useful portmanteau term. For the most recent discussion see the introduction by T.S. Brown to M. Bloch, *Feudal Society* (Routledge & Kegan Paul, 1990 edition), pp. xi–xxi.
2 This is Immanuel Wallerstein's phrase (*Historical Capitalism* (1983), p. 18).
3 Local difficulties militated against the completion of Andrew Butcher and Alan Cameron's papers. These précis are based on notes taken during the colloquium, and their content is solely the responsibility of the editor. They have been included in the absence of a written text, to maintain the balance of the discussion.
4 This paper complements Richard Britnell's 'The Pastons and their Norfolk', *AgHR*, 36 (1988), pp. 132–144.
5 *Historical Capitalism*, p. 18.

1

Were There Any Capitalists in Fifteenth-Century England?

Christopher Dyer
University of Birmingham

The intellectual gap that separates historians and social scientists is regrettably wide. Most historians of the fifteenth century are not fully aware of the interest taken in their period by sociologists, political scientists and economists who devise theories of historical change. On the other side the social scientists clearly do not read more than a few general historical works, and so their information is often out of date and inaccurate. The social scientists have the excuse that their surveys of history range over many centuries and even millennia, and often seek to compare the development of two or three continents, so that they cannot make themselves familiar with recent research on the details of the history of England or western Europe in a single century. But the barrier between the disciplines is much greater than a mere mutual lack of knowledge. All historians, and especially those educated in the British empirical school, are suspicious of theories that seem to have been plucked out of the air. To them the grand hypotheses launched by some of the sociologists seem both pretentious and ill-founded. The social scientists are bemused by the historians' refusal to generalize, and by their seemingly petty and narrow obsession with the minutiae of their data. This essay is aimed at bridging the gulf between the different academic traditions, in the belief that the practitioners of the social sciences are posing large and important questions about long-term change and the origins of our own society, and that historians should play a larger part in defining the problems It is important that historians should help to frame the questions, because of course they alone are in a position to gather the evidence that provides the answers. In a short essay it will be impossible to do more than refine the questions into answerable form, and to suggest some avenues for research.

Defining capitalism causes much difficulty for historians and social scientists alike. The word 'capital' was used in Italy in the thirteenth century to mean the money and goods used by a merchant in his trade,[1] but the idea of capitalism as a term embracing a whole social and economic system is an invention of the nineteenth century. The possible definitions are legion, but can be summarized under three headings. One emphasizes capitalism as a system of exchange relations, meaning an economic system dominated by the market, in which entrepreneurs are involved in specialized production and competition. Those who own capital use it to earn profits in the market place. Everything of utility – labour, land, credit – can be bought and sold. Secondly there is the more idealistic interpretation, originating in the work of Weber and Sombart, which stresses the mentality of capitalism. Economic activity is conducted in a rational spirit, by which producers and traders learn to appreciate the disciplines of the market, and develop habits of thought that will help them to maximize profit. Capitalism is therefore characterized by individualistic, acquisitive and thrifty attitudes. Thirdly, capitalism can be seen in the classic Marxist definition as a system of relationships in production, in which the ownership of the means of production is concentrated in the hands of entrepreneurs. They are able to employ a free labour force, who have themselves become separated from the means of production. Capitalists buy the labour of the workers, and sell the goods at a profit.[2]

The third definition has the great virtue of precision, and concentrates attention on specific economic enterprises which can only be found in particular places at particular times. The term 'capitalist system' could only be used to describe the western world in the last two hundred years, and if strictly applied, even, say, to nineteenth-century Britain, large areas of economic life would have to be regarded as falling outside the system. The problem with the definitions emphasizing exchange and mentality is that both trade and acquisitiveness have such a long ancestry that almost any age can be said to have had some capitalist characteristics. The search for a 'spirit' is especially difficult because of the vagueness of the concept. We might expect in any case that the mental climate of capitalism would follow from the establishment of the economic reality. Most social scientists would eliminate the second definition, and therefore ponder the dilemma of emphasizing either the broad notion of exchange or the narrower focus on production. Some have tried new formulations, like K. Tribe, who suggests that the key elements in a definition should be the separation of consumption and production, the competition between enterprises, and a national economy 'co-ordinated according to the profitability of the commodities sold by enterprises'.[3] This puts exchange in a prominent place, but aims to give it more precision. Some writers, including economic historians, have attempted to resolve the problem by defining different varieties of capitalism – agricultural, mercantile and industrial. Marxists can then regard the sixteenth and seventeenth centuries as an age of merchant capitalism, eventually to be succeeded by industrial capitalism.

In arriving at a definition we do not receive much help by turning to feudalism, often regarded as the preceding social system. If we characterize feudal society in the narrow traditional way, by the presence of peasant labour services, general self-sufficiency, and military service in return for the tenure of land, we find that its existence was confined to a short period in the early Middle Ages. Modern Marxist analysis stresses the more enduring features, such as the relationship between lords and peasants, based on the non-economic powers of compulsion exercised by the lords, which allowed them to extract rents and services from their tenants. Power is emphasized, because the peasants were economically autonomous – they did not need the lords, but the lords relied for their wealth on their share of the surplus product of the peasant. The level of rent was accordingly not fixed primarily by market forces, and land was possessed rather than owned. The basic unit of agricultural production was the peasant household, peasants being defined as small-scale cultivators. Production and consumption were mingled, and goods were often made or grown for use rather than exchange. A market existed, but its needs were satisfied by craft production in artisan workshops, and by a relatively minor urban sector.[4]

There are those who doubt the utility of the term 'feudalism' because its characteristics are so nebulous.[5] Many of the features detailed above would apply to any pre-industrial or peasant society, and derive from technical backwardness rather than a specific relationship between social classes. It would perhaps be most valuable to stress the landed hierarchy with its basis in political power, though of course this type of social organization stems from the weak market and self-sufficiency of the peasant household, which could only be controlled and milked by some form of compulsion. If the term 'feudalism' (itself a late coinage) had not existed, it would have been necessary to invent it. Like 'capitalism', it came into the language because of the need for a vocabulary to describe general types of human society. The occasional attempts to produce alternative terms ('pre-industrial', for example) have some value, but likewise are very imprecise.

In the period between the crises of the fourteenth century and the Industrial Revolution, say between 1350 and 1750, English society and economy cannot easily be described by means of the general labels available to us, hence the cliché that it was 'an age of transition'. It is generally recognized that this was a period of important changes – in the tenancy and ownership of land, in the size and intensity of the market, in the productivity of agriculture, in the scale of industry, in the transport network, in the size and composition of the wage-earning sector, in attitudes to economic life (the treatment of poverty, for example), and in the economic role of the state. These enabled a society in which units of large scale agricultural and industrial production, based on the ownership of land, machinery and buildings by entrepreneurs, employing a numerous workforce of wage earners, and selling their products through a complex and all pervasive commercial system, succeeded a mainly agrarian economy with much small-scale peasant and artisan production, and dominated by a landed aristocracy. The nature of the transition is a cause of debate. Some emphasize the evolutionary process by which capitalists emerged out of the interstices of traditional landed society; others see the birth of a new economic order as possible only with sharp conflicts, notably the subversion of the authority of the aristocracy, and the expropriation of the peasantry to create the new class of wage earners.

The proponents of the different theoretical schemes give the fifteenth century a varying degree of significance. The fashionable neo-classical approach accords primary importance to commercial growth, from which developments in agriculture and industry followed. In this view the fifteenth century was a period of limited significance, because the really creative episodes in European history lie in the much earlier birth of commerce and towns in the ninth, tenth and eleventh centuries. In a characteristic hyperbolic flourish, Hodges advances the belief that the ninth century saw the origin of the 'modern world economy' – he means a system of commercial exchange linked to the early emergence of state power.[6] Others, again following the logic that trade lay at the roots of all other changes, argue that the 'commercial revolution' of the thirteenth century (actually, 1160–1320) marks a breakthrough, and that it was then, not at any later period, that Europe established its economic supremacy over other continents, measuring their performance in terms of technology and living standards.[7] Such schemes will give the fifteenth century scant attention because it was well before 1400 that the course was set for commercial and colonial expansion, and ultimately industrial-ization. Indeed the depression in international trade of the fifteenth century seems to mark a setback, or at the very least a 'blip', in the progressive expansion of exchange from the early Middle Ages until modern times.

Another view of capitalist origins is even more dismissive of the fifteenth century. Followers of Adam Smith look for the 'take off', that is the upward spiral of production and consumption that lifts society out of rural drudgery on to a higher plane of intense economic activity. If such a transforming surge, associated with rapid technological innovations, is thought to be necessary for the advent of true capitalism, then not only the fifteenth century but also the seventeenth and a good part of the eighteenth would be regarded as pre-capitalist.[8]

While the Middle Ages might be treated as irrelevant by those who focus on the decisive phase of industrialization after 1750, there is some interest in the underlying structures which made society in Europe (or just in England) especially receptive to economic development.[9] Geographers point to the natural advantages of a continent with many opportunities for water transport, to a variety of regions that needed to trade their products with one another, or to the absence of natural disasters, such as earthquakes and floods, which regularly destroyed the investments of Asian societies. A prevalent interpretation of the history of the family identifies the simple household structure of Europeans (or north-west Europeans, or only the English) as predisposing the individual towards self-reliance, enterprise and profit. In other parts of the world large, extended families acted, it is said, as a drag on economic activity because, in protecting their members, they also stifled individual initiative. The nuclear family, far from cocooning its children, sent them out into the world to make their own living, and, together with systems of poor relief that depended on community rather than family charity, provided some of the preconditions of capitalism. Western families also practised prudential marriage, by which legitimate procreation was delayed until a couple could afford to set up an independent household. Thus the birth rate was limited to the numbers that the economy could support, and every advance in production or living standards was not immediately dissipated by another increase in population. This family system was firmly established by the sixteenth century, and it may be possible to trace it back to the fifteenth, or the thirteenth, or even earlier. In which case the medieval period gave rise to, or at least nurtured, social institutions that paved the way for the eventual emergence of the capitalist economy.[10]

In searching for the environment in which capitalism grew, much interest has recently been focused on the role of the state.[11] Did the western European states, which were varied, competing and relatively weak, give commerce and entrepreneurs the right circumstances in which they could flourish, while the monolithic despotisms of the east discouraged individual profit-making? Or did strong states help the growth of commerce, by protecting merchants, and by suppressing the excesses of aristocratic power? The emergence of a more centralized state in western Europe in the late fifteenth century seems to have aided recovery from the mid-century depression, as the renewed French monarchy put an end to the Hundred Years War, and a number of countries' governments pursued policies designed to foster trade and manufacture. Some of these measures, however, could act as a drag on efficient production, like actions to protect the peasantry, who were judged to be of fiscal and military value. In any case the power and resources of governments, however much they might seem to have expanded in the age of the new monarchy, were puny beside the bureaucracies and budgets wielded by their absolutist successors in the seventeenth and eighteenth centuries.

Why did economies change? The question can apply both to the fluctuations of any pre-industrial period, and to the great transformation of the Industrial Revolution. For some analysts, movement was generated internally, primarily by the slow and cumulative growth of the market. Others, who suppose that systems tend to reproduce themselves without much change, look to shocks from outside, like plagues or the climate. Recourse to such mechanical explanations as the weather are greeted with general scepticism, but the effects of demographic fluctuations are given a more prominent place in analysing social and economic change. Both the Industrial Revolution proper, and the commercial expansion of the high Middle Ages, coincided with population growth, which stimulated demand, and which in turn encouraged further increases in numbers of people. On the face of it, the later Middle Ages looks like a poor candidate for a period of economic development, because population declined and stagnated. Those who survived the epidemics may have enjoyed individual prosperity, but their collective purchasing power was below that of the more numerous thirteenth- or sixteenth-century population. As Postan put it, the fifteenth century was at the same time 'the golden age of the peasantry', and 'a time of economic decline'.[12] However, there is no need to discount the possibility that structural changes could occur in demographic troughs. One only has to think of the 'disappearance of the small landowner' in the late seventeenth century. Demographic fluctuations belong to a different order of historical change, being quantitative rather than qualitative, as is recognized by Le Roy Ladurie when he writes of the cyclical rise and fall of population (the 'respirations of a great organism') happening at the same time as the 'unlinear drift' towards capitalism.[13]

Another group of theorists who have problems with the idea of the fifteenth century as a period of growth are the monetarists. The supply of money increased, and its use penetrated deeply into every sphere of life, in the 'long thirteenth century', which was also a period of burgeoning commercial exchange. Similarly the sixteenth century is famed for its discovery of vast new sources of silver, and for its lively market for goods. The intervening period looks bleak by comparison, as silver and gold stocks were exported or gradually used up, without compensatory growth in mining of new supplies; this culminated in the great bullion famine of the mid-fifteenth century. Commerce also fell away, and the only ray of hope lay in the revival, albeit on a modest scale, in both the amount of money in circulation and in trade, in the last third of the fifteenth century.[14]

Marxists have traditionally assigned more importance to the fifteenth century in their accounts of capitalist origins than any of the schools of thought mentioned so far. Two episodes have been claimed as marking a significant stage in the development of capitalism – the enclosure movement in England, and the voyages of discovery by Europeans to other continents. Marxists are bound to give prominence to the antecedents of the fully developed capitalist economy, because of their expectation that the roots of a new system would be found in preceding social and economic structures. They depict medieval or feudal Europe as having many social and economic flaws. The agricultural sector predominated; the peasant and artisan producers were only capable of achieving low levels of productivity; the social structure was destructive of investment and efficiency, because the nobility took the surplus from the peasants and consumed it.

However, while many non-Marxists are content to dismiss the medieval period, consigning it to a pre-industrial limbo of gloom and inertia, Marxists are more willing to see the feudal centuries as containing elements of movement and even dynamism. Firstly, they share with Smith, Pirenne and others an appreciation of the period as one of expanding trade. This had initially been generated by demand from the nobility for imported luxuries and high-quality manufactured goods. From an original division of labour between townsmen and country dwellers developed a further differentiation of function between merchants and artisans within urban society. Urban growth encouraged advances in the rural economy, because the demand for foodstuffs led to commodity production (cultivation for sale) and primitive accumulation (the build up of property and wealth in the hands of the producers), both being regarded as pre-conditions for the emergence of capitalism.

Ideas have changed over the second source of dynamism in feudal society, social relationships. It was once believed that the main division of interest lay between the feudal nobility and the urban bourgeoisie. Towns had to struggle for their liberties and against the restrictive forces of lordship, and continued to be antagonistic to feudal privilege, because the economic life of the towns set them apart from the prevailing mode of production. In the long run the greater use of money – for example, when labour services were replaced by cash rents – was thought to have acted as a solvent on the traditional bonds of feudal society. Now it is argued that the merchants of the towns allied themselves with the nobility; the profits of lordship were used to buy the goods that the merchants supplied. On their side the merchants identified with the rural lords, sharing many of their tastes and interests, intermarrying with them, and some were able to buy land and give their descendants noble status.[15] The urban artisans, who worked in their houses with the help of family labour, bear some resemblance to the rural peasantry.[16] Indeed in small towns and throughout the countryside work in crafts was often combined with small-scale agriculture. There was a division of interest, and consequent social friction, between merchants and artisans, because the merchants dealt in the raw materials of industry, and in the finished goods, and consequently sought to reduce the artisans' remuneration in order to maintain competitive prices and to maximize their own profits. But the sharpest conflicts in the Middle Ages arose between lords and peasants. The lords lived on the surplus of the peasants, which they levied in the form of goods, labour and cash. The peasants, who were given a degree of self-confidence by the potential independence of their household economies, and derived some strength from their association in village communities, disputed their obligations and sought to keep as much of the surplus as possible. The class struggle was therefore centred on the issues of serfdom and rents.

These two sources of movement in feudal society acted together in the thirteenth century, when the growth of the market encouraged lords to step up their demands, and to use their powers over serfs to levy more cash. The peasants could pay more, the lords judged, because they could profit from the sale of corn, meat and wool. These demands met with a spirited but fragmented resistance. In the fourteenth century commercial growth suffered a check as markets became glutted. Partly because of the new economic and demographic situation after the Black Death of 1348/9, which improved the bargaining position and confidence of the peasants, and partly because the lords were increasingly allied with the state in the imposition of social discipline and extra taxation, social struggles reached a new stage of large-scale rebellion. They were unsuccessful in the short term, but the combination of peasant resistance and the realities of a shrinking market, especially the reduced demand for land, forced lords to make concessions. In the fifteenth century labour services were finally converted into cash payments, serfdom withered away, and rents declined. These changes had many consequences for the future structure of society. A liberated peasantry could form the basis of a force of 'free' wage workers. A peasant no longer fettered with burdens of servile dues and heavy rents had a better chance of producing effectively for the market and thereby accumulating capital. The loss of powers of private jurisdiction, and the reduction of rent incomes, weakened the traditional means of social domination by the lords.

One school of Marxists, led by Gunder Frank and Wallerstein, expresses limited interest in the Middle Ages, except in that the discoveries at the end of the fifteenth century mark the beginnings of the great age of European expansion.[17] They argue that in the global scene Europe and Asia were roughly equal in terms of social and economic development, until the colonial movement from the sixteenth century onwards gave Europeans world domination. The discoveries opened up new sources of raw materials and new markets, and made available to capitalists a more tractable workforce than had been available at home. In the new world economy or 'world system' the main inequalities lay not between the privileged and underprivileged classes within Europe, but between the European and non-European peoples. The first beneficiaries of the exploitation of the new system were the merchants who gained capital that was eventually invested in technological innovations and industrial production.

R. Brenner puts more emphasis on internal developments within Europe, and especially in England. He rejects demographic fluctuations and the growth of the market as the motive forces behind the changes of the later Middle Ages. Instead he lays stress on the struggle between lords and peasants, and the extent to which the peasants gained control of their holdings. According to Brenner, while the French peasantry were able to consolidate a degree of proprietorship that protected them from seignorial power, their English counterparts were still vulnerable to eviction in the late fifteenth century.[18] The enclosure and engrossing movement marked an important stage in the expropriation of the peasantry. As a result the gentry were able to create large farms appropriate for commodity production. This was all preparatory to the emergence of capitalist industry, as the loss of their lands separated the workers from the means of production, and so created a free labour force, while the new, large and efficient farms could supply foodstuffs for the workers in towns and industry.

A problem that poses some difficulty for the two lines of thought outlined here is the long period of time that divides the fifteenth-century origins of overseas expansion or the enclosure movement from the rise of industrial capitalism in the late eighteenth and nineteenth centuries. There is some agreement that the widely separated events are connected, yet some explanation is needed for the long delays between phases. Possible reasons might lie in the continued hegemony of the aristocracy, or the advent (on the continent) of the absolutist state, or the depression of the economy and the political crises of the seventeenth century. Whatever the reason, orthodox Marxists have long had to wrestle with the problem of an appropriate terminology for the 'early modern' centuries which seem to have been neither feudal nor capitalist. A related problem is the use of the concept of stages of history and of the possibility of a system developing piecemeal. The point of a 'system' is that it forms a coherent whole – in the case of capitalism the large farm feeds the workers in the factory, and their products are sold on the world market. Can one part of the system function before the other parts have been put into place? Can a system be reduced to its separate elements, when it works only as a whole?[19] Should we look therefore, not for a series of new inventions or developments, but for a short period of rapid innovation?

Another area of debate which concerns Marxist and non-Marxist historians alike is the relationship between town and country. In the last century it was assumed that towns played the key role as centres of innovation, and that the origins of capitalism would be closely related to the process of urbanization. Marx wrote of industrialization 'ruralizing' the countryside, and he was full of admiration for the urban bourgeoisie, who had, among other achievements, rescued mankind from the idiocy of rural life. Now that medieval towns are seen as deeply embedded in feudal society, and there is widespread recognition of an age of proto-industrialization in rural areas, we may begin to wonder whether, at least as far as industrial organization is concerned, the urban landscape was a hostile environment for early capitalism.[20]

This survey of ideas has been necessarily brief and superficial. Views have been oversimplified, and others omitted. I have naturally selected for inclusion those writers who believe in the significance of terms such as 'capitalism'. Those who do not accept the concept have not been included, though it ought to be said that there is a widespread view that acquisitiveness is an innate human trait, and that as this is the essence of capitalism, capitalism has always existed. Such views are incompatible with a thoughtful analysis of the past – the social scientists' obsessions with categories and phases may make historians impatient, but change is the preoccupation of all scholars, and they must make sense and order of the fragmented events of the past by depicting them in general terms.

Out of the mass of conflicting views presented above, certain questions can be extracted which are capable of being answered from our evidence. Firstly, on the basis of the strict definition of capitalism as a system of productive relations, can anyone in fifteenth-century England be described as a capitalist?

To begin to answer this central question, and in order to demonstrate that this is not a purely abstract subject, let us examine an individual with a claim to be considered a capitalist. His name was Roger Heritage, and he lived at Burton Dassett in Warwickshire. We know that he was an adult, but probably unmarried, in 1466, so he could have been born in the 1440s.[21] He died in 1495, having held the demesne of Burton Dassett on lease since 1480, and probably earlier.[22] His farm consisted of about 500 acres of land, with a rabbit warren and a windmill, for which he paid a rent of £20 per annum to the lords of the manor, who for most of his period as a farmer were Sir John Norbury and William Belknap, the nephews of the previous lord, and William's nephew who in turn succeeded him, Edward Belknap.[23]

Burton Dassett lay in south-east Warwickshire, not far from the point where the eastern boundary of that county meets both Oxfordshire and Northamptonshire. It could be described as lying on the eastern edge of the Warwickshire feldon, a clay plain famous for its champion husbandry; others would say that the hills rising to 600 ft (on which stand Burton Dassett church and the likely site of Heritage's house) mark the western edge of the wolds which stretched over much of Northamptonshire and Leicestershire. These wolds consisted of relatively high ground with clay soils which had in the remote past supported woodland and grassland, but which had over the centuries developed a champion landscape. In the thirteenth century both feldon and wolds supported a high density of nucleated villages, full of tenants with yardland and half-yardland holdings (10–40 acres of arable), who practised extensive cereal cultivation in open fields. Their lords exercised considerable discipline over them, and the majority held in villeinage, though not for very high rents.[24] A network of village markets (one was held at Dassett Southend, part of Burton Dassett) and towns gave the peasants opportunities to sell their produce in order to pay rents in cash and to buy goods that they could not grow or make for themselves. The area lay within the hinterland of the large town of Coventry.[25]

This homeland of the classic medieval peasantry had been transformed in the century before Heritage's birth. Villages shrank in size, and many of them were deserted. The power of the lords was weakened, and villeinage gradually disappeared, to be replaced by copyhold tenure. Although the fields continued to produce much grain, peasants increased the size of their flocks and herds, and in a minority of cases whole fields and village territories were totally converted into specialist pasture farms.[26] As the numbers of producers and consumers shrank, some of the smaller market centres decayed, though a number of Warwickshire towns flourished, including Coventry until the 1430s; even in decline in Heritage's time it was larger than it had been before the Black Death.[27]

It was in this world that Roger Heritage made his living. There are five reasons for describing him as a capitalist. Firstly, unlike the peasantry of the thirteenth century, or indeed most of those of his own time, he produced on a very large scale, using his hundreds of acres of land. His inventory taken in 1495 reveals that he owned 2 teams of oxen, 2 ploughs, 2 carts, 40 cattle, 12 horses and 860 sheep, suggesting that his farming operations were on a scale six, eight or even ten times greater than those of a normal peasant cultivator.

Secondly, he employed a considerable labour force. He had six living-in servants, judging from the six sets of bedding (sheets, blankets and coverlets) in the servants' chamber, but his total number of employees, both for farm and household work, was considerably higher. At the time of his death (in the autumn of 1495) he owed his servants £11 for their wages for the previous year, which leads to the conclusion that he employed about a dozen full-time workers at the prevailing rate of pay. No doubt he also made use of the labour of part-timers for such tasks as haymaking and harvesting.

Thirdly, Heritage was inevitably drawn into production on a large scale for the market. He had to find £20 rent money each year, and a great deal beyond that to cover his production costs and to make a profit. His arable cultivation had at the time of his death brought him crops worth £8, both the yield of the harvest of 1495, and some 'old wheat and old peas' left over from previous years. The hangover of unsold grain from one year to the next, which is attested in other fifteenth-century sources, reflects the slackness of the grain market; in a move again typical of his times Heritage left in his will pious bequests in the form of grain rather than cash.[28] Most of his grain production is likely to have been intended for internal consumption, that is for feeding his household and animals, and for providing liveries to employees as part of their pay. So the bulk of Heritage's cash income must have come from the profits of pastoral farming. His sheep would have yielded wool worth £12, and a surplus of animals was available for sale each year for at least £4. The milk and calves from twenty cows could have been worth £5 to £8, and there were enough beef cattle being fattened for market at a profit of 3s. to 4s. each to make another £2 or £3.[29] Rabbits were being bred in a warren and should be regarded as another product of pastoral husbandry. A payment of £6 for rabbits still owing in 1495 could represent all, or only a part of the income from the sale of these valuable delicacies. Together these sums would give Heritage an income from his pastures of about £30, and this estimate is confirmed by his debt to the vicar of Burton of 50s. 3d., presumably for wool, lambs, calves, and other small tithes, suggesting total production worth about £25. Other sources of cash included the hiring out of his plough teams, as four people owed him 21s. for 'tilling'. Perhaps he sold hay, or rented out pasture, as did other managers of demesnes in this period.

Heritage was able to make only limited profits. After he had paid his rent, servants' wages, and repairs of buildings and equipment he would have been fortunate to have made as much as £10 in cash for himself. He was labouring under the problems that faced all large-scale agricultural producers at that time – his large bill for wages, with servants receiving three or four times the amount of cash that their pre-Black Death predecessors earned, was hard to support in a weak market for crops. Grain prices, as we have seen, were so low that it was sometimes not worth carrying it to market, and wool, which he could probably sell for 4s. per stone, was fetching a shilling or two less than it did in the late fourteenth century. In order to make a profit in these difficult circumstances, he had to manage his farm to suit the shifts in the market. He had scaled down his arable farming because of the high labour costs and poor returns. His predecessors had planted as much as 200 acres each year in the fourteenth century; Heritage was equipped with enough ploughs to cultivate at least 150 acres, but probably confined arable crops to little more than a hundred acres, and hired out his spare ploughing capacity. He, or a predecessor, had noted that rabbits gave a good return for little expense, and had set up a warren on an area previously used for more conventional agriculture. He had decided, unlike some of his Midland contemporaries, to favour sheep rather than beef cattle, though he evidently saw advantages in dairying. He sold goods locally, not just in the chief market of the Warwickshire feldon, Stratford-upon-Avon, where he had joined the Holy Cross Guild and thus aided his commercial contacts in the town, but also in Coventry, Warwick and Kineton which he mentioned in his will. His trading also took him further afield; he had evidently sold produce to Richard Gibbons of Aylesbury (Buckinghamshire), as this man owed him money at the time of his death, and one of his daughters married a merchant of Witney (Oxfordshire).

Fourthly, Heritage invested in the buildings and equipment of the farm. His landlord, by the terms of the usual leasehold contract, would not have contributed to the upkeep or reconstruction of manorial buildings except in unusual circumstances. The inventory refers to a new farm building – evidently one erected by Heritage – which contained timber for four hovels. These were shelters of some kind, either for crops or livestock. The inventory values implements such as ploughs and carts because these also would have been bought and maintained by Heritage. He could well have spent money on the farm, for fencing for example, but these improvements would have been to the long term benefit of the lord and his successor in the farm, and would not appear in the inventory. The changes that had occurred on the Burton Dassett demesne in the later Middle Ages did not happen easily and naturally. True, grass would have grown on the disused arable land without much need of human intervention, but every management decision needed some innovation and investment. A large sheep flock had to be provided with a sheepcote or two – and these could be large and expensive buildings. Even the rabbits would have to be helped in their burrowing with artificial mounds, and the warren would need secure fencing to exclude vermin and poachers.[30] Changes in land use on the demesne would have implications for the remaining villagers' rights of common, and whether the changes were carried out by negotiation or imposition, new demesne pastures might well need to be fenced off. Pastoral farming was advantageous for lessees like Heritage because of its reduced labour costs, but this saving was achieved only by considerable capital investment.

Fifthly, Roger Heritage falls outside the conventional hierarchy of medieval society. He would have been known as a yeoman. Certainly his material possessions and income would have raised him well above the other inhabitants of his village. Not many of his neighbours, even those who were known as yeomen, would have lived like him in a six-roomed house or owned 60 lbs of pewter. He hob-nobbed with merchants, like Thomas Temple of Witney who married his daughter, and two other daughters were thought to be acceptable matches by local minor gentry families, who were no doubt willing to overlook the Heritages' lack of gentility because they brought plenty of money with them. One of his sons rose in the clerical hierarchy to become a fellow of Oriel College, Oxford, and rector of the wealthy parish of Hackney in Middlesex.[31] So we can locate Roger Heritage above the peasantry and below the gentry. He was socially mobile, and in a future generation, had the family survived in the male line, they would presumably have been accepted as gentry, as happened to those better-known east Warwickshire graziers, the Spencers.[32]

Heritage's will contains the usual conventional expressions of piety. For example, he admired the friars, and left them bequests of grain. He wished to beautify Burton church with a rood loft and images, and he hoped that his soul would benefit from two years of masses sung by a priest. An unusual passage in his will concerns the division of a sum of £40 among his sons. If one of them died, the share was to go to the others only if they were well-behaved: 'provided always that my executors and overseers . . . have a due consideration of the condition of my said sons, so that if they be wasters or of evil condition or disposition, that God forbid, that then they be only content with their part of the £40'. It would be tempting to see in this statement evidence of special concern for individual responsibility by a self-made man whose success depended on hard work and personal discipline, but such phrases can be found in other wills, and it would perhaps be dangerous to make too much of this insight into an early puritanism. Also the inventory of Heritage's possessions seems to reflect a modesty in his consumption of goods. The total valuation of the 'utensils' of his household such as furnishings and kitchen equipment amounted to a mere £15, compared with farm stock and equipment worth £109. A contemporary knight's goods and chattels would divide almost equally in value between domestic possessions and the grain, animals and implements of the demesne.[33] Heritage, unlike the gentry of his day, owned very little that could be called showy or luxurious. A hanging in the hall, the most prestigious item in the principal room of the house, was clearly an object of value, being worth 6s. 8d.; but eleven silver spoons seem to account for most of his plate. The bulk of his possessions were practical and utilitarian items necessary for accommodating and feeding a house-hold swollen by living-in farm servants. The explanation of his frugality could lie either in the low profit-margins of the Burton Dassett demesne, or in some temporary misfortune such as illness immediately before Heritage's death. If the inventory reflects a short-term episode of adversity rather than a lifetime of sobriety and thrift, it is still worth remembering that in hard times household goods had been relinquished more readily than farm stock. It could well be that a farmer did not need to maintain appearances for status reasons as did members of the gentry, and this helps to define the characteristic lifestyle and mentality of a capitalist farmer.

In any case, we do not need to use the stilted formulae of a will, or speculate about the missing items in an inventory, to establish Heritage's business-like outlook. He could never have made a success of fifteen years and more as a demesne lessee without the mental equipment that enabled him to invest, employ labour, and sell at a profit. And he did this in a harsh world, in which he lacked the social advantages of gentility, and where he needed to live on his wits to make farming pay despite low prices and high labour costs.

The reader may feel that although Roger Heritage changed and adapted his life to his environment, he was not sufficiently adventurous or innovative to merit the description of 'capitalist'. A real entrepreneur, it could be said, should have moulded his circumstances to suit his interests. In particular, we might note his reluctance to specialize, almost as if he continued in the peasant tradition of avoiding risk by practising arable cultivation, dairying, fattening beef cattle, keeping sheep, and raising rabbits. I doubt if heroic risk-taking and a bold, pioneering spirit are necessary prerequisites for the identification of capitalists. If these are essential attributes, many nineteenth- and twentieth-century businessmen would be found wanting. And if they are felt to be at least desirable qualities, then they can be found in other fifteenth-century farmers, for example John Heritage, Roger's son, who two years after his father's death did a deal with Edward Belknap, then the sole lord of the manor, to enclose land in the open fields, to convert 360 acres of arable land to pasture, and to remove the inhabitants of twelve houses. Roger must have been farming in the midst of a decaying village, in which the old distinction between arable and pasture was disappearing, while the remaining tenants demanded right of access to open-field strips and the common pasture. This must have constantly frustrated the demesne farmers' aim to use the land efficiently and intensively.[34] Perhaps the initiative to enclose came from the landlord, but implementing the scheme needed a partnership between Belknap and the new young farmer. One can imagine John Heritage waiting impatiently, like many farmers' sons in later centuries, for the chance to take over and wield a new broom. But the likelihood that John was more enterprising, and less caring of the interests of his poorer neighbours, cannot deprive his father of the description of 'capitalist farmer'.

Finally, we might expect capital to reproduce itself, and indeed we find that Heritage's farm, improved by Belknap and John, flourished in the hands of Heritage's great nephew Peter Temple in the 1540s and 1550s. He was by then paying nearly £100 in rent, but that was for 655 acres of enclosed land, unencumbered with tenants or peasants exercising common rights. The inflation of the sixteenth century had also raised livestock prices, and depressed the value of real wages. Temple was keeping on the pasture in the late 1540s as many as 220 cattle and more than 2,000 sheep; farmers had entered into a brave new world.[35]

The Heritages were characteristic of a small but significant group in fifteenth-century society.[36] Most demesnes on large estates, even on the manors of the middling and upper gentry, together with such assets as tithes and rectorial glebes, had been leased out in the late fourteenth century or in the decade or two after 1400. Some demesnes were let in fragments to a number of tenants, or en bloc to a village community, so that the land made modest additions to the relatively small resources of many peasant households. The same may have occurred, without our knowledge, in cases where there was apparently one farmer, who had decided that subletting was the best way of exploiting the resources of the demesne. Most demesnes seem to have been leased as single units, and occasional supplementary evidence, such as inventories, shows that the lessee exploited the land himself, or that cultivation was left in the hands of a bailiff or a single subtenant. The lessees included a good number of gentry, merchants and clergy, and they were most likely to have used indirect methods of management. The majority of lessees, and probably a near totality of subtenants, were of peasant origin. Usually we know no more about them than is written in the lease – their names, the assets conveyed, the length of the term and the rent, with clauses dividing responsibilities for the maintenance of buildings. When additional information can be gathered, it can sometimes tell us of agricultural improvements, such as enclosure or conversion to pasture, or of the market orientation of lessees who had interests in towns or contacts with the wool and cloth trades. The most innovatory of the farmers, the butcher graziers of the Midlands, used their lands as specialized pastures, often occupying large areas of former arable, including the whole of the field system of a deserted village. They fattened animals for the urban markets, which were expanding because of high per capita incomes which brought regular meat-eating to a greater proportion of households.[37]

Not every lessee changed the management or technology of his demesne, but the arrival of the farmer marks three important and enduring changes in late medieval England. Firstly, the management of agriculture slipped out of the hands of the landlords and their officials, to the advantage of a lower social stratum. The lords still creamed off the profits, but left the lessees with the chance to make something for themselves. Secondly, the demesnes changed their character, because leasing detached them from the peasant holdings to which they had been closely linked for many centuries. The demesne, instead of forming an integral part of a manor, became simply an area of land. No longer would production be supported or cushioned by the rents and services of the peasantry. To underline the growing divorce between demesne and village, some Midland farmers began that migration out into their fields which by the nineteenth century was to place the majority of farm buildings away from other settlements. And thirdly the whole structure of estates was transformed. The old estates had been based on the need in a pre-marketing age for scattered manors in different regions to give lords a balance of resources. Many of the new lessees held only one demesne, and those who acquired a number took them from different lords and organized them on fresh principles, often seeking to hold farms in a compact group for ease of management, and acquiring lands of the same type so as to be able to specialize – for example, in pastoral farming.[38] There were at least 5,000 farmers like Heritage, we can estimate, and they held as much as a fifth of the land in lowland England towards the end of the fifteenth century.

The gentry are worth considering as a second distinct group of possible fifteenth-century capitalists. It was once thought that the magnates of the thirteenth century ran their estates on capitalist lines, but the revelation that they invested relatively little, and relied heavily on 'feudal' revenues even at the apex of their 'high farming' phase, combined with their readiness to abandon direct management during the fourteenth century, has led us to concentrate more on the smaller landowners. Gentry sometimes continued after 1400 with the direct management of their demesnes, or took the demesnes of other lords on lease, or ran both their own lands and leaseholds simultaneously. Notable examples are John Brome of Warwickshire, the Catesbys of Northamptonshire, Thomas Keble of Leicestershire, the Townshends of Norfolk, and the Vernons of Derbyshire.[39] In many ways their activities are comparable with Heritage and the other non-gentry farmers. They produced for the market, specialized in pastoral husbandry, employed wage labour, and could invest in technical changes such as enclosures. We must, however, make some important reservations. For the gentry, agricultural production formed only one part, and then often a minor part, of their incomes. They could, and did, drop out of direct management of their estates, and resume it again when circumstances made it advantageous. They were not as heavily committed to the sale of produce as the yeoman farmers, because they maintained well-fed households who ate a high proportion of the grain and stock from their manors. For the yeomen farmers agricultural production was a way of life; the gentleman farmers regarded agriculture as a sideline, and were much more concerned with the usual aristocratic preoccupations of marriage, patronage, government and the law. Perhaps the main contribution that the gentry made to the development of capitalism lay in forming partnerships with yeomen farmers (like that between Belknap and the younger Heritage) in which the power of the lord was complemented by the entrepreneurial skills of the lessee to enhance profits for their mutual benefit. Such a cooperative alliance became the basis of many subsequent advances in English agriculture.

A third group to be considered are the peasants who accumulated larger holdings. They sometimes did this by taking all or part of a demesne on lease, but more commonly built up a complex holding by acquiring their neighbours' lands by marriage, purchase, or simply by taking on tenements that had been abandoned and 'lay in the lord's hands'. To take an example, successive members of the Cubbell family of Coleshill and Eastrop (Berkshire) gathered to themselves 3 or 4 yardlands (60–80 acres) of land, together with pieces of pasture and a mill.[40] They were able to run a hundred sheep, and employ three or four workers. They raised enough money by sales of produce both to pay rents, which for them and for most peasants by the middle of the fifteenth century were levied entirely in cash, and to spend on their own consumption. When the lord built houses for the Coleshill peasants his costs amounted to £7 or more on each building, which were equipped with stone walls and slate roofs. Presumably the peasants, who normally paid for their own buildings, also bought expensive materials and hired skilled labour. Some of the buildings, such as barns, represent considerable investments, and we know also of peasants who consolidated their holdings and enclosed their lands. As with the gentry, but for different reasons, there are difficulties in using the term 'capitalist' to describe the Cubbells and their like. Their large holdings were not always cultivated very effectively, and they often broke up after a short period. The Cubbells paid modest rents of 6d. per acre, and very low entry fines on acquiring new holdings; land could be obtained cheaply, and because of labour shortages and low prices, did not yield high profits. Wealthy peasants were inhibited in changing their techniques by the pressures of the community with whom they had to cooperate. They were unable to employ many workers because of the expense of wages. Their sources of labour were either the life-cycle servants (young people gaining work experience before going on to a more independent way of life) or smallholders earning wages part-time. We can recognize the capitalist potential of the Cubbells and the many thousands of comparable yeomen. It was from their ranks that the Heritages and their like emerged. And yet we must wonder, in view of the failure of many villages to polarize sharply between a few yeomen and numerous landless labourers, how many of the peasant elite really broke out of the economic and mental restraints of their communities.[41]

Fourthly, there were the merchants. Of course they can be regarded as capitalists in the sense that they risked large sums of money in buying goods, in order to sell them at a profit. There was nothing new about this in the fifteenth century; the merchant class had an ancestry of at least five centuries, and it was in the fourteenth century that English merchants extended their role in foreign trade and government finance. Although their mercantile activity resulted in high profits from long-distance trade and money-lending, they were neither specialized nor adventurous, even if some of them called themselves merchant venturers. Their business techniques, for example in accounting, lagged behind those of the continent, and especially the Italians. They traded in manufactured goods, but took little interest in industry. Their close social and cultural links with the landed gentry shows that they were not cut off from the aristocracy by a special mentality.[42]

One section of the merchant class deserves mention because they did emerge as a significant group for the first time in the late fourteenth and fifteenth centuries. These were the clothiers, the entrepreneurs who orchestrated the various cloth-making processes, and sold the finished products. They were often based in small towns or the rural areas in which woollen cloth was made. James Terumber, for example, rose from obscurity as a Bristol fuller to become a major figure in the 1460s in the Wiltshire industry from his base at Bradford-on-Avon, selling as many as 236 cloths in one year.[43] He was not untypical in his specialization, not just in the trade in woollen cloth, but in particular types of cloth. Clothiers sometimes acquired sheep pastures and fulling mills, showing their aim of gaining an interest in all stages of the lengthy production process. Indeed some clothiers, especially in East Anglia, in parallel with continental entrepreneurs, took the first tentative steps towards an early form of industrial capitalism, because they owned spinning houses and dye pans, and were employing workers on their own premises rather than merely coordinating the separate activities of artisans working in a state of semi-independence at home.[44]

As is clear from the many qualifications needed in discussing the various groups of capitalists, proto-capitalists and those caught up in a capitalist tendency, no one could allege that England in the fifteenth century had a capitalist economy. The aristocracy still lived largely from rents that were fixed by custom, not by market forces, and their culture of chivalry and 'good lordship' influenced the thinking and behaviour of the rest of society. The middling peasantry survived in sufficient numbers to refute any notion of a generally polarized peasant society, or of wholesale removal of the peasants from the land. Wage labour seems not to have grown in use during the fifteenth century, and the preponderance of young servants and part-time smallholding labourers in the workforce prevents us from identifying a proletariat of any significant size. Although the fifteenth century saw much individual wealth, and industries such as iron and cloth expanded to satisfy the rising demand, there was no upward spiral of consumption and production. The generation of new industries and a decisive extension of home comforts for the middling sort came in the sixteenth century. Social attitudes were shifting – for example, a more corrective attitude to poverty was gaining ground, but this was still not enough to shatter the old community cohesion, even in the most commercially-minded districts.[45]

The pace of change was slow. We cannot sum up a complex society like that of fifteenth century England in a single phrase. It retained many traditional characteristics, but society was open and varied enough to contain the likes of Heritage, the Cubbells and Terumber.

In conclusion, two supplementary questions require at least brief discussion. Was the fifteenth century an important period for the emergence of capitalists? And what were the mechanisms of social change?

On chronology it is of course true that the urban and commercial growth of the ninth to thirteenth centuries provided the preconditions for a future world dominated by exchange, in the sense that an urban hierarchy and a market network were then established. However, the crises of the fourteenth century broke the continuity in the economy. The thirteenth century ended in stagnation. Many of the smaller markets disappeared and some larger towns declined. The aristocracy were shaken by falling incomes, rising costs, war and rebellion. The social structure of village communities was disrupted by the combination of famine, epidemics and migration. Of the groups identified above as showing capitalistic characteristics, the merchants and gentry can be traced back before 1300. There were peasants with large holdings who profited from the expanding market of the thirteenth century, but they were less numerous and their holding generally smaller than those of their fifteenth-century successors. And their accumulations of land were even more fragile. A numerous body of yeomen, farmers and clothiers were produced by the peculiar combination of low population, falling landlord incomes and expanding rural cloth-making that occurred after 1348/9 and especially after 1400. The thirteenth century had been a period of high economic pressure, in which any innovation might have been dangerous. In the fifteenth century there was more opportunity and incentive for lords, tenants and entrepreneurs to experiment. But the disadvantages of the fifteenth-century economy for market production are manifest. It was a hard school, in which profit-making was only possible for those who judged the market carefully, and made the most efficient use of expensive labour.

On the sources of social change, the idea that the growth of commerce would in itself lead to capitalism is not supported by the English experience of the thirteenth century, when serfdom and other seignorial institutions were strengthened by the rising market. Brenner believes that the key episode in the later Middle Ages was the expropriation of the peasantry to create larger units of production. There is insufficient evidence that this happened on a general scale. Brenner was right to see the formation of larger farms as an important trend, but he misunderstood the cause. Weakened lordship and cheap land provided the environment for the engrossing of holdings. The landlords who expelled tenants in the decades around 1500 were merely tidying up and completing a process that had been begun by the peasants themselves. Brenner underestimated the capacity of peasants to run their own lives, and to take the initiative in reorganizing their holdings. Was the birth of capitalism painless, then? Engrossing was easy when peasants voluntarily abandoned their holdings, or when, if they were pushed out, they could obtain land elsewhere; the agony came in future generations when their more numerous sixteenth-century successors found that the old holdings were not available for new tenants, and that the enclosure of common fields and pastures was irreversible.

To sum up, capitalists and potential capitalists lived in fifteenth-century England. The appearance of these people was made possible by the earlier commercial revolution, and the crises of the fourteenth century. Structural change, especially in rural society, preceded the enclosure movement and the voyages of discovery. Early capitalists appeared in a context of struggle and adversity, not because they depended on the expulsion of the weak and poor, but because they had to organize production in the midst of a market recession.

Notes

This is a very controversial topic, and this paper raised a good deal of criticism and comment from those who heard it at the Liverpool colloquium, and at a seminar on pre-industrial economic and social history at the Institute of Historical Research in London. My final version will not satisfy all of those who contributed to the discussions, but they will see that I have introduced a number of qualifications and passages that take account of their views. I am grateful to Dr N.W. Alcock, who drew my attention to Roger Heritage's will.

1   R. de Roover, *Business, Banking and Economic Thought in Late Medieval and Early Modern Europe* (Chicago, 1974), pp. 28–9 (introductory chapter by J. Kirshner).
2   M. Dobb, *Studies in the Development of Capitalism* (rev. edn., London, 1963), pp. 4–8; R.H. Hilton, 'Capitalism – what's in a name?', in idem, *Class Conflict and the Crisis of Feudalism* (London, 1985), pp. 268–77; R.H. Hilton (ed.), *The Transition from*

Feudalism to Capitalism (London, 1976), pp. 11–18; J. Baechler, *The Origins of Capitalism* (Oxford, 1975), pp. 29–50.

3   K. Tribe, *Genealogies of Capitalism* (London, 1981), p. 38.

4   R.H. Hilton, *The Transition from Feudalism to Capitalism* (London, 1976), pp. 9–30.

5   E.A.R. Brown, 'The tyranny of a construct: feudalism and historians of medieval Europe', *American Historical Review*, 37 (1974), pp. 1063–88; M.M. Postan, 'Feudalism and its decline: a semantic exercise', in T.H. Aston et al. (ed.), *Social Relations and Ideas* (Cambridge, 1983), pp. 73–87.

6   R. Hodges, 'Anglo-Saxon England and the origins of the modern world economy', in D. Hooke (ed.), *Anglo-Saxon Settlements* (Oxford, 1988), pp. 291–304.

7   J. Abu-Lughod, 'The shape of the world system in the thirteenth century', *Studies in Comparative International Development*, XXII (1987–8), pp. 3–25.

8   W.W. Rostow, *How it all Began. Origins of the Modern Economy* (London, 1975), pp. 1–32.

9   E.L. Jones, *The European Miracle* (Cambridge, 1981), especially pp. 3–41; J.A. Hall, *Powers and Liberties. The Causes and Consequences of the Rise of the West* (Oxford, 1985), pp. 111–44; M. Mann, *The Sources of Social Power*, vol. 1 (Cambridge, 1986), pp. 373–517.

10 E.A. Wrigley, *People, Cities and Wealth* (Oxford, 1987), pp. 4–13.

11 E.R. Wolf, *Europe and the People without History* (Berkeley and Los Angeles, 1982), pp. 101–25; Hilton (ed.), *Transition from Feudalism to Capitalism*, pp. 169–87; Mann, *Social Power*, pp. 430–7.

12 M.M. Postan, *The Medieval Economy and Society* (London, 1972), p. 142.

13 E. Le Roy Ladurie, 'L'histoire immobile', *Annales E.S.C.*, 29 (1974), pp. 673–92; idem, 'A reply to Robert Brenner', in T.H. Aston and C.H.E. Philpin (eds.), *The Brenner Debate* (Cambridge, 1985), pp. 101–6.

14 J. Day, 'The great bullion famine of the fifteenth century', in *The Medieval Market Economy* (Oxford, 1987), pp. 1–54; P. Spufford, *Money and Its Use in Medieval Europe* (Cambridge, 1988), pp. 363–77 (the latter author writes with great authority on the history of money, but is not a monetarist).

15 Dobb, *Development of Capitalism*, p. 120; R.H. Hilton, 'Towns in English feudal society', in *Class Conflict*, pp. 175–86.

16 R.H. Hilton, 'Popular movements in England at the end of the fourteenth century', in *Class Conflict*, pp. 152–64, especially p. 157.

17 A. Gunder Frank, *On Capitalist Underdevelopment* (Oxford, 1975); I. Wallerstein, *The Modern World System. Capitalist Agriculture and the Origins of the European World Economy in the Sixteenth Century* (New York, 1974), especially Chapters 1 and 2.

18 R. Brenner, 'Agrarian class structure and economic development in pre-industrial Europe', and 'The agrarian roots of European capitalism', in Aston and Philpin (eds.), *Brenner Debate*, pp. 10–63, 213–327.

19 Mann, *Social Power*, pp. 16–18; P. Glennie, 'In search of agrarian capitalism; manorial land markets and the acquisition of land in the Lea Valley, *c.* 1450–*c.* 1560', *Continuity and Change*, 3 (1988), pp. 11–40.

20 J. Merrington, 'Town and country in the transition to capitalism', in Hilton (ed.), *Transition from Feudalism to Capitalism*, pp. 170–95.

21 J.H. Bloom (ed.), *The Register of the Gild of the Holy Cross . . . of Stratford-upon-Avon* (London, 1907), p. 135.

22 PRO PROB 2/457 (inventory); PROB 11/10, fol. 231v. (will); Northamptonshire CRO, Temple Stow Box 6/2.

23 Shakespeare's Birthplace Trust Record Office, ER 1/66/538; *Victoria County History of Warwickshire*, V, p. 70; N.W. Alcock (ed.), *Warwickshire Grazier and London Skinner 1532–1555* (British Academy Records of Social and Economic History, new series, IV, 1981), pp. 27–37.

24 R.H. Hilton, *Social Structure of Rural Warwickshire in the Middle Ages* (Dugdale Society Occasional Paper, No. 9, 1950); J.B. Harley, 'Population trends and agricultural developments from the Warwickshire Hundred Rolls of 1279', *EcHR*, 2nd series, XI (1958/9), pp. 8–18; H.S.A. Fox, 'The people of the wolds in English settlement history', in M. Aston et al. (eds.), *The Rural Settlements of Medieval England* (Oxford, 1989), pp. 77–101.

25 R.H. Hilton, *A Medieval Society* (2nd edn., Cambridge, 1983), pp. 168–83.

26 C. Dyer, *Warwickshire Farming 1349–c. 1520* (Dugdale Society Occasional Papers, no. 27, 1981).

27 C. Phythian-Adams, *Desolation of a City. Coventry and the Urban Crisis of the Late Middle Ages* (Cambridge, 1979), pp. 7–50.

28 C. Dyer, 'A small landowner in the fifteenth century', *Midland History*, 1 (1972), p. 6.

29 Calculations are based on the figures in T.H. Lloyd, *The Movement of Wool Prices in Medieval England* (*EcHR* Supplement no. 6, 1977), pp. 38–44; Dyer, *Warwickshire Farming*, p. 20; C. Dyer, 'Farming techniques, the west midlands', in E. Miller (ed.), *The Agrarian History of England and Wales*, III (Cambridge, 1991, forthcoming).

30 M. Bailey, 'The rabbit and the medieval East Anglian Economy', *AgHR*, 36 (1988), pp. 1–20; D. Austin, 'Excavation and survey at Bryn Cysegrfan, Llanfair Clydogau, Dyfed, 1979', *Medieval Archaeology*, 32 (1988), pp. 130–65.

31 Alcock (ed.), *Warwickshire Grazier*, pp. 11–17, 21–2.

32 M.E. Finch, *The Wealth of Five Northamptonshire Families* (Northamptonshire Record Society, XIX, 1956), pp. 38–9.

33 C. Dyer, *Standards of Living in the Later Middle Ages* (Cambridge, 1989), p. 76.

34 Alcock (ed.), *Warwickshire Grazier*, pp. 27–38; idem, 'Enclosure and Depopulation in Burton Dassett: a sixteenth-century view', *Warwickshire History*, III (1977), pp. 180–4.

35 Alcock (ed.), *Warwickshire Grazier*, pp. 37, 39–99. John Heritage had expanded his operations in the first decade of the sixteenth century, as he appears as a tenant of Moreton-in-Marsh (Gloucestershire) and had a share in a lease of a pasture at Upper Ditchford in the same county: Westminster Abbey Muniments 8362 and Hereford and Worcester County Record Office, ref. 009:1 BA 2636/37 (iii) 43806, ff. 23–4.

36 F.R.H. Du Boulay, 'Who were farming the English demesnes at the end of the Middle Ages?', *EcHR*, 2nd ser., XVII (1965), pp. 443–55; B. Harvey, 'The leasing of the abbot of Westminster's demesnes in the later middle ages', *EcHR*, 2nd ser., XXII (1969), pp. 17–27; B. Harvey, *Westminster Abbey and its Estates in the Middle Ages* (Oxford, 1977), pp. 148–63; J.N. Hare, 'The demesne lessees of fifteenth-century Wiltshire', *AgHR*, 29 (1981), pp. 1–15.

37 R.H. Hilton, 'A study in the pre-history of English enclosure in the fifteenth century', in *The English Peasantry in the Later Middle Ages* (Oxford, 1975), pp. 161–73; Dyer, *Warwickshire Farming*, pp. 17–22.

38 H. Thorpe, 'The Lord and the Landscape', in *Volume Jubilaire M.A. Lefèvre* (Louvain, 1964), pp. 97–101.

39 Dyer, 'Small Landowner', pp. 1–14; idem, *Warwickshire Farming*, pp. 18–21; E.W. Ives, *The Common Lawyers of pre-Reformation England* (Cambridge, 1983), pp. 345–53; K.J. Allison, 'Flock management in the sixteenth and seventeenth centuries', *EcHR*, 2nd ser., XI (1958), pp. 98–112; S. Wright, *The Derbyshire Gentry in the Fifteenth Century* (Derbyshire Record Society, VIII, 1983), pp. 19–21. For a general comment on the economic activities of gentry, see C. Carpenter, 'The fifteenth century English gentry and their estates', M. Jones (ed.), *Gentry and Lesser Nobility in Late Medieval Europe* (Gloucester, 1986), pp. 36–58.

40 R. Faith, 'Berkshire: fourteenth and fifteenth centuries', in P.D.A. Harvey (ed.), *The Peasant Land Market in Medieval England* (Oxford, 1984), pp. 116–17, 146–9, 152–74.

41 Hilton, *English Peasantry*, pp. 37–53.

42   S. Thrupp, *The Merchant Class of Medieval London* (Ann Arbor, Mich., 1948), pp. 234–87.

43   E.M. Carus-Wilson, 'The woollen industry before 1550', *Victoria County History of Wiltshire*, IV, pp. 128–47.

44   E. Power, *The Paycockes of Coggeshall* (London, 1920); D. Dymond and A. Betterton, *Lavenham: 700 years of Textile Making* (Woodbridge, 1982); A. Derville, 'L'héritage des draperies médiévales', *Revue du Nord*, 69 (1987), pp. 715–24.

45   M.K. McIntosh, *Autonomy and Community. The Royal Manor of Havering, 1200–1500* (Cambridge, 1986), pp. 221–63.

2

Landlord and Tenant: the Paston Evidence

Colin Richmond
University of Keele

I have dithered over how to begin this paper. Should it be with a grand statement, an apt quotation such as 'Political toleration is a by-product of the complacency of the ruling class. When that complacency is disturbed there never was a more bloody-minded set of thugs than the English ruling class'? Or, should I start with the backs of Paston letters? I have opted for the backs of three letters of September 1461.

The letters[1] were written to John Paston by three of his servants, John Pampyng gentleman, James Gloys priest, and James Gresham gentleman. Another of John's servants, Richard Calle (neither gentleman nor priest), used the backs of these letters to do some rough accounting. Richard Calle is still sometimes called the Pastons' bailiff, though he was far more than that; the tasks he performed were those of receiver, superviser, steward, and cofferer[2] (it is evidence of John Paston's stinginess that he employed one man to do the work of four). On the backs of his colleagues' letters, sometime after Michaelmas 1461, Richard carefully numbered as well as named the estates for which he had to account. We may ponder how he came to be in possession of the letters, whether they were kept for their fronts or their backs, and why a fourth and probably a fifth letter, whose dorses were part of his sequence, were not. I know, I believe, which were the estates on the missing dorses, numbers vii and viii and x and xi. Professor Norman Davis rarely nods: he does so only over the backs of letters. From the dorse of John Pampyng's letter he omitted to record the xii in the top left hand corner.[3] Because item xii comprises foreign receipts (though Richard does not say so) and thus closes the sequence, because vi is Richard's number for the Matlask estate accounts on the dorse of James Gloys' letter, and because estates i to v and ix are on the dorse of James Gresham's letter, it has become a fairly simple matter to deduce the identity of estates vii and viii, x and xi.

I have bothered to excite you with my discovery of the estates which are not there, because these eleven estates of John Paston's in 1461 were the extent of his landed property, if we exclude the Fastolf lands, just about in John's hands at this date but soon almost all save Caister itself to be lost to the family. If I list the eleven – Snailwell, Cressingham, Sporle, Palgrave, Sparham, Matlask, Bessingham, Fritton, Mautby, Swainsthorp, Gresham – many of them will be unfamiliar, for these (Gresham and perhaps Sporle apart) were not major Paston manors. Those up in north-east Norfolk – Cromer, Oxnead, Paston itself – John's mother Agnes had for life (along with, of course, her own Barry estates, Marlingford in Norfolk, Stansted in Suffolk, and Horwellbury near Royston in Hertfordshire). John's two younger brothers held other property: Clement had Winterton near Yarmouth, William Holwellhall at East Tuddenham in central Norfolk. East Beckham, a manor John's father, Judge William Paston, thought he had bought in 1434, the family did not finally acquire until 1503: it cost them dear, possibly as much as forty times its annual value.[4] If John's brother Edmund had not died in 1449 allowing Snailwell, Cambridgeshire, to come to him, John certainly would have had the worst rather than the best of the patrimony. Sporle, Swainsthorp, which ought to have provided a daily 4d. for a monk of Norwich Cathedral priory to pray for Judge William's soul but did not, Cressingham and Palgrave were not 'ryche juelle[s]'[5] in the Paston coronet. Moreover, Gresham was John's because it was his wife's jointure. The remaining five estates, Sparham, Matlask, Bessingham, Fritton, just over the Norfolk border in Suffolk, and Mautby were part of his wife Margaret Mautby's inheritance – the other part, the four manors of Kirkhall in Salle, Briston, Flegghall and West Beckham, Margaret's Mautby uncles held for life; Margaret only got them on the death of Edward who was the last to die in 1479, five years before she died and thirteen years after John had.

The point I may seem to be labouring is an important one. The Paston estates in 1461 are really not what one would expect them to have been. John resented what little they were; that little was somewhere around or something over £200 per annum. That they were not all that they might have been was due, of course, to the human predicament, in this case John's father's, as at his death Judge William left a young widow, Agnes, and young children to be taken care of; the youngest of them (in an unusual overlapping of generations) only as old as his eldest grandson, that is two years old. The young widow, typically for the fifteenth century, was generously dowered; she outlived her eldest son by thirteen years: John Paston never lived at Paston, nor at Oxnead, nor, for that matter, at Gresham after it had been severely damaged by Lord Moleyns in 1448/9. He never lived (we might say) at home. Moreover, he and Agnes did not get on; she considered he had treated his younger brothers and sister abominably – she was right – and seldom wrote to him in later years; he *never* wrote to her – unless, of course, she did not keep his letters. This discord meant that none of the revenue of her lands – dower, jointure, inheritance (annual value £100) – was ever, so far as I can tell, put at the disposal of John or his sons when in turn they became head of the family. None the less, it would be wrong to regard John Paston's circumstances in 1461 as abnormal, as (I nearly said) a predicament, for the general point I wish now to labour is simply that: that the human condition is a predicament.

This may be why historians are not good interpreters of it. We are not, or do not tend to be, nominalists. What we are, what we cannot help but be, is humanist realists. Our intellectual baggage consists of benign models of the state, society, the family, of the individual – the bank manager, the motor mechanic, the policeman, and so forth. We even, I assume, have a Platonic notion of the landed estate: efficiently managed, smoothly run, thoughtfully administered. But has there ever been such, any more than there has been a benevolent state, an harmonious society, a happy family, an integrated individual? It is not that the world is closer to hell than heaven – to say so would be to be dualist about it – but I do think we might save ourselves a great deal of Olympian tut-tutting at how imperfect things were, if we took more account of the imperfectability of men and women since their dismissal from Eden. Redeemed we may be, but unregenerate we manifestly remain. It is, I suppose, psychologically impossible to have non-benign models; even ideological freaks like National Socialists, Stalinists, or Free Market conservatives believe they are improving man's lot while demonstrably damaging it. Still, historians might be more helpful expositors of the past if they presented its mishaps as par for the course. I am not only referring to human relations. Death, disease, natural disasters (telling phrase), and bad weather were both too random and too regular for life to have been comfortable or calculable. Perhaps it is the engulfing imagery of western society which leads us astray: the ubiquitous commercial, after all, cannot do other than picture a benign universe. Thus, our imaginations overpowered by what might be, we have become inadequate interpreters of historical suffering. The great historians are east Europeans. In other words, what would be unthinkable for a graduate of Harvard or Yale has been the experience of graduates of Vilna or Lvov. By way, therefore, of the Ukraine, Lithuania, and White Russia I return to Norfolk.

The Pastons of Norfolk were as normal a gentry family of the fifteenth century as the Wilkinses of Reading are a typical urban family of the twentieth. Both families 'take on board' the vicissitudes of their lives (many of them self-induced) because they are, so to say, life itself. We never hear any more of the child Margaret Paston was carrying in the mid-1450s, which she hoped John would want to 'be named Herry in remembrans of your brother Herry'[6] – unless it did survive and was christened Walter – than we ever hear a word of John's brother Henry. This is not because (absurd idea) these folk lacked feeling – Margaret's comment shows they did not – but that still-born or dead children were regarded as part of life: bearable, but not taken for granted. No more did John Paston I or John Paston II rail against their mothers for living too long. Only once did John Paston II express feelings which may have been bitter, and the occasion of that was exasperation at what one once mistakenly would have called his mother's feminine logic: she had not helped him get his most valuable manor of Sporle out of a crippling mortgage, yet was considering not leaving him her property because he might have to 'late goo the maner off Sporle'.[7] Remember: she on John Paston I's death had carried off her five Mautby manors and Gresham, her jointure reducing the head of the family's total to a paltry five. It seems to me this silence is neither reticence nor stoicism but simply the well-observed fact, well-observed not only by anthropologists, that people do not talk about the obvious.

If there is an actual, that is an historical, model historians have in mind when discussing landed estates and their management it is that of the ecclesiastical corporation. But the monastic or cathedral estate was as unlike a secular estate, noble or gentle, as say a state collective farm was (or 'an agro-industrial centre' is) from that of a kulak. The fluidity of a family's property is what is most striking. I do not mean so much its acquisition by purchase or marriage, or its dispersal through sale, gift in exchange for prayers, or by failure of male heirs, important and insufficiently stressed as this sort of mobility is – land in the later Middle Ages was like the sea, always in motion – but its movement within the family, as we have seen in the case of the Pastons. Who had which manor when takes some finding out where they are concerned, as I expect it does for most secular estates even where account and court rolls survive. One of the consequences of such shifting landlordship – and landladyship – may have been that it was a lighter burden for tenants to bear because it could not be exerted so strenuously as when there was continuity of ownership. I say 'may have' because, on the one hand there are no estate documents to demonstrate it in the case of the Pastons, and on the other I am aware that there was frequently stable estate management where there was a rapid turnover of owners. Do not mistake me here: I am not thinking of the transfer of an estate from one family to another or a manor's decomposition among two or three heiresses, for evidence (not Paston evidence) suggests a new owner was often like a new broom: sweeping more cleanly in obvious areas, reaching into parts other brooms recently had not. At Haveringland in Norfolk, for instance, in 1424/5 when Sir Henry Inglose, Sir John Fastolf's comrade in arms and principal councillor, bought the manor from the executors of Sir John Geney, a farm of £18 and woodsales of £4 (in 1419/20) were turned into cash liveries of £41 and woodsales of £23; the sale of wool also fetched £23. The situation did not last. Nor did the rigorous accounting procedures. Which was cause; which effect?[8] No, it is the chopping and changing within a family, or rather among the members of allied families, which might have made an impact on rent rolls.

Take the Mautby manor of Kirkhall in Salle, for example, which, when it returned to the main stem of the family, in the person of Margaret Paston, in 1479, she leased out. The lease, along with other Kirkhall estate documents, escaped the eighteenth-century destruction of such unromantic but combustible material (at least ten boxes full at Oxnead in 1735[9]), because Sir William Paston had sold Kirkhall in 1643.[10] The history of Kirkhall between the death of Margaret's grandfather Robert Mautby in 1418 and her inheritance of it in 1479 is after this fashion.[11] Eleanor, Robert's widow, held it and other Mautby manors to maintain herself, Robert's four younger sons, and his daughter. When the boys reached twenty-one each was to have a manor for life and as each died his manor was to descend to the surviving brothers – a tontine in which the survivor was to have all. So it was, but only eventually. Robert's eldest son John, Margaret's father, died fairly young in 1433 leaving a widow and the twelve-year-old Margaret. There were now two Mautby widows (both remarried) to be dowered and a granddaughter to be provided for. Such a situation was tailor-made for Judge William Paston: he stepped in to sort everything out and to claim the heiress for his son. On paper, halves and thirds of manors feature, and whatever happened to other Mautby manors, Eleanor Chambre, as she had been since 1422, took a third of the revenues of Kirkhall until she died in 1444 or 1445. The other two-thirds ought to have been Walter Mautby's, but he (and another brother, Peter) were dead by September 1442 when the two remaining brothers, Thomas and Edward, made an agreement with John and Margaret Paston, who had had their first son the previous April. Probably, though it is not certain, the final surviving brother, Edward, who died in 1479, got Kirkhall: two-thirds in 1442, the whole in 1445. Yet, if between 1428 and 1433 it was John Mautby who actually received half the revenues of Kirkhall (and Eleanor Chambre the other half), was it actually Edward who got two-thirds of them between 1433 and 1445? I expect it was, but (as you can see) it is hard to tell. Moreover, Edward was an absentee landlord: he lived in London. He had a receiver at Kirkhall but his niece Margaret kept an eye on things for him there.[12] Edward's London wife made shirts for Sir John Paston in the 1470s; to that cosmopolitan courtier his aunt Maud appeared a *bürgerliche Hausfrau* and he wrote in a very superior tone to his mother about her after Edward's death.[13] Margaret, none the less, gave her a six mark annuity out of Kirkhall, between a fourth and a fifth of what the joint property of Kirkhall-Briston was clearly worth: to that degree, therefore, the Pastons still did not have all of Kirkhall forty years after John had married Margaret for it.

This has been confusing. It has not been my intention to make Kirkhall's history simple, because it was not. It may be argued that the difficulties arise only out of the evidence; at the time everyone knew exactly where the silver ought to go. So it should be argued, as I am sure that, so far as the landlord and his agents were concerned, this was very much the case. It is my case, however, that the amount of silver they collected may have been reduced by the discontinuity (and division) of lordship: four Mautbys, at least, in thirty years. Arrears, apparently *the* problem of fifteenth-century estate administrators, had greater opportunity of faster growth under such conditions. There must have been intervals and gaps in rent collection; for instance, John Mautby died in 1433 and it was not until 1435 that, with the intervention of Judge William Paston, an agreement was reached by all those with an interest in his lands. I have to hypothesize, for this possible contribution to the hazards of estate management at an unfavourable time for landlords cannot be distinguished from others, long term and short, particular and general. The net annual value of Kirkhall (with Briston) was more often below £20 than it was above it before 1470; during the 1470s the reverse appears to be the case. Then, in 1480, Margaret leased it to Thomas Brigg, gentleman, who owned two other manors in Salle, for a 'mere' £18,[14] and may have continued to pay Maud Mautby's annuity of £4. The profit (*profectus*) of Kirkhall was sometimes recorded at the foot of the annual account. It is difficult to grasp now how it was arrived at. The Kirkhall accountant knew; so did Thomas Gnateshall, an estate officer of Margaret's who was the 'eye' she kept on Kirkhall in the 1450s:

> I have ben att Salle and enqueryd ther, and my Mayster Edward is clerly answeryd of xviij li. be yere and more vij or viij s., and so hath it be thes iiij yere, and all the londys leton ther. As for Bryston, Thyrnyng, and Owleton, as I am enformyd, leton also, the wheche are perteynyng to the seyd maner of Salle, etc. And so is he clerly answeryd yerly att ij termys in the yere, withowte ony costys or expensys att London, as it is seyd beforn, besyde the fees, that is to seye the receyvour xxvj s. viij d., the styward xx s., and the baly xxvj s. viij d., and all here costys.[15]

Yet, did they know, could they know anymore than we do, whether the revenues of Kirkhall had fallen because the changes of lord and lady over sixty years had made the running of the property less than smooth? They may not have cared; nor may it have occurred to them to care. That was my original point: most enterprises do not run smoothly and everyone except historians expects them not to. We are chasing a chimera if we believe landlords, any more than leaders of commerce, government ministers, or vice-chancellors, manage other than on a day-to-day, hand-to-mouth principle. In that sense it may be said fifteenth-century landlords did not know what they were doing. Certainly they did not know where they were going; but that is an unfair comment, as forward planning, if the phrase is anything more than propaganda, was not a medieval concept save eschatologically.

There was more than their fragmentation which made rent collection on the Paston estates a tiresome, troublesome, and close to unrewarding business. For example, when ownership was in contention competitive rent-collecting ensued. This occurred at Gresham in 1448/9 when Robert Hungerford, Lord Moleyns, claimed the estate,[16] at Marlingford and elsewhere in the 1480s when John Paston III and his uncle William were in expensive conflict over the estates Agnes had held between 1444 and her death in 1479,[17] and most dramatically (and famously) at the ex-Fastolf manors of Drayton and Hellesdon near Norwich and Cotton in Suffolk in the 1460s when Fastolf's other executors challenged John Paston's possession. Such competition led to tit-for-tat distraints of the animals of tenants and farmers. At Drayton in 1465 the Duke of Suffolk's bailiff confiscated a Paston loyalist's plough-horse; the Pastons countered by taking two plough-horses and the plough of a tenant who was thick with the Suffolk party; that party retaliated by carrying off two of the parson's plough-horses and a plough of a tenant.[18] The foldcourse sheep flocks at Drayton and Hellesdon and the tenants' cattle at Drayton were also on the move: first distrained, then repleved.[19] What was the cost of this and to whom? The husbandry of the tenants was undoubtedly interrupted: beasts driven away, barn doors sealed, ploughing delayed, fields unsown.[20] When, in January 1469, 'in the grey mornyng iii men of my lord of Norffolk . . . with longe sperys' took away three horses of the Titchwell farmer, William Cotting, the humane rector of nearby Brancaster who twenty-five years before had been a youthful clerk of Judge William Paston's, was in no doubt of the harm done: 'Thise pouere fermores are liche to be undo; wherfore atte vertu of God sende tidynges in hast what we shall do [he wrote to Richard Calle], for swiche an opyn wrong unremedied knew I never, ne good and trewe men so unkyndely vexed.' William ended his letter with the home truth for landlords who found themselves in such a situation: 'And ye helpe not this matier I holde a man more than wood [mad] that wolde outher hold lond of yow or do for yow.'[21] In 'normal' circumstances landlords, including the Pastons, frequently used the threat of distraint, or distraint itself, to coerce tenants and farmers to pay arrears; when landlords were at war with one another they used distraint as a conventional weapon. Tenants confronted by household ruffians with 'longe sperys' were constrained to pay, as they did at Cotton in 1461; Richard Calle reported that William Jenny had collected more than £24, 'for the tenauntes myght not cheese but they moste nedes paye, for they distreyned on my lordes of Suffolk fee, my lordes of Norwich fee, and on all men grounde so that they myght not have her catell in reste, weche cauced hem to pay her money. I knowe weele j-nough who payed and wo paied not. All the grete fermours have payed.'[22] Violence against tenants themselves was unusual, although the Sporle tenants once wrote to Sir John Paston that they had been manhandled and that 'our servauntys wer bete at the plowe in Sporle felde, and somme of then be lyke to dey . . . we arn grevously troubled and not lyke to kepe oure tenourys the whiche we holde of you but yf ye helpe us',[23] and once, returning from Yarmouth, Margaret's Mautby farmer was shot at by the Duke of Norfolk's desperadoes who were occupying Caister – though their shooting sounds as if it were more sporty than serious.[24]

As the Pastons' troubles over property rights were only an extreme case of what was commonplace throughout England, we are not dealing with a side issue. While there had to be winners and losers among landlords, or rather while most landowners won some and lost some, were tenants and farmers always losers, or rather were they losers at all? We have noticed that there is ample evidence for the temporary dislocation of their husbandry; there is no evidence, however, that they paid twice on a disputed manor. I presume they might have been turned out for non-payment of rent by the party to whom they had not paid, as Richard Calle once suggested Titchwell farmers who were paying their rents to William Yelverton should be replaced by 'other folkes',[25] but in mid-fifteenth century England and in such a situation, were replacements likely to be found? As we have heard William Cotting explain: if a landlord did not stick up for his tenants he was likely to lose those he had and deter others from coming forward – as happened at Titchwell.[26] Turning tenants or farmers out who did not pay their rents was, even in ordinary circumstances, a very last resort. What seems to have happened on a disputed estate was for the tenantry to split: each contesting lord got some rents until the conflict simmered down, while during an impending arbitration rents were paid to a third party. Farmers and tenants who were behindhand when a property dispute was 'settled' were not to be threatened, Henry Heydon advised John Paston III after the ten- or twelve-year war between him and William Paston had been concluded: they had only to be 'warned kurtesly'.[27]

That indeed is the heart of the matter in the fifteenth century, in Norfolk, where the Pastons are concerned: farmers and tenants, being so hard to come by or playing so hard to get, had to be decently treated; the landlord had 'to gett in fayernesse', as Henry Heydon phrased it. To establish this commonplace one needs only to read Richard Calle's letters to John Paston between 1460 and 1465,[28] and those of other Paston servants (and friends) who worked but less single-mindedly as rent collectors, stewards, and overseers: James Gloys, John Russe, William Barker, Thomas Gnateshall, William Cotting, and numerous other rural vicars.[29] I urge this course upon you. Here I will draw your attention to two aspects of the landlord–tenant relationship: the importance attached to getting and keeping a farmer, that is a good farmer, and the extended negotiation and bargaining required to get one. Here is Richard Calle on Robert Cole of Bessingham:

> Item, William Smythe shal occupie hes ferme this yere [of Bess-ingham], and Croumer; and as for the yeres aftre, I have founde a meane that all your londes schall be letten as weele as ever they weere in that maner [Bessingham], with helpe of on Robert Coole, weche Robert fereth hym sore of the affence weche he ded a-yenst John Herlyng; for he is informed that your maistreschip hath taken an axion a-yenst hym . . . Wherfore that it like you to withdrawe if any axion ye have a-yenst hym, for he will abide any ij men award ther-aboute; and more-over he is the moost able man to take a ferme of lond that I knowe in your lordeschip, and he schal be a gret fermour of youre the next yere.[30]

Here also is Agnes to John on farmer Gurney at Holwellbury:

> Item, as for Holwelbury I sende you a bill of all the reseytes syn the deth of youre fadere, and a copy wrete on the bak how youre fader lete it to ferme to the seide Gurnay. I wulde ye shulde write Gurnay and charge him to mete wyth you fro London warde, and at the lest weye lete him purveye x li., for owyth be my reknyng at Myhelmesse last passed, be-syde youre faderes dette, xviij li. xiiijs. viijd. If ye wolde write to him to brynge suerte bothe for youre faderys dette and myn, and pay be dayes so that the man myte leven and paye us, I wolde for-geve him of the olde arrerages x li., and he myte be mad to paye xx marc. be yere. On that condicion I wolde for-geven him x li., and so thynketh me he shulde han cause to preye for youre fader and me . . . I fele be Roberd his wif is right loth to gon thens; she seide that sche had lever I shulde have all here gode after here day than their schulde go out there-of.[31]

Alas, the compromise failed; a few months later Agnes wrote: 'speke sadly for j another farmer'.[32] As for bargaining with prospective tenants, John

Paston III writing to his father about former Fastolf property at Earlham provides an admirable illustration:

Plesyt yow to have knowlage that I have spoke wyth Warwyk and Stwkle fore the plase and the londys in Arleham, and they wyle not geve but vjd. for an acre, and they to kepe the reparacion of the plase; but so I wold not lete heme have it. But Stwkle hathe promysyd me that all the londys schalle be purveyd for as for thys yer. Warwyk was wyth my modyr as thys day, and he desyiryth to have the londys in Arleham for vij d. an acre as for thys yer. And in as myche as Stwkle had promysyd me to purvey for the londys for thys yer, I cownselyd my moder that he schuld not have heme wyth-owt he wold tak hem for a longer terme. As for Kook, he wole no lenger hold the plase and the xviij acrys nowthyr for vij nor viij d. an acr and to kepe the reparacion of the plase. He wole geve but vj d. for an acr, and he to kepe the reparacion of the plase; and yet he wole not be bownde to repare the plase. And so he wole no lenger have it but he may have it for vj d. [33]

The three elements of a lease are present here: cash rent, term of years, and maintenance. [34] To juggle these to everyone's satisfaction was a form of art as skilful as that exercised by W.C. Fields.

While it is clear that in East Anglia, as elsewhere in fifteenth-century England, it was farmers and tenants who had the upper hand, there was also, as there was bound to be, a good deal of variation from place to place, and from person to person. Cromer, like Bessingham, was a place where lands were successfully let, although in 1453 there was a problem which William Reynolds, Agnes's bailiff there, explained to her:

I have late a place of youre in quiche John Rycheman duellyd, for it stode at a grete dyspeyre; and I have late it for xv s., but up youre good grace, for the lockes of the dores arn pulled of and born a-waye, and the wyndowes ben broken and gone and other bordys ben nayled on in the stede of the sayd wyndowes. Also the swynysty ys doun and all the tymbyr and thacche born a-way. Also the hedge ys broken and born a-wey quiche closed the gardeyn, querethorgh the place ys evyl apeyred to the tenaunt. On Sent Marckes Daye I entred the seid place and lete it to youre Ge-hove, and on the day after cam Henre Goneld and seyd my latyng schald not stond, and went and seled the dores; querfore I beseche youre graciows favore that my latyng may stond, for I have late alle youre londes everychon. I know not oon rode unlate, but alle ocupyed to youre profyghte. The tenaunt quich by youre lycens schuld have youre place to ferme by my latyng ys gretely be-hated with oon Johane the wyfe of Robert Iclyngham, chapman, quich ys voysed for a mysse governyd woman of hyr body by the most parte of owre town wel recordyth the same, and sche duellyth al by youre seyd plase. And by-cause this seid tenaunt ys gretely a-gens hire for hire ungoodly governaunce, therfor sche mad menys to on Abraham Whal, quiche ys on of hire supportores, and he hath spoke with the seyd Henre Gonelde that he myght seke a remedy to cause this seyd tenaunt to be a-voydyd and kept oute youre seid place and not come ther-inne.[35]

Sex, politics, and religion (as well as administrative inefficiency)[36] all had a role to play in the landlord–tenant relationship. Here is politics:

And as for gadyryng of mony [Margaret wrote to John in January 1462, when local as well as central politics were in a queasy state] I sey nevyr a werse seson, for Rychard Calle seyth he can get but lytyll in substans of that is owyng, nowthyr of yowyr lyvelod nor of Fastolfys. And John Paston seyth they that may pay best, they pay werst. They fare as thow they hopyd to have a newe werd [world].[37]

And here is religion (and marriage as well):

Please it you to wete [James Gloys wrote to Sir John Paston on 10 November 1466] that I was at Snaylwell on Sonday last past, and it fortuned so that the most part of your tenauntes wern ought, summe at Caunterbery and summe at othere places at mariages, and of them that wern at home I asked mony in your name.[38]

James Gloys in this illuminating letter goes on to offer the new head of the family some advice. He and Richard Calle were to be at Snailwell again in ten days time,

to take a direccion for the ferme and to set in a fermour, for there is a thrifty man wuld have it that dwellith be-syde Bery, and he shall be there the same day to have an answere there-of and to take it if so be that ye wull lete hym have it worth the mony and that he may leve thereon. All the town seth that it hath un-don the fermour that had it last; therefore telle Calle how ye wull do in the matere and lete hym be there at that day . . . And lete your lond that your fermour may leve and pay you, and than shall your lordshepes ben good and your lond wele teled; and if ye undo your tenauntes with over-charging of your fermes it shall distroy your tenauntes and lordshepes.

The caution to treat one's tenants well is familiar from some well-known sixteenth-century examples,[39] when landlordly restraint was, one supposes, less common because less required by economic circumstance. In the fifteenth century it was essential. After all, if arable was not let, it soon lost its condition and its value; Richard Calle makes this point:

> as for the ferme that Cheseman had in Boyton, that is to sey xl acre lond erable, j medwe, and other smale parcelles, payng yerly for it iiij li., weche I can not lete the xl acre lond a-bowe xl comb barly or xls., and ye to bere al charges of the reparaucion and fense aboute the place, weche shulde be gret cost. The londe is so out of tylthe that a-nedes any man wol geve any thyng for it. Ther can no man lete it to the walwe that it was lete be-fore.[40]

It was Margaret Paston who was most articulate on the need to treat tenants with consideration; in her case, I think, there was more than self-interest in her concern; she told her eldest son in 1470 when they thought they had seen off the bad years: 'your lyffelod hath stond this ij yere in such trobill that ye myght right nought have of it, ner yet can take of it wyth-ought ye shuld hurt your tenauntes. Thei have so ben vexid be on-trewe meanes be-fore this tyme.'[41] Was she indicting her dead husband, who was keener to impose obligations[42] on farmers and tenants to pay than, possibly, she thought proper? Perhaps he had not responded to her plea to him in 1465:

> ther be dyvers of your tenauntrys at Mauteby that had gret ned for to be reparyd, but the tenauntys be so pore that they are not a power to repare hem; wherfor yf it leke you I wold that the marche that Bryge had myght be kept in your owne hand this yer, that the tenauntys myght have ruschys to repare wyth her howsys. And also ther is wyndfall wod at the maner that is of noo gret valewe, that myght helpe hem wyth to-ward the reparacion yf it leke you to late hem have it that hathe most need therof.[43]

It was Margaret who remembered in her will all her tenants: every household on her estates and in the Paston parish of St Peter Hungate in Norwich was to have 4d., 6d., 8d., or, at Mautby itself, a shilling.[44]

Mautby was not like Cromer or Bessingham: it was not easy to lease successfully. Margaret, in an oft-quoted passage, thought she might be compelled to take it 'in myn owyn hand and to set up husbondry ther, and how it shall profite me God knowyth. The fermour owyth me lxxx li. and more; whan I shall have it I wote never.'[45] Demesne farming for the Pastons was a desperate expedient. I know of no estate where they kept a demesne farm; even Paston itself Judge William leased out.[46] The Mautby farmer's arrears were exceptional; yet as Mautby was worth not less than £20 a year he was no more than four years behindhand. Four years, in other words, was exceptional: panic measures were to be contemplated. Almost all other Paston farmers and many of their tenants were in arrears; my impression, however, is that collection was on the basis of a year's grace: Sir John Paston wrote of 'the olde arreragys ore ellys off the last yere', for example.[47] At Titchwell the farmer, Simon Miller, was fully paid up at Midsummer 1464 and had adequate excuses for his failure to pay the 19s. 10d. lacking from his farm of £10.[48] None the less, most letters dealing with the collection of rents are gloomy, if not positively doom-laden, and William Paston's memorandum on rent collection of August 1477 had as many entries of 'Sele doris and distrayne' as 'Gadir the rente' or 'Aske the ferme'.[49] 'As for mony, it cometh slauly jn' is a constant refrain,[50] but I do not detect desperation, other than in Margaret's letter about Mautby and possibly in some of Sir John Paston's letters of the early 1470s (and then, particularly to his mother, I discern him writing for effect). In this agriculturally rich and commercially prosperous region of England there were farmers – no doubt 'economically vigorous' ones[51] – and tenants to be found, drivers of hard bargains though they might be. And, after all, on the score of 'As touchyng any recept of monay, truly I can noon gete', while bearing in mind the century's chronic cash-flow problem,[52] even the avaricious (or should we say ambitious) John Paston in his London prison could break into verse to his wife:

Item, I shall telle yow a tale:
Pampyng and I have piked your male,
and taken out pesis v,
for upon trust of Calles promise we may sone onthryve.
And if Calle bryng us hedir xx li.,
ye shall have your peses ayen good and round;
or ellis if he woll not pay yow the valew of the peses there,
to the post do nayle his ere,
or ellis do hym some other sorough,
for I woll nomore in his defaut borough;
and but if the reseyvyng of my livelod be bettir plyed,
he shall Cristes curs and myn clene tryed.[53]

I have said the family had no demesne farm. They did, however, take rents in kind. These meat and grain rents were important, not only for household consumption (which is where the beef went),[54] but also, and this needs to be stressed, for sale – in Yarmouth and, particularly where Mautby and Caister malt was concerned, in London.[55] One grain-rent story, because it made the writer of it chuckle on paper, deserves repeating here; this is John Paston III to John Paston II in January 1467:

> Also I undyrstand by your lettyr sent to my modyr and me that ye wold have your lyvelod gadyrd as hastyly as we myght do it. Syr, as to that, and othyr folk do no wers ther dever in gaderyng of othyr manerys then we have don in Caster, I tryst to God that ye schall not be long unpayid; for thys day we had in the last comb of barly that eny man owyth in Caster towne, not wyth standyng Hew Awstyn and hys men hathe crakyd many a gret woord in the tym that it hathe ben in gaderyng. And twenty comb Hew Awstyns man had don cartyd, redy for to have led it to Yermowth, and when I herd ther-of I let slype a sertyn of whelpys, that gave the cart and the barly syche a torn that it was fayne to take covert in your bakhous systern at Caster Halle; and it was wet wyth-in an owyr aftyr that it cam hom, and is nye redy to make of good malt ale, ho ho. [56]

Many – most – other aspects of landlord–tenant relations are illustrated in the *Letters*: the far from trivial issue of bond tenure, for example. The Pastons themselves were charged with being of servile origin; the charge was, I believe, correct. Even if it was not, John Paston suffered in purse, property, and person. [57] Also, the issue of communal pasture rights under pressure is beautifully articulated in a letter of Elizabeth Clere; [58] and in a letter (the only surviving letter) of William Paston IV, this Cambridge undergraduate and his tutor listened to the Snailwell bailiff and farmer telling them 'that all the comun shuld a be takyn a-way butt for Master Cotton and the vecur of Fordan [Fordham]'. [59] The interest of the vicar of Fordham in the common rights of the Snailwell tenants raises a matter which I have no time for here: the social conscience of the parish clergy. [60] There are, I am sure, other matters relevant to our theme touched on in the *Letters*; one needs to be 'Funes, the Memorious' to register and unravel them all.

We should recall that John Paston was a second-generation landlord. His grandfather Clement had been a tenant, 'a good pleyn husbond'; Clement was a typical kulak, for he had 100 or 120 acres, married ambitiously, and sent his son to school. [61] I am uncertain whether it is the historical fashion to be sympathetic or antagonistic towards kulaks; it is always in fashion to be critical of landlords. With reason. The remarkable sequence of picky letters from John to Margaret in 1465 reveals a man similar to John Clare's unforgettable Farmer Saveall:

> And if twas but of worth we might suppose
> He'd even save the droppings of his nose.

But early nineteenth-century Northamptonshire was a long way, a world away, from fifteenth-century Norfolk, and John Paston is too complicated to be typecast, as his prison poem discloses. If, on the one hand, he did John Kendal of Filby out of 10 acres of arable for nine years,[62] on the other, he reduced John Herling of Bessingham's rent by an annual 5d.[63] Yet, is that the measure of the man: taking 16s. 8d., giving 5d.? I like to think so: nailing the unjust landlord is a religious duty. It is also a pleasure.[64] As it is to observe grain being stolen from the obsequious miller of Paston by his fellow tenants.[65] Such role reversal shows that the temper of the tenantry, as well as its economic position, was of the best: their spirits were high. I am not thinking here of friction between tenants or between tenants and farmers, largely unavoidable and therefore a constant of rural life,[66] but of tenants standing up for themselves against landlords. Christopher Dyer, notably among others, has enlightened us on this subject. At Paston we can put names to a couple of such bloody-minded fellows and their wives: Mr and Mrs Warin King and Mr and Mrs Warin Harman. The saga of road-diversion and wall-building at Paston by those jumped-up lords, the Pastons, and of the resistance of the Harmans and Kings to such gentrification deserves a Thomas Hardy to describe it. I have tried to do so elsewhere. Meanwhile read Agnes's four letters of 1451.[67] It epitomizes Warin Harman (and the fifteenth-century tenantry) to discover that in 1451 'he hath dayly fyshid hyre [Agnes's] watere all this yer'.[68] We are indeed a long way from John Clare's Helpston or George Sturt's Farnham; when a footpath was closed at Farnham, George Sturt wrote of 'that servility to wealth which is so conventional as to be almost unconscious in England'.[69] In fifteenth-century East Anglia Old Hodge was not Old Hodge yet. That is why I find it such an attractive place to work.

Notes

1   Norman Davis (ed.), *Paston Letters and Papers of the Fifteenth Century*, 2 vols. (Oxford, 1971–6), II, nos. 644, 645, 703.

2   See, for example, ibid. II, no. 650.

3   BL Add MS 27444, f. 103.

4   See the third chapter of my *The Paston Family in the Fifteenth Century: the first phase* (Cambridge, 1990).

5   'A ryche juelle yt ys at neede for all the cuntre yn tyme of werre', is what William Worcester considered Caister (Davis, II, p. 355).

6   Davis, I, p. 255.

7   Ibid., I, p. 466.

8   BL Add Chs 9333, 9335. This short series of manorial accounts (BL Add Chs 9327–9355) with a handful of letters from Sir Henry Inglose attached deserves closer study. I wish I could trace the whereabouts of the Bylney of Haveringland cartulary

(G.R.C. Davis, *Medieval Cartularies of Great Britain: a short catalogue* (London, 1958), no. 1,209) sold at Sotheby's in June 1965 to S. Crowe, bookseller, of Bloomsbury.

9 Davis, I, p. xxvi.

10 W.L.E. Parsons, *Salle* (1937), p. 8, citing Blomefield.

11 I have dealt with the Mautby marriage in chapter four of *The Paston Family in the Fifteenth Century*.

12 Davis, II, No. 730.

13 For the shirts, see Davis I, p. 351; for the snobbery, see Davis, I, p. 513: 'She is in many thyngys full lyke a wyffe off London and off Londone kyndenesse, and she woll needys take advise off Londonerys, wheche I telle here can nott advyse her howghe she scholde deele well wyth any body off worshyp.'

14 Davis, I, No. 229; *Salle*, pp. 10–14.

15 Davis, II, p. 337.

16 The troubles at Gresham feature in chapter two of *The Paston Family in the Fifteenth Century*.

17 For this debilitating dispute see ibid., pp. 195–207.

18 Davis, I, pp. 294, 295–6.

19 Ibid., I, pp. 297, 301–2, 304–5.

20 Ibid., I, pp. 286, 336, 664; II, p. 583.

21 Ibid., II, p. 571. For William Cotting as a clerk of Judge William's, see ibid., I, p. 627.

22 Ibid., II, p. 370.

23 Ibid., II, p. 411.

24 Ibid., I, p. 366.

25 Ibid., II, p. 299.

26 The 'no-go' conditions at Titchwell in 1470, when William Wainfleet received the estate for Magdalen College and (in this way) brought to an end the conflict there, are described by William Worcester (ibid., II, p. 583, cf. p. 585).

27 Ibid., II, p. 470.

28 Ibid., II, Nos. 614, 618, 632, 647, 649, 650, 653, 661, 669, 670, 678, 683, 685, 690.

29 The way in which all sorts of folk, including vicars, oversaw the running of the Paston estates is too large (and complex) a topic to deal with here. For vicar's 'estate' letters see, for instance, Davis II, nos. 470 (the vicar of Sporle); 488, 721, 903 (William Cotting); 731 (Thomas Hert, vicar of Stalham); and nos. 735 and 783 (the vicar of Paston). The informal nature of John Paston's administration is caught in his note to Margaret: 'Item, if on man may not attende to gader silver, sende a-nother' (ibid., I, p. 130, line 131).

30 Ibid., II, p. 223.

31 Ibid., I, p. 38.

32 Ibid., I, p. 39. William Cotting's attempt to persuade a man to take on the farm of Snailwell failed: the man knew all about the debts of the previous farmer and (besides) said he was going to retire: 'he seythe that he shall dwelle with his wyffes fader and fynden hym for his good as longe as he levyth, and he will no forther medill in the werde [world]' (ibid., II, pp. 81–2).

33 Ibid., I, p. 521.

34 Repairs were also the issue in Davis, I, p. 349. For terms and rents, see also John Paston II on Sporle in 1473 (ibid., I, pp. 470, 471).

35 Ibid., II, p. 17.

36 Ibid., I, p. 187: 'for I understond be jow that ther was no rent gaderid this xv ar xvj yer for deffawth off a rentall'. This was, I think, at Paston, as William Paston wanted Warin King [of Paston] to 'make the rentall be hart'. The date was 1479: the fifteen or sixteen years would take the inefficiency back to before the death of John Paston in 1466.

37 Ibid., I, p. 279. That certain rents were not at all 'economic' is shown by Davis, I, p. 27: 'And there is a man in Truntche hyght Palmere to, that hadde of vowre fadre [Judge William Paston] certein londe in Truntche on vij yere ore viij yere agoone for corn, and

trwli hathe paide all the yeris; and now he hathe suffrid the corne to ben withsette for viij s. of rentte to Gymmyngham, wich yowre fadre paide nevere. Geffreie axid Palmere why the rentte was notte axid in myn husbonddis tyme, and Palmere seyde, for he was a grete man and a wyse man of the lawe, and that was the cawse men wolde not axe hym the rentte.'

38 Ibid., II, p. 376. Sub-letting was a more serious hindrance to businesslike rent collection (ibid., I, p. 129, line 90; II, pp. 146–7).

39 I have in mind the striking passage on Sir John Gostwick of Willington in A.G. Dickens, *The English Reformation* (London, 1964), pp. 161–3; cf. idem, 'Estate and Household Management in Bedfordshire, *c.* 1540', *Publications of the Bedfordshire Historical Record Society*, XXXVI (1956), pp. 38–45.

40 Davis, II, p. 256. Richard wrote two months later (ibid., II, p. 261): 'Plese you that ye remembre the bill I sent you at Hallowmesse for the place and londes at Boyton weche Cheseman had in his ferme for v mark. Ther wol no man have it a-bove xlvj s. viij d. Alblastre and I have do as moche therto as we can, but we can not go a-bove that; and yet we can not lete it for this yere with-owte they have it for v or vj yere.'

41 Ibid., I, p. 356.

42 See, for example, the tough policy described in John Russe's letter of 1456 (ibid., II, no. 551), *but* (it must be said) this was on Sir John Fastolf's lands in the old man's lifetime.

43 Ibid., I, pp. 292–3.

44 Ibid., I, p. 385.

45 Ibid., I, p. 351.

46 The lease of 18 September 1422 is at the Norfolk Record Office: Phillipps MS 532; the accompanying inventory is Davis, I, no. 11 (Bodleian Library, Douce charters 18).

47 Davis, I, p. 413, lines 8–9. A two year cut-off point seems to be indicated in Davis, II, no. 922.

48 Ibid., II, p. 348 (cf. II, p. 299, lines 17–30; this dates William Cotting's No. 721 to 31 July 1464): 'Plese it yow to wete that I have receyved this day of Simond Miller, your fermour at Tichewell, ix li. ij d. for midsomer payment last passed, whiche I sende to yow . . . Ye shulde now have had x li., but the seid Symond hath paied to the fyndyng of a man to the Kyng for the toun of Tichewell v s., and ne had I ne be ye shulde have payed a marke. He hath payed also for rente vj s. viij d. He hath paied for other costes atte shreves turne and atte hundred for the seid maner xviij d., and he kepith stille vj s. viij d. for his gowne, whiche he is wont to take of this payment.' For prompt paying tenants, see also ibid., II. no. 673, lines 1–4.

49 Ibid., I, no. 98.

50 Ibid., I, p. 246, lines 19–20. See also: ibid., I, pp. 237, 346–7, 557, 558; II, pp. 327, 395, 412.

51 The phrase is Christopher Dyer's, *Warwickshire Farming, 1349–c. 1520. Preparations for Agricultural Revolution*, (Dugdale Society Occasional Papers, no. 27, 1981), p. 22.

52 N.J. Mayhew, 'The Monetary Background to the Yorkist Recoinage of 1464–1471', *British Numismatic Journal*, XI (1974), pp. 62–73.

53 Davis, I, p. 145.

54 Ibid., II, p. 258, lines 35–6.

55 Ibid., I, pp. 130, 142, 222, 292, 372, 375; II, no. 669 (which is wholly about the sale of malt), and pp. 306, 421, 423. It may be that the mouse-eaten wheat John Paston had at Mautby *c.* 1445 was from a demesne farm (ibid., II, pp. 26–7), but tenant rents at Mautby were in 'barly and greynes' (ibid., I, p. 142, lines 83–7). The Pastons had sheep in various foldcourses; the wool was sold locally (ibid., I, pp. 136, 259, 314; II, p. 359).

56 Ibid., I, p. 532; the 'ho ho' was a second thought (fn 3).

57 See *The Paston Family in the Fifteenth Century*, Chapter 1.

58 Davis, II, no. 500.

59 Ibid., I, p. 670. The problem was a long-standing one (ibid., II, p. 377, lines 35–43).

60 William Cotting was conscientious, even punctilious (ibid., II, no. 721, lines 13–16, 20). His will displays this trait particularly strongly (Norfolk Record Office, NCC Register A Caston, f. 244 (dated 26 April 1484 and proved 5 October 1485)). In Blomefield's day William's brass survived in the chancel at Brancaster; its inscription also shows the man, 'qui hic nunc pulvere dormit expectans adventum redemptoris sui' (F. Blomefield, *Topographical History of Norfolk* (Kersfield and Lynn, 1739–75), V, p. 1256). The vicar of Quinton, Warwickshire, was also (as we would now say) communally-minded. Dr Christopher Dyer has quoted from his letter of *c.* 1480 to the President of Magdalen College ('Deserted Medieval Villages in the West Midlands', *EcHR*, 2nd series XXXV (1982), p. 29) and has pointed out to me that the letter is printed in full by the Revd W. Denton, *England in the Fifteenth Century* (London, 1888), note D, pp. 318–20.

61 Davis, I, p. xli-ii.

62 Ibid., II, pp. 408–9.

63 Ibid., II, p. 353. John Herling's letter to Margaret is full of complaints, mainly about the wrongs done to him by other tenants at Bessingham; he and Robert Cole had been at loggerheads for sometime (ibid., II, p. 223).

64 To bring at least one gentleman to book see Tony Harrison's poem 'National Trust'.

65 Davis, II, no. 704.

66 See, for example, Davis, II, p. 367, note 63, and the early part of this paper.

67 Davis, I, nos. 21–4. My attempt to tell the story is in Chapter 1 of *The Paston Family in the Fifteenth Century*.

68 Davis, I, p. 244. For Warin Harman throwing his weight about, see ibid., I, p. 38, lines 7–9; for Warin King throwing his, ibid., II, p. 367.

69 Quoted by Jan Marsh, *Back to the Land. The Pastoral Impulse in Victorian England from 1880 to 1914* (1982), p. 61.

3

Coping with Uncertainty: Women's Tenure of Customary Land in England *c.* 1370–1430

Richard M. Smith
University of Oxford

Students of the manorial court, apt to use its proceedings for the investigation of social and economic conditions in the English countryside for the period after 1250 when these records first become widely available, have to date paid relatively limited attention to its development as a *curia*. Its links to other echelons within the wider legal system have been rarely studied with the intensity that students of landlord–tenant relations, peasant land markets and historical demography have heaped upon it. Recently there have been signs of a growing interest among social and legal historians in developments affecting the instruments at the disposal of manorial tenants on those occasions when they established their rights in, and publicly registered their transactions of, customary land.[1] This paper is largely concerned with the involvement of female tenants in those courts in the late fourteenth and early fifteenth centuries and represents an extension of previous work that focused on the period from *c.* 1250–1350.[2] Throughout this and the early study runs a desire to discover something of the material circumstances of women both within and outside of marriage. This particular interest is intensified by an awareness of a fundamental feature of Eurasian societies that Jack Goody has persistently emphasized – that property from conjugal estates devolved on both men and women through inheritance or pre-mortem endowment.[3] This awareness has come to influence the thoughts of a growing number of historians in their writings on various aspects of the political and economic consequences of property holding within all sections of society in the European Middle Ages.[4]

A number of changes in English manorial courts between *c.* 1250 and *c.* 1330 led to quite profound alterations in the way women functioned in those tribunals in matters concerning land. First, the clarification of the wife's acceptance of land transfers made by the husband during the course of the marriage was one noteworthy development on a number of manors that have been surveyed.[5] This change followed in the wake of the emergence under common law in the late twelfth century of the fine levied in the king's court by husband and wife as the essence of the process whereby the wife's land came to be conveyanced to a third party and her subsequent right of dower barred.[6] In the majority of the earliest manorial court rolls from the 1240s to 1270s no such regularity of procedure is detectable; land transactions are rarely recorded as being undertaken by conjugal pairs and no written record was preserved of the wife's attitude to such transactions that concerned land to which their rights in dower were attached. In the late thirteenth century some, and by the third decade of the fourteenth the majority, of manorial courts had adopted the practice of formal examination of the wife to establish her agreement to the sale or granting of land in which she and her husband had concurrent rights. A noticeable decline in pleas of dower seems to have been one result of this development and another was the increased frequency with which women were brought into view in the proceedings of the manorial court as formally recorded conjoint participation in land transfers grew in significance. Conjoint land transfers in a number of manors in southern and eastern England have been shown to have tripled or quadrupled in number in the fifty-year period between the last quarter of the thirteenth and the first quarter of the fourteenth centuries.[7]

Secondly, it has also been noted that at approximately the same time as jointure became a practice among the more substantial freeholders in the course of Edward I's reign it was also detectable among certain sections of the customary tenantry.[8] These devices frequently created a joint life tenancy for the donor (usually, but not invariably, the husband) and the donor's spouse, with provision for the remainders and reversions to a named child of the marriage or a more general provision for the heirs of the couple's bodies.[9] Less commonly encountered before the end of the fourteenth century were transactions that simply created a joint tenancy for the donor and the wife with no specific remainder clause.[10]

Another development that can in some places be documented from the earliest decade of the fourteenth century was the so-called 'deathbed transfer' which occurred when a tenant 'languishing near death' (*languens in extremis*) or 'on his deathbed' (*in mortali lecto*) gave specific instructions to a 'third party' who was sometimes a manorial officer (usually the reeve or bailiff) or other persons who were likely to be witnessed by other tenants, concerning the disposal of his landed assets following his death. At the subsequent court, the 'third party' was to ensure that the tenement was granted to the recipient by the process of 'surrender and admittance'. In effect, seigneurial interest in this procedure continued to be strong as the surrender and admittance ensured that the court roll entry concerning the transactions made it clear that the land was held, usually at the lord's will, and that seigneurial levies were taken. As a recent study concerned largely with the legal theory of this device has noted, the most distinctive feature of such transfers is that they occurred outside the court and seem to have been an acceptance of a villein's right to make an oral will relating to his or her customary property.[11] Indeed, unlike other *pre-mortem* arrangements for the transfer of property, they allowed an individual to delay the decision on the devolution of his property to almost the last possible moment and to avoid the operation of 'the custom of the manor', on the property of which the tenant was seised at death. It should be added that customary tenants, certainly from the 1290s, had employed the entail which allowed individuals to grant land to another or others and the heirs of the grantees' or grantors' bodies, which would in default of issue revert to the heirs general of the original grantors or donors.[12] While this might be used by an individual to fulfil very specific wishes with regard to the devolution of the property after his or her death and although remainder might go to the donee after the donor's death, thereby not depriving him of the enjoyment of the land in his own lifetime, it did not facilitate a 'change of heart'.

In jointure, entail and the deathbed transfer we can observe customary tenants by the close of the fourteenth century increasingly able to deploy devices which students of the later medieval nobility and gentry have come to regard as fundamental in any discussion of family strategies concerning both the provisions made by men for their wives and children and maintenance over the longer term of the integrity of the estate – two interests which were always potentially in conflict with each other.[13]

This paper is primarily concerned with the implications of these developments for women's participation in the various forms of land exchange that are encountered in manorial court proceedings in the sixty years from approximately 1370 to 1430. It cannot be stressed too greatly that the chronology depicting these changes may have been spatially uneven, with the earliest manifestations of all the devices mentioned above proving to be more distinctly associated with the Home Counties and East Anglia than central-southern, western and midland England. To date systematic work on the court rolls of the Midlands and the western counties of England directed specifically towards these issues has been limited and much research in the unpublished court rolls remains to be done before conclusions can be drawn with confidence.[14] By the late fourteenth century it has been suggested that jointure and examination were to be found in most regions, although our understanding of the deathbed transfer, which has only recently attracted the serious attention of social and legal historians, currently lacks any clear sense of its actual geographical extent in that period.[15]

Initially we will consider the proportional presence or frequency of women in the processes by which property was redistributed and how this might have changed by the early fifteenth century. It is possible to consider this matter in very simple terms by viewing the patterns displayed by a sample of land transactions that have been taken from the proceedings of seven manors – all located south and east of a line drawn from the Wash to the Thames valley. The more detailed samples relate to Redgrave, a manor of the Abbot of Bury St Edmunds in the extreme north of Suffolk, Barnet in Hertfordshire, which was a manor of the Abbot of St Albans, Winslow in Buckinghamshire and also within the estate of the Abbot of St Albans, Martham, a manor of Norwich Cathedral Priory, and the manor of Crictot Hall in Hevingham – both the last two mentioned being situated in east Norfolk. Two smaller samples confined to the first decade of the fifteenth century are taken from the manorial court proceedings of the manor of Great Waltham in central Essex and Holkham, Boroughhall, on the coast of north Norfolk – both lay manors.[16] The statistics presented in Table 1

Table 1
CUSTOMARY LAND TRANSFERS:
INTER-VIVOS AND POST-MORTEM

	Men both Parties	%	Women one Party	%	Husbands/ Wives together	%
Winslow						
1368–77	148	67.5	30	13.7	41	19.8
1422–33	151	60.0	42	16.8	57	23.2
Redgrave						
1368–77	85	42.9	63	31.8	47	25.3
1400–09	59	45.0	40	30.5	32	24.5
Barnet						
1372–81	67	57.3	24	20.5	26	22.2
1413–22	69	43.7	45	28.5	44	27.8
Gt. Waltham						
1400–09	53	49.1	33	30.6	20	20.3
Holkham						
1400–09	17	37.7	17	37.7	11	24.6
Martham						
1370–99	343	59.7	137	23.8	95	16.5
1403–38	231	58.3	63	15.9	102	25.8
Hevingham						
1382–1416	161	46.0	91	23.0	98	31.0
1425–1500	296	47.0	88	14.4	229	39.0

For sources see note 16

are by themselves rather coarse and potentially ambiguous in their meaning but they do show just how frequently by the early fifteenth century women were participating, whether passively or actively, in both *inter-vivos* and *post-mortem* land transfers. By that period, in only two manors did the proportion of land transfers involving males as both 'parties' approach 60 per cent. In the remaining five places 'all-male' transactions accounted for fewer than half of those which were registered concerning customary land. In one important respect there might seem to be an obvious explanation for these patterns, at least as they relate to the matter of inter-generational or *post-mortem* transfers; the demographic conditions that prevailed in the later fourteenth and early fifteenth centuries made it more likely that men would not have male offspring alive at their own death to serve as 'heirs'. In contrast, however, simple modelling reveals that under the more buoyant demographic conditions characteristic of the later thirteenth century it is likely that between 10 and 15 per cent of men would have had no surviving direct heirs whatsoever, 70–75 per cent would have had at least one son and of those without sons at least a further 13–15 per cent would have had a daughter.[17] At that time female opportunities to fulfil the role of heiress, while not wholly inconsequential, were somewhat limited.

With the demographic decline that can reasonably be supposed to distinguish the period extending through the late fourteenth and early fifteenth centuries more than 30 per cent of men would have been without surviving sons or daughters at their deaths and over 50 per cent of men would have reached the end of their lives without a son to receive the inheritance. However, four in every ten of those without a son would have had a daughter who could have been the beneficiary of the inheritance.[18]

Table 2
POST-MORTEM TRANSFERS (EXCLUDING HEVINGHAM)

	Deceased Males	%	Deceased Females	%	Both Sexes	%
Heir		%		%		%
Son(s)	104	50.2	39	38.2	143	46.3
Daughter(s)	27	13.0	15	14.7	42	13.7
Other Kin	37	17.9	25	24.5	62	20.0
No Heir	39	18.9	23	22.6	62	20.0
Total	207	100.0	102	100.0	309	100.0

For sources see note 16

In Table 2 we can observe that only 143 out of 309, or 46.3 per cent of *post-mortem* transfers in the sample, involved inheritance from parent to son; father-to-son transfers represent 50.2 per cent of inheritances when the deceased was a male, confirming the somewhat perilous state of that particular pathway. But it is also evident that daughters did not inherit in accordance with the opportunities theoretically available to them. This may well have been an important factor accounting for one in every fifth death yielding no heir whatsoever. A further 20 per cent of deaths involved inheritances by kin other than direct offspring of the deceased.

It would seem that access to property through inheritance channels that reflected the operation of the 'customs of the manor' was not the primary means by which women secured a significant influence upon the tenurial patterns of customary land in these manors. Consequently, it would seem that it was through *inter-vivos* transactions that their tenures were achieved. It is possible, indeed probable, that the distinction between *inter-vivos* and *post-mortem* transactions is over-drawn and far too categorical, for a further 137 individuals, overwhelmingly males, made 215 deathbed transfers in six of the manors, details of which are shown in Table 3. These transfers were directed primarily to kin although persons probably not immediately recognizable as close kin or kin of any kind were notable among the beneficiaries and accounted for 36 per cent of the recipients of property via such transfers.

Table 3

DEATHBED TRANSFERS (EXCLUDING HEVINGHAM)

	By Males	%	By Females	%	Both Sexes	%
Beneficiary		%		%		%
Widow	58	31.0	–	–	58	27.0
Widow (+son(s))	11	5.9	–	–	11	5.1
Widow (+other(s))	6	3.2	–	–	6	2.8
Son(s)	16	8.6	5	17.9	21	9.8
Daughter(s)	20	10.7	6	21.4	26	12.1
Other Kin	15	8.0	1	3.6	16	7.4
Unrelated(?)	61	32.6	16	57.1	77	35.8
Total	187	100.0	28	100.0	215	100.0

For sources see note 16

Deathbed grants to their wives accounted for 75 of the 187 (41.1 per cent) transfers made by males, although in 17 of these transfers the widow was a co-recipient with another person who was in only 11 of these instances a son. In only 21 cases (9.8 per cent of the total) are sons singled out by their father or mother as an immediate beneficiary of a deathbed transfer, which stands in marked contrast to their prominence as heirs when the parent died intestate and property descended according to the 'customs of the manor'. A very noticeable reluctance on the part of those making deathbed transfers to dispose of property to daughters is also apparent. In only 26 out of 215 instances (12.1 per cent) are daughters recorded as acquiring property in this way.

Younger women, whether married or spinsters, do not appear to have entered into property at moments in the cycle of their families of birth that were clearly associated with parental death. Yet widows were singled out most frequently by husbands as the beneficiaries of property that they 'willed' at this point in time. These transactions are especially interesting for in marginally more than half of the instances of this type of deathbed transfer the widow either held the property jointly with sons and other persons (thirteen) or had use of the property for her life with remainders to others (twenty-five instances). Sons were the most frequent recipients of these remainders (seventeen) and a daughter was mentioned as eventually to succeed to land temporarily under her mother's control in only one case. Sometimes persons who were either more distant kin or unrelated executors for the deceased person's will were listed as beneficiaries after the widow had died. Thirty-seven deathbed transfers were by the husband to the widow, who then possessed full powers over its subsequent disposal. The sizes of these deathbed transfers varied greatly in each case and the dimensions of the tenements are rendered in a form that makes a strict quantitative analysis difficult, if not wholly impossible. In the majority of those instances when the widow received this unqualified control there was no other deathbed transfer by her husband mentioning additional beneficiaries.

In a minority of instances it is possible for us to observe how complex the arrangements might become; this is especially apparent when the deathbed transfers can be observed alongside the evidence bearing upon testamentary devolution of chattels and the 'intestate' inheritance of property according to manorial custom that had not previously been redistributed.[19] For example, in one case from Winslow the relatively affluent virgator John Jankyn in 1430 gave half an acre of meadow to his widow Alice, and granted a further half an acre to his son William, to whom in 1423 he had given a virgate and messuage by 'surrender and admission'; the remainder of his estate, which included a virgate of land, a toft and a further half an acre, of which John Jankyn died seised, passed according to manorial custom to his son John, who paid the heriot of a horse valued at a mark.[20] In the proceedings of the same court John Jankyn's will had been enrolled. This specified that 6 bushels of grain were to go to his daughter-in-law, a further 2 bushels to his granddaughter Matilda. His sons, William and John, were made their father's executors.[21]

It is noteworthy that in the above case the widow received only a small grant of property as a result of the husband's deathbed transfer. In fact it equalled that given to Jankyn's son William, who was not the lawful heir according to manorial custom, although he had earlier received land amounting to half the area of his father's estate. His daughter-in-law received a bequest of grain, as did the granddaughter, but the bulk of the estate devolved to the 'customary' heir. A similar pattern of devolution seems to have characterized the 'estate plan' of Thomas Erl of Martham, who in the course of eight deathbed transfers made bequests amounting to almost 6 acres to ten different individuals, one of whom was his wife Katherine, who received just one acre; his two daughters, one of whom was married, received jointly a gift of 1 acre and 1 rod. In this case the majority of the deathbed transfers went to persons whose familial relations with Thomas appear not to have been close or indeed extant. Like John Jankyn, the bulk of Thomas Erl's property, 23 acres, passed by intestate inheritance to his son Robert.[22] We are unable in the case from Martham to establish whether a will was made or has survived and consequently we cannot establish whether bequests of moveables might have further benefited Erl's wife and daughters.

The pattern of transfers displayed by Erl is far from atypical. In the samples from Martham, Redgrave and Barnet it appears that of the ninety-six persons making at least one deathbed transfer, thirty-nine (40.4 per cent) also allowed part of their estate to devolve according to manorial custom to heirs who were in almost three-quarters of the cases their sons. In fact twenty-three (59 per cent) of these individuals allowed the greater part of the property in their possession at or close to their death to pass according to manorial custom. This is a feature consistent with the overall quantities of land devolving via deathbed transfers and intestate means in all six of the sample manors (see Table 4). It is, of course, impossible to obtain a precise measure of the relative importance of the two devices, owing to the failure of the court record to provide detailed measurements of plots that were often described somewhat imprecisely as 'toft', 'croft', 'pightle' or 'curtilage'. None the less, when measurements are given it would seem that, in the sample, marginally more than 25 per cent of the land acreage constituting post-obit transfers was made up of those directed by the deceased on his deathbed. This most likely represents an underestimate, for 33.5 per cent of deathbed transfers and only 17 per cent of *post-mortem* (intestate) transfers were lacking specific areal measurements.[23] We can perhaps be no more precise than to suggest that, in the manorial sample upon which this study is based, by the 1420s between one quarter and one third of customary land transferred at or close to the death of males was achieved through deathbed transfers.[24]

Table 4
QUANTITIES OF LAND (RODS) TRANSACTED
BY TYPE OF TRANSACTION

Recipients		Post-Mortem		Deathbed Transfer*		Inter-Vivos		
		Male	Female	Male	Female	Male	Female	Husband/ Wife
Winslow	1368-77	1126 (4)	708 (2)	134	10 (1)	2119 (41)	-	669 (13)
	1422-33	1748 (3)	128	337 (3)	340 (2)	2550 (30)	3 (2)	731 (16)
Redgrave	1368-77	91 (8)	37 (2)	15 (13)	8 (2)	199 (34)	76 (9)	78 (15)
	1400-09	128 (3)	160	74 (12)	115 (7)	92 (15)	-	136 (17)
Barnet	1372-81	172 (8)	52 (5)	20 (1)	12 (2)	364 (42)	40 (1)	24 (6)
	1413-22	190 (10)	12 (3)	143 (7)	267	226 (32)	44 (1)	252 (19)
Martham	1370-1402	871 (1)	354	109	198 (1)	855 (6)	62 (4)	190
	1403-1438	600 (1)	280 (1)	130	160	622 (1)	24	276
Waltham	1400-09	130 (1)	-	56 (4)	88 (3)	590 (20)	61	220 (5)
Holkham	1400-09	75	83	1	15 (1)	104 (1)	2	91 (2)

* The volume of land going to males by deathbed transfer includes that granted to widows with reversions to sons after the widow's death.

Note: Figures in parentheses relate to transactions whose area is difficult to estimate.

For sources see note 16

Statistics such as these might be interpreted to suggest that while widows may have been quite frequently chosen as beneficiaries of their husband's deathbed bequests of land, their shares were always quite strictly limited to small proportions of the total estates. Of the fourteen instances in this sample of widows receiving full powers of disposition of land they acquired by deathbed transfer concurrently with a son or sons who simultaneously inherited land according to the custom of the manor, only five appear to have obtained a majority share of the *post-mortem* inheritance, although the absence of any search through surviving will registers requires that caution is exercised in accepting this conclusion. In some cases the *de facto* situation may have emerged as more favourable for the widow than is implied by the husband's estate plan. For instance, in 1378 in Martham,

William Blakeman on his deathbed transferred 1 acre and 3 rods to his wife Alice but 3 acres to Nicholas Curson and Nicholas Haldayn, who in the very same court transferred the 3 acres to Alice through a conventional surrender and admittance, although we do not know whether money passed between the parties.[25] In 1415 Thomas Pope of Barnet, as his dying wish, granted 8 acres of arable and woodland to his wife.[26] In a court held a few weeks later his death was reported and it was noted that he had died seised of an inn called the 'Swanne on the Hope', attached to which was a curtilage and a croft of 3 acres. A heriot was taken and it was confirmed that his heirs were unknown. At the same court Thomas's widow Joan, by then remarried to Alan Gaythorpe, entered the holding with her new husband. That holding had escheated to the lord abbot, from whom they held it for the duration of their lives. After their deaths the holding was to revert to the abbot as landlord.[27]

In considering all deathbed transfers to widows it would seem that the sizes of the property in cases when it was specifically stated that the land and buildings should revert at the widow's death to a named heir were larger than those which went to the widow granting her full powers of disposition. Of the 37 cases in the latter category, over two-thirds appear to have been 1 acre or less in area, whereas in excess of two-thirds of those in the former category exceeded 1 acre.

In some cases it is clear that fathers were striving to provision more than one son and in certain instances other persons who may or may not have been kin. John Hened of Barnet made four deathbed transfers in 1418, two to his widow Elena, who received a little over 4 acres of land (1 acre, 1 rod of which was to go on her death to their son Thomas and 3 acres to their son Richard).[28] John Hened also granted 3 acres to one Henry Bulshrawe and 1 rod to John Wendon.[29] In Redgrave in 1408 Walter Clark made deathbed transfers of a cottage to his daughter Isabel, a stall in the local market at Botulesdale to his son Thomas, a cottage in the market to one John Slawe and a messuage and stall in the market to be held by his widow Cristina which would on her death revert to Thomas and John.[30]

Differences of family composition might have had much bearing upon the social practices responsible for the under-representation of daughters as recipients of land at the moment of parental death. While sons, in cases in which the deceased father died 'intestate', were the principal beneficiaries (56.5 per cent of cases), this pattern would seem not to apply to those women whose deaths show the custom of the manor applying to the land of which they died seised (see Table 2). Kin other than offspring were more likely to inherit from women than men. Furthermore, escheats to the manorial lord because of the complete absence or in some cases reluctance or refusal of heirs to come forward were more frequently encountered among female than male death entries in this sample of manorial court proceedings. In fact inheritance by more distant kin and escheats accounts for 50 per cent of these cases and indicates that many of these women may have been in possession of property and consequently at risk to appear in the court record on their death either because they were widows of men who lacked sons or were spinsters. They were marginally more likely to have had daughters who inherited from them than were males, although the differences with samples of this size may not be statistically significant. The very small number of females who made deathbed transfers (twenty-eight) in three-quarters of the cases 'willed' their land to persons who were possibly distant kin or more likely neighbours and who were also more frequently found to be female than in the deathbed transfers made by males.

A feature worthy of more detailed attention than is possible in this present discussion concerns the women whose deathbed transfers involved a gift and a request to executors to sell all the property that they possessed for the benefit of their soul.[31] Katherine Neweman of Barnet exemplifies such behaviour when in 1419, *jacens in extremis* she granted her cottage and its attached curtilage to her executors John Lyons and Richard Bosiler so that it could be sold for the sake of her soul and the benefit of the Chapel of St John the Baptist.[32] Isabel Sexteyn of Redgrave in 1400, on her deathbed, out of court and through the auspices of Adam Ode and witnessed by Robert Murgate, John Norton and Thomas Nase and others of the homage, willed that her cottage and curtilage should be sold and the money used for the benefit of her soul and that of her late husband John Sexteyn.[33]

It is a striking feature of these cases that there is little concern to benefit more distant kin (nieces, nephews etc.) but rather to focus attention on those pious bequests with spiritual benefits for the widow herself and/or her late spouse. Even in those cases where the deathbed instructions are apparently indicative of a more complex familial situation we find the deathbed grants directed to a narrow range of kin. For instance, Ralph Wengrave of Winslow in 1433 also on his deathbed gave his wife Emma a croft of half an acre and granted her the substantial rump of his property containing a messuage with its adjacent land of 2 acres, a toft, half a virgate, a cottage and 2 acres, another messuage and 2 acres, and 20 acres along with $1\frac{1}{2}$ acres of meadow until her son John came of age. He also specified that if John were to die then the property was to go to Joan his eldest daughter, who, if she died, was to be succeeded by Joan his youngest daughter, who, in her turn, was to be succeeded by Emma, the widow, if by then she was still alive. If Emma should outlive the specified heirs then she or her executors were instructed to see that the property at her death was sold for the benefit of the souls of Ralph and his family.[34] Essentially similar principles of confining kin recognition to spouse and immediate offspring distinguish the actions of the much more humble tenant of the Abbot of Bury St Edmunds, Robert Littlebury of Redgrave, whose cottage and its adjacent curtilage he granted in 1404 to Matilda, his widow, and after her death to John, their son. However, if he were to die before Matilda, she was to arrange to have the property sold at her death for the benefit of his and her own souls.[35]

The creation of specific provision for the wife by the dying husband might be thought to have been unnecessary if it can be assumed that her customary dower right would have applied. Or was it that the deathbed transfer served to downgrade the importance of dower among the customary tenants of the later fourteenth and early fifteenth centuries? For instance, in the case of John Jankyn of Winslow considered above we know nothing of any dower provision for his widow in the land that passed according to manorial custom to his son John. In another particularly revealing case from Barnet in 1424 concerning Henry Mudsprot, a customary tenant with a substantial property in the market at Chipping Barnet, we can see how the deathbed transfer to his wife of a messuage, shop and curtilage with 8 acres, from which (unusually) a horse was taken as heriot, was made by the husband on the condition that she did not claim her dower on any of his lands. If she did, the land was to be sold by the executors and the money so raised was to be used to the benefit of Henry's soul. There is no mention of other heirs in this case and the very substantial remainder of Henry's property, four messuages, one with a garden attached, three with curtilages and crofts and six shops on which a heriot of two two horses valued at two marks was taken was to be sold by his executors, John Lyons and Hugh Langeford, for the benefit of his soul.[36]

Right to dower, if applied, we know to have been one third in Winslow and Barnet, one half in Redgrave and the whole of the late husband's land as free bench at Waltham. It would, however, be unwise to treat such rights as automatic and customary in all cases. The court proceedings of these manors are certainly not devoid in the late fourteenth and early fifteenth centuries of entries specifying the widow's dower right, although this tends to be mentioned in the context of a record of rights attaching to land in gifts or sales such as when in 1373 William atte Dane of Barnet and Joan, his wife, having been formally examined, transferred to Richard Kymbell a third part of 3 acres which had been Joan's dower through her previous marriage to one John Gyrder.[37]

How, we may ask, did deathbed transfers co-exist, if at all, with dower rights? Our evidence, such as that revealed in the case of Henry Mudsprot mentioned earlier, seems to indicate that dower was effectively displaced as a customary right and that the grant by the dying husband may have served as a substitute or alternative. A first reading of a case from Barnet in 1379 might suggest such an interpretation as very wayward indeed. The case concerned Cristiana, wife of John Nicol, who was able to retrieve one third of the property that her husband had previously granted *in vita sua* to his four daughters and to Richard Nicol.[38] However, it seems that the dower plaint initiated by Cristiana was successful because these extra-curial grants were not made on John's deathbed nor was formal examination of the wife undertaken.[39] The evidence from the deathbed transfers suggests that wives were treated equitably by their husbands as part of the overall provision they made for their children, or specifically their sons when they had survived. We have seen that in certain instances, as a consequence of deathbed transfers by their husband, wives had possession of the whole holding rather than a third or a half which would have been her share under her customary rights. In a far from inconsequential share of these grants quite frequently the widow's rights were not restricted by any lifetime interest or remainders to children. It would seem too that in many, perhaps the majority, of these deathbed transfers to wives heriot was not taken, which would have been particularly valuable to small-holders, thereby limiting capital depreciation of the holding and erosion of its total assets.[40]

There is, of course, a danger in exaggerating the incidence of these arrangements and their quantitative importance in determining the amount of property actually held by widows on these manors in the period from 1370 to 1430. We should, however, note that they grew sharply in importance after 1400 when, as we have suggested above, they most likely accounted for at least a third of the land that devolved in association with deaths of customary tenants. Only further research will reveal whether their incidence continued to grow over the course of the fifteenth century and whether the principal beneficiaries continued to be widows.

Another set of developments may have been far more important in undermining the importance of dower and this had already made an impact as early as the late thirteenth century, although it was to become a much more important influence in and after the last two decades of the fourteenth century in the manors in this sample. But before this issue is considered it is appropriate to give some attention to influences that bear upon the transfer of property by married couples utilizing the procedure of 'surrender and admission'.

There are clearly visible signs that married women were increasingly to be found participating in *inter-vivos* transactions achieved by the procedure of surrender and admission in those manors that adopted a system of formal examination of the wife in the early fourteenth century. An investigation of 5,512 'parties' in *inter-vivos* land transactions on the manor of Redgrave between 1260 and 1319 revealed 618 (approximately

11 per cent) to have been conjugal pairs.[41] In addition, Carolyn Clarke discovered that on the manor of Chesterton, close by the city of Cambridge, 606 of the 6,334 parties in land transactions between 1277 and 1325 were undertaken by husband and wife pairs (approximately 9–10 per cent).[42] Judith Bennett's sample of the court proceedings of the crown manor of Brigstock – a forest community in Northamptonshire – shows approximately 8 per cent of what she terms the 'actors' in a sample of land transactions taken for the years 1301–45 were married couples.[43] We cannot be precise about the ways that the clarification of the woman's right in the matter of her dower claim may have served to intensify the exchange of property in which an individual's rights were more securely specified. But it was striking that the adoption of formal exmaination and a growth in the turnover of land through *inter-vivos* transfers moved in tandem. Disentangling what were the causes and effects in these matters is, however, by no means straightforward.

Redgrave is the only one of the manors in this sample studied in detail in the early decades of the fourteenth century for which we can currently observe the pattern of women's land transfers in a period one century later. At Redgrave between 1368 and 1377 20 per cent of the 205 parties in *inter-vivos* transfers were married couples, increasing to 34 per cent between 1400 and 1410 (see Table 5). In the manor of Winslow in the ten-year period after and including 1368 11.0 per cent of parties were husbands with their wives, rising to 21.6 per cent between 1422 and 1435. In Barnet the proportion of all parties who were married couples increased from 15 per cent in the years 1372–81 to 31 per cent from 1413 to 1422. The proportions for Waltham and Holkham in the first decade of the fifteenth century were 20 and 31 per cent respectively. On the two east Norfolk manors in this sample growth in the frequency of conjugal pairs as parties in land transactions was less impressive but in both places by the early fifteenth century one in five of all parties in *inter-vivos* transfers were married couples.

The proportional significance of married couples participating in land transactions by the means of surrender and admission had certainly risen by two- to threefold in Redgrave over the fourteenth century and the rate of change seems to have been particularly rapid at the beginning of the fifteenth century. The pattern detectable in the seven-manor sample suggests that by the early fifteenth century between one in five and one in three of the parties in *inter-vivos* land exchanges were married couples. If the incidence of such transfers had been as in Redgrave in the late thirteenth century, when only one in ten or one in twelve transfers involved married couples, then the changes that had taken place by 1420 were indeed very great.

It is reasonably clear that in the majority of places so far studied in the

Table 5
'PARTIES' IN *INTER-VIVOS* LAND TRANSFERS

	All Parties	Husband/Wife Parties	%
Winslow			
1368-77	354	39	11.0
1422-33	352	76	21.6
Redgrave			
1368-77	205	42	20.5
1400-09	130	45	34.6
Barnet			
1372-81	139	22	15.8
1413-22	173	54	31.2
Great Waltham			
1400-09	130	26	20.0
Holkham			
1400-09	58	18	31.0
Martham			
1370-1399	870	110	12.6
1403-1438	596	108	18.1
Hevingham			
1382-1416	554	107	19.3
1425-1500	1156	251	21.7

For sources see note 16

early fourteenth century couples acting as donors, grantors or sellers of land greatly exceeded in number those couples who received property in the ratio of between three and four to one. In the case of Redgrave in the period 1295–1319, 72 per cent of the conjoint transactions involved married couples acting as grantors; this represents a pattern quite widely encountered at this date.[44] In Brigstock 80 per cent of the *inter-vivos* transfers made by married couples show them disposing of property rather than acquiring it.[45] In Redgrave we see a shift in this pattern by the closing years of Edward III's reign, although well over half of the conjoint transactions showed husband and wife partnerships in the role of grantor – a pattern also encountered in Winslow and especially Barnet for roughly comparable dates.[46]

By the early fifteenth century there had been a striking transformation in the trend. We have already seen that over the last third of the fourteenth century there had been a notable growth in the proportional significance of these conjoint transfers. However, there was an even greater growth in the incidence of conjoint transfers in which husbands and wives were acquiring property together. In fact, almost seven out of every ten conjoint transfers in all seven of the manors in the sample reveal married couples in the role of grantee or purchaser by the early decades of the fifteenth century (see Table 6).

Table 6

INTER-VIVOS LAND TRANSFERS OF MARRIED COUPLES

	Grantors	%	Grantees	%	Grantors/ Grantees	%
Winslow						
1368-77	21	56.7	13	35.1	3	8.2
1422-33	23	34.3	32	47.8	12	17.9
Redgrave						
1368-77	23	56.1	17	41.5	1	2.4
1400-09	5	13.9	22	61.1	9	25.0
Barnet						
1372-81	15	71.4	5	23.8	1	4.8
1413-22	11	28.9	21	55.3	6	15.8
Gt. Waltham						
1400-09	6	26.1	14	60.9	3	13.0
Holkham						
1400-09	5	29.4	11	64.7	5	5.9
Martham						
1370-99	51	52.6	41	42.3	5	5.1
1403-38	31	26.3	77	65.3	10	8.4
Hevingham						
1382-1416	37	36.6	55	54.5	9	8.9
1425-1500	49	21.9	152	68.2	22	9.9

For sources see note 16

Taking up land conjointly may have offered a number of advantages to the conjoint holders. Indeed, when compared with the position of the dowager, that of the female who had acquired land conjointly serves to emphasize the advantages of holding jointly. A grant of land to both husband and wife could fulfil much the same function as the free bench for the widow, or curtesy in the case of the widower, once death terminated the marriage, although the benefits might prove to be greater. In joint tenure the surviving spouse would take over the property previously held jointly with no liability to pay a new entry fine or heriot. However, an entry fine or heriot was often, although not invariably, exacted from individuals claiming free bench or curtesy.[47] Furthermore, most holders of free bench, dower or curtesy possessed no more than a life interest in the land whereas conjoint tenants could often hold the land heritably with full powers of alienation, if no restraints had been specified in the original grant. The advantages gave the surviving widow or widower a less ambiguous tenure, which she or he could sell or transfer as conditions required. In fact this may help to explain the heavy predominance in the manorial courts of the late fourteenth and early fifteenth centuries of women acting alone as grantors or sellers of property. In this feature we may be able to identify another possible shift in pattern when comparisons are made with the earlier years of the fourteenth century. For example, in Redgrave between 1260 and 1319 391 females were identified making *inter-vivos* transactions in the Redgrave courts but they were disproportionately found to have been acquiring property.[48] In fact over two-thirds of these women appear to have acquired more property than they granted or sold and were the beneficiaries of transactions made very largely within their families. Many of these transactions were grants of land to unmarried daughters. However, the practice of granting landed dowry to daughters is only rarely observable in the manor courts of our sample in the early fifteenth century. In the smaller two-decade sample for 1368–1377 and 1400–10, relating, it should be stressed, to a much reduced manorial population in Redgrave than existed prior to 1320, thirty-one *inter-vivos* transactions involving females reveal them in 70 per cent of the cases to have acted alone as one of the parties as sellers or grantors. While the role played by solitary female participants in land exchanges in the other manors in the sample for the early fifteenth century has not been compared with the earlier period, it is clearly evident that the pattern resembled that which had come to distinguish Redgrave. Of the 118 instances in this sample of women acting by themselves in *inter-vivos* transfers (not including Redgrave) only thirty-eight (32 per cent) show them to have been acquiring property.

Although it is not always easy to be certain, these women, so frequently selling or granting land, would seem disproportionately to have been widows rather than females at an early stage in their adult lives. For instance, Juliana, widow of John Ilsent, in 1430 surrendered a cottage, a toft and $6\frac{1}{2}$ acres to Thomas Stretele in exchange for four marks, to be paid each year in four quarterly payments of 3s. 4d. for a period of four years. In addition, Thomas Stretele was to maintain Juliana in food and to provide her with accommodation within the property she had sold to him. If such an arrangement proved impossible to implement she was to have a part of the messuage to do with as she liked for the remainder of her life.[49] Likewise, Matilda, widow of John Dory of Botulesdale, a market centre within the manor of Redgrave, in 1409 sold a messuage and curtilage to John Bretonn, who was to pay her in four annual installments of unequal amounts, the first sum being £6, followed by three further payments each of five marks. Matilda was to retain two rooms in the messuage for the remainder of her life for which she agreed to pay John Dory an annual rent of 10d.[50] Rosa, widow of John Mandevyle of Winslow, over a period of seven years following her husband's death in 1418, transferred by surrender and admission 8 acres in four transactions to three different persons.[51] Margaret, widow of Richard Swalwetayl of Botulesdale, in 1404, five years after her husband's death, first sold a barn to John Louden, then a cottage to Walter Gyleys for eight marks and proceeded in 1405 to undertake two extra-curial transfers, one of which concerned a stall in the market to John Pyntyle and his wife Marjorie, and the other a cottage and three shops to Henry Reve, who was to see that the property was sold and the proceeds distributed for the benefit of Margaret's soul after her death.[52]

What developments may have facilitated this increasing tendency of women, and widows in particular, to loom so large in the evidence as 'sellers' of land? In the early fourteenth century a relatively high proportion of the quite small number of grants to husbands and wives had, in fact, been grants in fee tail, that is to 'A and B and the heirs of their bodies'. For instance, at Winslow during the first twenty-two years of Edward III's reign, ninety-five out of 487 permanent grants contained entails.[53] Leon Slota estimates that at Park and Codicote, both manors of the Abbot of St Albans in Hertfordshire, twenty-six and forty-one respectively, of 303 and 299 permanent transfers between 1285 and 1349 were entailed.[54] These consequently placed restrictions on the freedom of the parental grantee or grantees subsequently to alienate such property away from heirs contrary to the intentions of the grantor, clearly representing a development in the manorial court that owes a great deal to the influence of the statute *De Donis* of 1285.[55] While protecting the wife from alienations of land that the couple held jointly in their marriage, it also restricted her range of options with respect to its use in her widowhood if at that phase in her life she possessed surviving offspring. At approximately the same period, as we have already mentioned, we can begin to detect the formal execution of jointure, although always on a modest scale.[56] Such an agreement, like the entail, commonly erected a joint tenancy for the donor and the donor's spouse, with provision for remainders to the children or specified child of the marriage. Far less common was a jointure arrangement that simply created a joint tenancy for the donor and his wife with no specific remainder clause. Such jointures are certainly still detectable in the late fourteenth century; five were made in Barnet between 1372 and 1381 and five at Winslow between 1368 and 1377. However, they seem, like entails, to have remained a relatively rare arrangement in the early fifteenth century, with only seven identifiable in the six sample manors after 1400. They were, then, of minimal significance compared with the conjoint acquisition and the less frequent, but highly noteworthy, deathbed transfer.

The increasingly common conjoint type of acquisition seems to have omitted any specific reference to it as a tenancy held by 'X and Y and the heirs of their bodies', which therefore ensured that the survivor of the marriage possessed freedom to dispose of property without reference to the legally constituted claims of offspring or other kin. Jointure had served to bar the wife's right to dower because through the employment of joint tenancies no dower arose since the husband lacked the sole and separate seisin that alone gave his widow his estate. This would seem to apply with equal force to formally constituted jointure and to conjointly acquired property involving married couples.

Can we observe in the move towards joint tenure the process by which a formally recorded grant, in which there was no acknowledgement or specification of the dower, served to undermine the latter's centrality as the basis for the wife's security in her widowhood? It has more than once in this discussion proved difficult to disentangle cause and effect and in this regard this issue is no exception. For instance, Barbara Harvey, who has identified the emergence of jointure on certain manors within the estate of Westminster Abbey in the late fourteenth century, explains it by what she sees as a need to protect widows in a climate in which there was a growth in life tenancies, which would mean that if wives were not specifically mentioned they would in theory have beeen allowed nothing in their widowhood. She sees the emergence of life tenancies, indeed the growth of land markets that disturbed customary procedures for the transference of holdings, as potentially damaging to the material circumstances of the widow but she also suggests that the jointure that in consequence arose led to her gaining a 'more honourable estate'.[57] While such an argument appears to fit the specific circumstances of certain Westminster Abbey manors, jointure can be less easily explained in that way on manors that have been the focus of this paper.

It has been hestitantly suggested in this and other work that the evidence seems more consistent with an interpretation that sees manorial courts rapidly moving to employ instruments that originated under common law that were strikingly reminiscent of entails, jointures and arrangements akin to uses.[58] Such an argument implies a greater degree of integration of legal cultures relating to common and customary law than is sometimes supposed. There are certain very obvious difficulties with this position as it might be thought to be treating law and legal institutions as exogenous or autonomous in their relation to social and economic change.

It would also be unwise to expect that the strategies adopted by the later medieval nobility with respect to their own properties would have any detectable bearing upon those undertaken by customary tenants managing holdings that ranged from a miniscule rod with an attached cottage hovel to a full virgate or two. With regard to jointure and entail we are familiar with arguments about the possible contradictory influences they might have had; on the one hand disadvantaging the widow as a more equitable distribution of property is made by the landholder between his wife and all of his surviving offspring and on the other providing the means to place control of property in the hands of a dowager, who, if young when widowed and not restricted in her freedom to alientate, could seriously damage the material lot of the children to the original marriage.[59] It has, furthermore, in discussions of the later medieval nobility been suggested that the use may have served to disinherit women, in particular the heiress.[60] There is no doubt that the evidence from this, as yet, small sample of marginally more than two hundred, primarily early fifteenth-century, deathbed transfers from the six manors which have served as the focus of this study, shows little favour bestowed upon their daughters by men as they arranged for the disposal of their property after their death. What is more, dowries in land to daughters, as already noted, were at this date an increasingly rare event and the cash gift or portion, even within this group, as among the gentry and nobility, may have become a more normal form of marital endowment, although this is far from easy to establish using manorial court proceedings. Wills too, most likely under-report the full extent of the practice, which was not necessarily held back until the moment of parental death.[61]

Adopting a quantitative perspective on the 3,150 transactions that have been considered in this sample leads us to suppose that more land was acquired by women, disproportionately from persons who were not their kin in *inter-vivos* transfers, which they held conjointly with their husbands, than was received either in the form of *post-mortem* inheritance or post-obit gift (see Table 4).[62] This was land of which they could for the most part dispose without reference to legal restraints designed by the family, although whatever they did was ultimately subject to the influences which the landlords and their officials might seek to impose upon their own curia.

It is obviously tempting to reflect upon the implications of these changes for the material circumstances of women in these communities. This is by no means an easy task because there were over the period covered by this study certain diverging and potentially contradictory forces at work in the rural economy. The land that women held in widowhood, and *ipso facto* more likely in later life, had become an asset with substantially reduced value by the early fifteenth century. These women were frequently in familial circumstances in which children had not survived or had migrated and so were unable to assist in the cultivation and management of land. Furthermore, labour was scarce and costly. It was, and this is in sharp contrast with the early fourteenth century, becoming increasingly uncommon to find an elderly female entering into a maintenance contract with her own children.[63] Much more common as a basis for her income was the lease by the widow of her land for a term of years or a land sale registered with very strict and increasingly elaborate terms to do with non-compliance on the part of the purchaser and with reservation of right of re-entry on the part of the widow seller.[64] How far we should see the use of the deathbed transfer to the widow with reversions to named sons as a 'defensive strategy' employed by fathers who were seeking to bind together the generations when economic forces may have been pulling them apart is a question that can and should be asked, although not easily answered. How far too, we might ask, did the husband and wife pairing become more important in a peasant economy that by the late fourteenth century was itself deficient in labour and far more pastoral in its emphasis? Did such moves away from arable farming perhaps increase the wife's contribution to the combined household and farm economy and consequently serve to increase the motive behind conjoint acquistion of land by married couples?[65] While it is difficult to provide a confident answer to any of these questions, the evidence considered in this essay raises the possibility that the lot of married women within certain sections of the customary tenantry in the early fifteenth century may have improved relative to the widowed members of their sex when compared with their respective situations a century earlier.

Notes

1 J.S. Beckerman, 'Customary Law in Manorial Courts in the Thirteenth and Fourteenth Centuries' (Ph.D. thesis, University of London, 1972), pp. 117–83; R.M. Smith, 'Some Thoughts on "Hereditary" and "Proprietary" Rights Under Customary Law in Thirteenth and Early Fourteenth Century England', *Law and History Review*, 1 (1983), pp. 95–128; L.A. Slota, 'Law, Land Transfer and Lordship on the Estates of St. Albans Abbey in the Thirteenth and Fourteenth Centuries', *Law and History Review*, 6 (1988), pp. 119–38; L. Bonfield, 'The Nature of Customary Law in the Manor Courts of Medieval England', *Comparative Studies in Society and History*, 31 (1989), pp. 514–34.

2 R.M. Smith, 'Women's Property Rights Under Customary Law: Some Developments in the Thirteenth and Fourteenth Centuries', *TRHS*, 5th series, 36 (1986), pp. 165–94.

3 J. Goody, 'Inheritance, Property and Women: Some Comparative Considerations', in J. Goody, J. Thirsk and E.P. Thompson (eds.), *Family and Inheritance: Rural Society in Western Europe 1200–1800* (Cambridge, 1976), pp. 10–36; *Production and Reproduction: A Comparative Study of the Domestic Domain* (Cambridge, 1976); *The Development of the*

Family and Marriage in Europe (Cambridge, 1983); *The Oriental, The Ancient and the Primitive: Systems of Marriage and the Family in the Pre-industrial Societies of Eurasia* (Cambridge, 1990).

4 For example, E. Searle, 'Women and the Legitimization of Succession in the Norman Conquest', *Anglo-Norman Studies: Proceedings of the Battle Conference*, 3 (1980): pp. 159–70, 226–9, and in greater detail in *Predatory Kinship and the Creation of Norman Power 840–1066* (Berkeley, 1988); S.D. White, *Custom, Kinship and Gifts to Saints: The Laudation Parentum in Western Europe, 1050–1150* (Chapel Hill, 1988); S.L. Waugh, *The Lordship of England: Royal Wardships and Marriage in English Society and Politics 1217–1327* (Princeton, 1988), especially Chapter 1; R.M. Smith, 'Monogamy, Landed Property and Demographic Regimes in Pre-industrial Europe: Regional Contrasts and Temporal Stabilities', in J. Landers and V. Reynolds (eds.), *Fertility and Resources* (Cambridge, 1990), pp. 164–88.

5 Smith, 'Women's Property Rights', pp. 181–4.

6 J. S. Loengard, '"Of the Gift of Her Husband": English Dower and its Consequences in the Year 1200', in J. Kirshner and S.F. Wemple (eds.), *Women of the Medieval World*, (Oxford, 1985), pp. 223–4.

7 Smith, 'Women's Property Rights', pp. 181–86

8 K.B. Macfarlane, *The Nobility of Later Medieval England* (Oxford, 1978), p. 65; Smith, 'Women's Property Rights', p. 190.

9 Smith, 'Women's Property Rights', pp. 190–91.

10 Ibid., p. 191.

11 L. Bonfield and L.R. Poos, 'The Development of the Deathbed Transfer in Medieval English Manor Courts', *Cambridge Law Journal*, 47 (1988), pp. 403–27.

12 Smith, 'Women's Property Rights', pp. 186–9; L.R. Slota, 'The Village Land Market on the St. Albans Manors of Park and Codicote 1237–1399', (Ph.D. thesis, University of Michigan, 1984), pp. 120–22; L. Bonfield and L.R. Poos, 'Law and Individualism in Medieval England', *Social History*, 11 (1986), pp. 298–9.

13 C. Given-Wilson, *The English Nobility in the Late Middle Ages*, (London, 1987), pp. 143–4.

14 These issues are discussed at greater length in Z. Razi and R.M. Smith, 'The Manorial Court Roll and the Study of English Medieval Society: Past, Present and Future', in Z. Razi and R.M. Smith (eds.), *The Manor Court and English Society: Studies in the Evidence* (Oxford, forthcoming).

15 Smith, 'Women's Property Rights', p. 193, and Bonfield and Poos,'The Development of the Deathbed Transfer', p. 427.

16 The manuscript sources are: Winslow Court Book, Cambridge University Library (CUL) MS Dd 7 22; Redgrave Manor Court Rolls, University of Chicago Library (UCL), Bacon Manuscripts 24–5, 30–2; Barnet Court Book, British Library (BL) Add MS 40167; Holkham Hall, Norfolk, Boroughhall Manor Court Rolls, Holkham Deeds (HD) 97; Great Waltham Manor Court Rolls, Essex Record Office (ERO) D/D Tu 239; Martham Court Rolls, Norfolk and Norwich Record Office (NRO) 11312 26 B3, NNAS 5924–40; Hevingham Manor Court Rolls, Crictot Hall, Norfolk and Norwich Record Office (NRO) NRS 14486 29 C1, 14637 29 D2, 14772 29 D4, 19558 42 D2, 19559 42 D2. I am extremely grateful to Dr Bruce Campbell, Department of Economic and Social History, The Queen's University, Belfast, for allowing me to consult his transcriptions of land exchanges in the proceedings of the manor courts of Martham and Hevingham.

17 R.M. Smith, 'Some Issues Concerning Families and Their Property in Rural England 1250–1800', in R.M. Smith (ed.), *Land, Kinship and Life-Cycle* (Cambridge, 1984), pp. 45–7, and E. A. Wrigley, 'Fertility Strategy for the Individual and the Group', in C. Tilly (ed.), *Historical Studies of Changing Fertility* (Princeton, 1978), pp. 235–54.

18 Smith, 'Some Issues', p. 51.

19 For revealing indications of the strategies that can be identified when court roll entries and wills relating to the same individual are combined see Bonfield and Poos, 'The Development of the Deathbed Transfer', pp. 422–36.

20 CUL MS Dd 7 22: Courts held at Winslow 7.6.1423 and 12.6.1430.

21 CUL MS Dd 7 22: Court held at Winslow 12.6.1430, '. . . *Item [lego] Johanne uxori Johannis Jankyn vj buselli ordei. Item Matilde filie Johannis Jankyn ij buselli ordei, ad omnia ista bene faciendum constituto Johannem filium meum et Willelmum filium meum esse executores . . .*'

22 NRO NRS 5928

23 A real precision in such calculations is hard to achieve. Deathbed transfers frequently lack detail on the exact linear measurements of landholdings that are being exchanged. A fairly typical entry is that made in the Redgave manor court of 11.5.1405 (UCL Bacon MS 30): '*Johannes Clerk super lectum suum mortalem sursum reddidit in manus domini per manus Thome Mildynhale et testimonium homagio j cotagium cum curtiliagio de alba firma ad opus Isabelle uxoris eius tenendum sibi et heredibus suis . . .*'

24 These figures may underestimate the exact areal proportion because both Barnet and Redgrave contained locally important market centres. As a consequence, in these two manors a sizeable number of the deathbed transfers relating to valuable properties such as shops and stalls lacked precise dimensions.

25 NRO 11312 26 B3.

26 BL Add MS 40167: Court held at Barnet 23.7.1415.

27 BL Add MS 40167: Court held at Barnet 30.9.1415.

28 BL Add MS 40167: Court held at Barnet 27.12.1418, '*Johannes Hened jacens in extremis sursum reddidit in manus domini unum croftum cum gardino et duas acras terre . . . Et dominus concessit dictum toftum gardinum et terram cum pertinenciis Elene relicte dicto Johannis tenendum sibi et suis ad terminum vite tenendum in villenagio ad voluntatem domini per servicia et post decessum dicte Elene dictum crofum gardinum et terram cum pertinenciis remaneat Thome filio predictorum Johannis et Elene tenendum sibi et suis in villenagio ad voluntatem domini per servicia et dicta Elena dat domino de fine xijd et fecit fidelitatem etc. . . . Johannes Hened jacens in extremis sursum reddidit in manus domini unum croftum terre continentem in toto tres acras terre . . . Et dominus concessit dictum croftum terre Elene relicte dicti Johannis tenendum sibi et suis ad terminum vite sue tenendum in villenagio ad voluntatem domini per servicia. Et post decessum dicte Elene dictum croftum terre cum pertinenciis Ricardo filio predictorum Johannis et Elene cum pertinenciis remaneat tenendum sibi et suis etc. . . . Et predicta Elena dat domino de fine xijd et fecit fidelitatem etc. . . .*'

29 BL Add MS 40167: Court held at Barnet 27.12.1418, '*Johannes Hened jacens in extremis sursum reddidit in manus domini tres acras terre jacentes in uno crofto . . . Dominus concessit dictas tres acras terre . . . Henrico Bulshrawe tenendum sibi et suis in villenagio ad voluntatem domini per servicia etc. Et dat domino de fine xxd et fecit fidelitatem etc. . . . Johannes Hened jacens in extremis sursum reddidit in manus domini unam rodam terre jacentem inter regiam viam ducentem de Southmymmys versus London ex parte una et boscum domini vocatum le Ffolde ex parte altera. Et dominus concessit dictam rodam terre Johannis Wendon tenendum sibi et suis in villenagio ad voluntatem domini per servicia. Et dat domino de fine vjd.*'

30 UCL Bacon MS 31: Court held at Redgrave 1.3.1409.

31 See Bonfield and Poos, 'Deathbed Transfer', p. 425, and a much fuller discussion in E. Clark, 'Charitable Bequests, Deathbed Transfers and the Manorial Court in Late Medieval England', in Razi and Smith (eds.), *The Manor Court.*

32 BL Add MS 40167: Court held at Barnet on 23.11.1419.

33 UCL Bacon MS 30: Court held at Redgrave 1.7.1400. This case is of further interest as Adam Ode was amerced for failing to come to court to implement Isabel Sexteyn's request. The court moved to seize this property and subsequently granted it to Adam Ode with specific instructions that he should sell it and thereafter distribute the proceeds for the benefit of the souls of Isabel and John Sexteyn. ('*Juratores presentant*

quod Isabella Sexteyn super lectum suum mortalem sursum reddidit in manus domini j cotagium cum curtilagio per manus Ade Ode et testimonium Roberti Murgate, Johannis Norton, Thome Nase et aliorum de homagio ad vendenda et distribuenda pro anima eius et pro anima Johannis Sexteyn viri sui et quia dictus Adam non venit ad dictam terram reddendum ideo in misericordia. Et preceptum est seisire in manus domini. Postea dominus concessit predictum cotagium cum curtilagio predicto Ade Ode ad vendendum et denarios inde provientes distribuendos ut supra cui liberatum sub condicione supradicta. Et dat de fine. Et fecit fidelitatem.') In the following year (UCL Bacon MS 30: Court held at Redgrave 17.9.1401) Adam Ode sold the cottage called 'Sexteyns' to John Sexteyn and Agnes his wife.

34   CUL MS Dd 7 22: Court held at Winslow 5.10.1433.

35   UCL Bacon MS 30: Court held at Redgrave on 4.5.1405, '*Item quod Robertus Littlebury super lectum suum mortalem sursum reddidit in manus domini per manus Johannis Foulere senior et testimonium Henrici Baxtere et aliorum de homagio j cotagium cum curtilagio de alba firma ad opus Matilde Littlebury tenendum sibi ad totam vitam suam. Et post eius decessum predicum cotagium remaneat Johanni filio suo . . . Et si contingat predictum Johannem obire sine herede de corpore sue legitime procreato ante decessum predicte Matilde tunc predictum cotagium vendeat per predictam Matildam vel per attornatum suum. Et denarios inde provientes distribuenda per animabus predictorum Roberti et Matilde et benefactorum suorum.'*

36   BL Add MS 40167: Court held at Barnet 9.5.1424.

37   BL Add MS 40167: Court held at Barnet on 22.12.1373, '*Willelmus atte Dane et Johanna uxor euis examinata reddidit sursum in manus domini terciam partem trium acrarum terre quam quidem terciam partem dicta Johanna tenuit nomine dotis post mortem Johannis Gyrdeler nuper viri sui. Et dominus concessit dictam terciam partem terre cum pertinenciis Ricardo Kymbell tendendum sibi et suis in villenagio ad voluntatem domini pro servicia debita et coinsueta. Et dat domino de fine xviijd.'*

38   BL Add MS 40167: Court held at Barnet on 3.5.1379.

39   Ibid., '*Cristiana que fuit uxor Johannis Nicol in propria persona sua petit versus Johannem Martyn et Julianam uxorem suam Ricardum Fferour et Johannam uxorem suam Johannem Cosyn at Margaretam, uxorem suam et Elenam filiam Johannis Nicol nomine dotis terciam partem unius tenementi nuper viri sui. Et predicti Johannes, Juliana, Ricardus, Johanna, Johannes, Margareta et Elena presentes in curia nichil pro se habent nec dicere sciunt quare executionem inde habere non debeat. Ideo consideratum quod predicta Cristiana recuperet seisinam tercie partis predicte nomine dotis . . . Cristiana que fuit uxor Johannis Nicol petit versus Ricardum Nicol in placito terre terciam partem unius messuagii unius gardini unius gravette cum duabus croftis adjacentes et cum pertinenciis in Cheppyngbarnet post mortem Johannis Nicol nuper viri sui. Et predicta Ricardus presens in curia nichil sit dicere quare excecutionem habere inde non debet. Ideo consideratum est quod predicta Cristiana recuperet seisinam tercie partis predicte . . .'*

40   Smith, 'Women's Property Rights', p. 191. For further reflections on seigneurial interests see Bonfield and Poos, 'Deathbed Transfers', p. 417–19.

41   R.M. Smith, 'Familes and Their Land in an area of Partible Inheritance: Redgrave, Suffolk 1260–1320', in R.M. Smith (ed.), *Land, Kinship and Life-cycle* (Cambridge, 1984), p. 187.

42   C. Clarke, 'Peasant Society and Land Transactions in Chesterton, Cambridgeshire, 1277–1325' (D. Phil. thesis, University of Oxford, 1985), p. 183.

43   J.M. Bennett, *Women in the Medieval English Countryside: Gender and Household in Brigstock Before the Plague* (Oxford, 1987), pp. 112–13.

44   Smith, 'Women's Property Rights', p. 185 n. 72.

45   Bennett, *Women in the Medieval English Countryside*, p. 113, Table 5.3.

46   A preliminary analysis of this matter using the land transactions in the court book of the Abbot of St Albans manor of Codicote in Hertfordshire suggests that already prior to 1349 conjoint acquisitions by husbands and wives exceeded sales or grants. Develop-

ments in other manors in the first seventy-five years of the fourteenth century obviously need considerably greater consideration than they have received in this present discussion.

47 See n. 40 above.
48 Smith, 'Families and Their Land', p. 167, Table 3.13(b).
49 CUL MS Dd 7 22: Court held at Winslow on 12.6.1430.
50 UCL Bacon MS 31: Court held at Redgrave on 7.5.1409.
51 CUL MS Add Dd 22 7: Courts held at Winslow on 8.5.1424, 23.7.1425, 12.6.1430 and 7.5.1431.
52 UCL Bacon MS 30: Courts held at Redgrave on 17.6.1404 and 17.9.1405.
53 Smith, 'Women's Property Rights', p. 188.
54 L.A. Slota, 'The Village Land Market', p. 121.
55 Smith, 'Women's Property Rights', p. 188.
56 Ibid., pp. 190–1.
57 B.F. Harvey, *Westminster Abbey and its Estates in the Middle Ages* (Oxford, 1977), pp. 277–98.
58 Smith, 'Some Thoughts on "Hereditary" and "Proprietary" Property Rights', p. 128, and 'Women's Property Rights', pp. 193–4. However, for some justifiable doubts see Bonfield, 'The Nature of Customary Law', pp. 520–1, but see P.R. Hyams, 'What Did Edwardian Villagers Mean by Law', forthcoming in Razi and Smith (eds.), *The Manor Court*.
59 See n. 13 above.
60 Ibid., pp. 190–1.
61 See an important discussion of this matter as it relates to the early modern period with very considerable relevance to the later medieval centuries in L. Bonfield, 'Normative Rules and Property Transmissions: Reflections on the Link Between Marriage and Inheritance in Early Modern England', in L. Bonfield, R.M. Smith and K. Wrightson (eds.), *The World We Have Gained: Histories of Population and Social Structure* (Oxford, 1986), pp. 155–76.
62 This estimate most likely represents a minimum measure of the extent to which women received land via this route. It should also be noted that, because so much of the property concerned houses, cottages, buildings, gardens and closes, these crude proportional calculations may greatly underestimate the proportional significance of the actual value of property transferred by this mode of transaction.
63 This matter is the subject of a forthcoming study based on almost one thousand 'contracts' concerning elderly tenants. See R. M. Smith 'The Manor Court and the Elderly Tenant in England in the Later Middle Ages', in Razi and Smith (eds.), *The Manor Court*. See too, E. Clark, 'Some Aspects of Social Security in Medieval England', *Journal of Family History*, 7 (1982), pp. 307–20 and 'The Quest for Security in Medieval England' in M.M. Sheehan (ed.), *Aging and the Aged in Medieval Europe* (Toronto, 1990), pp. 189–200.
64 These arrangements took the form of the transactions discussed above in notes 49 and 50. They are considered in greater detail in Smith, 'The Manor Court and the Elderly Tenant'.
65 Research on the position of women in the late medieval rural economy, in contrast to their activities in towns, has been rather limited, but there are signs of a stirring of activity. See S.C.A. Penn, 'Female Wage-earners in Late Fourteenth-Century England', *AgHR*, 35 (1987), pp. 1–14; P.J.P. Goldberg, 'Women's Work, Women's Roles in the Late-Medieval North', in M.A. Hicks (ed.), *Profit, Piety and the Professions in Later Medieval England* (Gloucester, 1990), pp. 34–50. For more general considerations over both medieval and early modern centuries see R. M. Smith, 'Women's Work and Marriage in Pre-industrial England: Some Speculations' in S. Gavaciocchi (ed.), *La Donna Nell' Economia Secc. XIII–XVIII* (Prato, 1990), pp. 31–55.

4

'To oure losse and hindraunce': English Credit to Alien Merchants in the Mid-Fifteenth Century

Wendy Childs
University of Leeds

The subject of credit in English trade, internal and international, is not an unexplored one. Professor Postan drew historians' attention to it most clearly in 1928,[1] and, although published specialist work on credit in England remains limited, writing on medieval trade since then has assumed the presence of credit at all levels. The present debate is not so much over the existence of credit, but over its scale and importance, especially at times of bullion shortage. Was there enough credit allowed, and were bills flexible and transferable enough to help offset the shortage of hard cash? In the light of recent monetarist work, well encapsulated in the collection of John Day's essays, and in the syntheses by Peter Spufford,[2] it seems useful to re-examine the use of credit in a period of bullion shortage.

Two related sources in the Public Record Office allow a glimpse of credit in London in the late 1450s, at the end of what was probably the most severe bullion shortage of the Middle Ages. The Exchequer Memoranda Rolls for the last years of Henry VI's reign, and especially for 1459–69, suddenly record a large number of prosecutions of Englishmen for allowing extended credit to alien merchants for their purchases of wool, cloth, and tin, in contravention of the statutes of 8 and 9 Henry VI; and linked with them, and probably present in the Public Record Office because they were used as evidence in preparing the prosecutions, are two debt registers kept by two London scriveners, William Styfford and John Thorpe, for the period 1457–9.[3] These documents are not unknown to historians of English trade, but until recently have not received detailed attention.[4] Yet they provide a cohesive group of cases for analysis at a time of particular significance in the history of money and credit. They do not resolve the debate on the overall importance of credit, but they do allow some observations to be made. The reasons for bringing the prosecutions show something of the attitudes to credit then, and the content of the accusations themselves illustrates some aspects of the working of credit transactions in overseas trade.

The prosecutions took place against a long-term background of general acceptance that credit was necessary in trade, but against a medium-term background of increasing unease or irritation on the part of some groups over its unrestricted extension to alien merchants. Widespread acceptance of credit from the thirteenth century is shown by the legislation passed under Edward I to protect creditors; by the late thirteenth- and early fourteenth-century Letter Books and recognisance rolls of London which show widespread use of credit by buyers and sellers in all branches of England's overseas trade; and by studies of the Italian involvement in the wool trade which have emphasized the frequency of advance sales.[5] In the later fourteenth century Gilbert Maghfeld's account book showed some 75 per cent of his business was done for credit; in 1424 the will of William Lynn showed that as well as £965 in cash and £899 in goods, he also left £3,027 in debts owed to him, while himself owing £1,637; the extent of credit in the fifteenth-century wool trade and in the Cely family dealings is very well known, and any historian dipping into the documents of Early Chancery Proceedings finds many examples of obligations at all levels.[6] Professor Day has insisted that such credit instruments were supplements to the money supply not substitutes for it, and that even up to the eighteenth century the money in circulation was 90 per cent in coin and only 10 per cent in paper,[7] but, although bills and obligations did not move as freely as in later centuries, they were clearly readily transferable within the merchants' world, as wills and lawsuits show. Many were transferred on trust, others were transferred with formal registration. For instance in August 1458 William Ketweigh, a German merchant, arranged to pay Richard Payn, a London draper, £43 1s. 9d. by handing over seven obligations amounting to this sum due to him from London skinners; and if, unlike this case, the obligation offered was larger than the sum owed, other obligations could be given back as 'change', as when William Bruwel in 1447 received an obligation of £97 18s. 4gr. Flemish and gave various obligations worth £78 Flemish in return.[8] Trade for credit was also done with no written record at all and the extent of this will never be known. At the village and local level many small purchases might well have been made on tick or with a handshake before witnesses. This happened in international trade too: merchants of all nationalities bought and sold on credit without getting written obligations and had to rely on witnesses to prove their cases. Even Italians did so and they above all should have known better, given the admonitions of their merchant manuals and the need to keep good accounts for their superiors and partners. Niccolo and Raffaello Lomellini sinned in this way by selling black velvet and bales of woad to William Bukket of Salisbury without taking 'especialty in writyng', and later found that Bukket refused to pay a penny.[9] There is no doubt about the longevity of credit in English trade, nor, in the long term, about its total acceptance in the mercantile and administrative worlds.

However, in the fifteenth century there is also evidence of increasing disquiet about the extent of credit in the economy, especially in relation to aliens. This disquiet was no doubt brought on by the bullion shortages and by the perceived problems in English trade. Bullion shortages appeared in England as well as the rest of Europe, especially between 1395 and 1415 and again in the 1440s and 1450s; at the same time the English trade in wool was steadily shrinking, and the cloth export trade went through difficulties in 1405–25, in 1436–9, and in the 1450s.[10] England's plight was not as dire as that of other countries, since the overseas trade balance seems to have remained overall in her favour, and the shortage of silver was not extreme enough to undermine the currency. None the less, the government was worried and responded to the difficulties with restrictive legislation. Not only were the fourteenth-century prohibitions on the export of bullion confirmed in the fifteenth, but new arrangements were made with the Staple in the bullion and partition ordinances of 1429/30 to force alien customers to pay at least part of the wool price in bullion.[11] As usual, economic difficulties had brought increasing resentment against alien merchants and in the same year legislation was passed to restrict the credit allowed to aliens in general trade as well as in the wool trade. The statute of 8 Henry VI cap. 24 forbade any Englishman to sell any goods to any alien merchant whatsoever except for ready money. The reason given for this was not however the need for bullion but rather that aliens, having received goods on credit, had fled with them and never paid.[12] Neither attempt to restrict credit was successful. The terms of the bullion ordinance plunged the wool trade into chaos and brought on a ten-year slump, and the total restriction on credit in general trade proved immediately unworkable. In the next parliament early in 1431 a commons petition claimed that English merchants were now quite unable to sell any cloth to alien merchants so that the king lost his customs duties, and the cloth-workers and English merchants were greatly damaged. Accordingly the act was amended to allow up to six months credit but no more. Opinion about credit for aliens was clearly divided. Resentment was strong enough among some, probably the Staplers and the cloth exporters wishing to limit alien competition, for another petition to be presented in the parliament of 1433 asking for a return for a period of three years to the total prohibition of credit for alien merchants; but the petitioners recognized that not everyone agreed with them, because they also asked for legislation to prevent collusion between English sellers and alien buyers. The government did not accept the petition and credit continued to be allowed for six months.[13] Clearly the government's advisors, no doubt including the wool and cloth producers who welcomed alien buyers, recognized that trade simply could not go on without credit, although some probably agreed with the *Libelle of Englyshe Polycye*, written in 1436, that certain aspects of it were regrettable. The anonymous author's dislike was kept especially for the Venetians, whom he accused of manipulating credit to the detriment of English merchants. As 'ane emsampelle of deseytte', he complained that the Venetians rode around the Cotswolds 'borrowing' wool. They sent it to Venice, sold it, and sent the proceeds by letter of exchange to Flanders; there they lent the money to Englishmen to buy goods and received the loans back from them by exchange again in England, at a charge of 12d. in the pound for immediate repayment, 2s. for one month and so on. This, he said, was usury, 'to oure losse and hindraunce'. Certainly the practice of buying large amounts of wool from Cotswold producers and exporting it on long-term credit is exactly what is revealed twenty years later in the prosecutions of 1459. As 'anothere exemple of disceytte' he further complained that the Italians bought or 'borrowed' wool at Calais for payment one or even two years later. This he accepted as 'fayre lone' whatever the bullion ordinance laid down, but he objected to the way that they took the wool to Bruges, sold it immediately even at £50 in the £1000 loss, then lived comfortably on the proceeds, making yet more money from lending and letters of exchange until the time came to pay for the wool and buy more.[14] None the less, it was not precisely this that the preamble to the statute complained about, but rather a fear of eventual loss through non-payment.

Despite the activity of a pressure group against credit for aliens between 1429 and 1433, and the general antipathy to aliens which surfaced from time to time, there is no evidence that the limitation in the statute 9 Henry VI was well enforced, or even enforced at all at first. There were no prosecutions in the Exchequer, even though it seems unlikely, given the sharp division of opinion over the need for credit, that all merchants complied exactly with the statute. Indeed the well informed author of the *Libelle* complained publicly that they did not, but were still allowing credit for terms of up to two years. Why then, nearly thirty years after its first appearance, was there such a purge against offenders? What brought this particular statute back to the attention of the government? Part of the answer is that a number of long-term financial and commercial problems were becoming acute by 1459, focusing government attention on revenue and trade. The government, always short of cash and with income further shrinking during the trade slump of the 1450s, was in increasing need of income in a period of civil war. Professor Griffiths has shown that Henry's advisors were squeezing every last penny from the royal estates at this time,[15] and Dr Jenks, whose study of the debt register of John Thorpe led him to look at these prosecutions, sees them as another of Henry's stratagems for raising cash. He emphasizes that in the summer of 1459, when the prosecutions reached their peak, Henry VI desperately needed money as he mustered troops against the Yorkists.[16] That the king's advisers should look closely at the state of international trade, although not necessarily immediately at the matter of credit, was not surprising. In the first place, the bullion shortage had become severe, indeed the period of the 1440s and 1450s was probably the worst bullion famine ever experienced in Europe,[17] and the blame for such occurrences was usually put on the export of silver by merchants or the Church. Secondly, an obvious slump in cloth exports after 1448, and the visible disruption of trade after the loss of Gascony in 1453, not only deprived the Crown of customs revenue but probably also seemed to confirm the contemporary view (certainly wrong) that continued high imports, often handled by aliens, were draining bullion away.[18] Anti-alien feelings reached a peak with anti-alien riots in 1456–8. Resentment against the Italians was particularly acute, at first shown against the Venetians and Florentines for their financial dealings and their import of luxury goods, but extending to the Genoese in 1458 when the fate of Robert Sturmy's venture to the Mediterranean became known.[19]

Yet, while all these points are important, they still do not quite explain why the government became conscious of the possibilities of this particular statute after thirty years, and suddenly in 1459 initiated 104 prosecutions in two law terms alone. It is possible that awareness came gradually as a few cases were brought to the attention of the Exchequer from 1455 by informers sympathetic to the wool Staplers, and prompted perhaps by resentment of Italian competition which was encouraged by the Gloucestershire wool producers. In June 1455 two prosecutions occurred, apparently the first under the statutes.[20] John Sewer, one of the London woolpackers, accused John Nichol of Stow-on-the-Wold and John Briddock of Northleach of selling wool to Rinaldo Baroncelli for payment in a year's time contrary to the statutes of 8 and 9 Henry VI, but this did not unleash a general enquiry or a flood of accusations, although later prosecutions certainly show that other offences were occurring at this time. Not until May 1457 did another prosecution take place, when John Judde, a mercer and also customs collector at Chichester, accused John Townsend, similarly of Gloucestershire, of selling 140 sacks of Cotswold wool to Antonio de Camela and others for £800 payable in three instalments at six months, eighteen months and two-and-a-half years.[21] Shortly after this a few more cases were thrown up by the great Guildhall enquiry into breaches of the Staple regulations, which began in December 1457. The terms of the enquiry were broad enough to cover breaches of other statutes, too, and this time five country woolmen were prosecuted for allowing extended credit to Italians.[22] John Lenard of Chipping Campden had sold sixteen sacks of wool to Francesco di Michele for £112 repayable over twenty-one months; John Townsend of Lechlade had sold 147 sacks to Eduardo Cattaneo and Raffaello Doria for £1,078 repayable over twenty-two-and-a-half months; Henry Bishop of Burford had sold thirty sacks to Giovanni de' Bardi for £225 payable over two years and seven months; John Stokes of Chipping Norton sold fifty-two sacks to Giovanni da Ponte of Venice for £372 13s. 4d. payable over a similar period; and John Briddock of Northleach again found himself accused, this time of selling seventeen sacks to Bartolomeo Shyatis (degli Sciatti?) of Lucca for £205 6s. 8d. payable over twenty-three months. How far these cases, brought to the Exchequer court early in 1458, stimulated a general investigation is impossible to say, but if thoughts were turning that way they must have been powerfully encouraged by the withdrawal from England by October 1458 of Francisco Dyas, a Spaniard who left behind him many large debts to notable and angry Londoners. This, I think, was the final stimulus to Henry VI's attempt to raise money from breaches of this statute, and it was a classic case of an alien withdrawing with debts unpaid exactly as envisaged in the preamble of the original act.

Dyas arrived on the English scene as suddenly and dramatically as he left it. On 3 November 1453 he bought a safe-conduct for himself and three servants for five years.[23] This in itself was unusual for Spanish merchants, who usually came without servants and bought safe-conducts for only one or two years at a time. He met immediate trouble when he was accused of breaching the safe-conduct on his first arrival at Rochester by entering a walled town before he had been given licence to do so by the bailiff. Dyas was not amused, claimed this was a trumped-up charge, and sued the bailiff for damages for a half-day and a night in prison, for a forced payment, and for a further 3s. 4d. he alleged he had been compelled to pay for wine.[24] After this his business seems to have gone more smoothly. Dyas had close connections with the Italian trade: he exported on a Florentine galley from Southampton in 1456; he bought goods from Homobono Gritti and Giovanni de' Bardi in 1457; he stood surety with eleven Italians for Gritti and another Venetian in May 1458; and he used two Centurioni merchants to pay off debts of £499 in July that year.[25] He also acquired safe-conducts for two large Basque ships of 400 and 450 tons in 1456 and 1457, which were almost certainly involved in the Mediterranean trade, although they may have been going only to Andalusia.[26] His credit was obviously good: between 1455 and 1458 he was allowed credit by John Derby, Thomas Wattes, Amoneus Bertet, William Brogreve, and

Thomas Cooke, all London drapers; by Robert Colyns, merchant; and by Homobono Gritti of Venice, Giovanni de' Bardi of Florence, and Galioto and Leonello Centurioni of Genoa, for terms of between one and three years.[28] Whether through planned fraud, as Thomas Cooke later claimed, or some personal disaster, Dyas was known to have disappeared by October 1458, leaving bad debts behind him. On 19 October the Centurioni began a suit for £400 before the mayor and sheriffs in London, and had attached as Dyas's two fardels of silk valued at £1,000 then on a Venetian galley in the Thames. On 23 October Brogreve and on 29 October Bertet also began suits in the mayor's court. All three cases were considered in the Guildhall and it was decided that the attachment of the silk for the Centurioni was invalid since the galley had then been lying outside the jurisdiction of the City, but the attachment of it for the Londoners was valid because by then it had been brought ashore to the parish of All Hallows by virtue of the attachment made for the Italians. The Centurioni were at liberty to start their suit again and this they did on 26 November, but on 29 November all the documents in the case were called in from the City courts to the Exchequer.[29] The reason for this transfer of the cases was probably the Crown's realization that, since Dyas's safe-conduct had by now run out, he was an enemy alien, and therefore the Crown itself had a claim on the valuable silk as enemy goods. The case had no doubt been brought to its attention by the impatience of Thomas Cooke, the London alderman, who, rather than vie with others in London courts for the silk, paid for royal letters direct to the Spanish king asking him to ease the hearing of a case in Spanish courts. These letters were dated 2 December and information about the case must have been in the government's hands during the last week of November.[30]

Although the first prosecutions for breach of the credit regulations were not until the following May, given that the Crown would need time to gather evidence and have it all ready for such a large number of cases at once, it is quite likely that Dyas's default was the trigger for them. Dyas's disappearance was clearly seen as deliberate fraud, echoing the preamble to the statute exactly; those harmed included Thomas Cooke and others rich enough to make a very public fuss; the case was certainly known to officials in both the Exchequer and Chancery by November and December of 1458; and possibly those suing Dyas even drew attention to the registers of debts, which were to be the source for later Crown prosecutions against English merchants. Some of those, such as Thomas Wattes and John Derby, who had dealt with Dyas had every reason to feel aggrieved: not only had Dyas absconded with their goods but they were to make further losses through being prosecuted for the credit they had allowed him.

The scale of prosecutions in 1459 was very different from the previous ones. In comparison with eight cases in the previous four years, 110 cases were heard in 1459/60, 104 of them in the two terms of Trinity and Michaelmas 1459 alone. The rate then dropped away nearly completely with only a further six in the first three terms of 1460.[31] All cases but one were presented by William Notyngham, the king's attorney, underlining that the actions were the result of Crown policy and planning. The presentation of the cases was standard, generally giving the date and place of the offence, the parties concerned, the commodities, price, and length of credit involved. For instance on 8 June 1459 Notyngham, after citing the relevant clauses of 8 and 9 Henry VI, stated that William Brogreve, London draper, on 8 August 1455 in the parish of St Edmund Langbourne had sold to Francesco Guinigi twenty-eight coloured broadcloths for £112, half payable at the following 8 April (1456) and the rest on the following 8 October, thus allowing fourteen months for Guinigi to pay. Similarly, on 11 June he accused Henry Bishop of Burford, woolman, of selling to Giovanni de' Bardi on 12 February 1458 at Westminster thirty sacks of Cotswold wool for £220, with £40 payable at the following Pentecost (21 May 1458) and £60 at each subsequent Pentecost until 1461 (thus providing over three years and three months credit).[32] To the 110 cases in 1459/60 more can be added. The government had needed information and seems to have acquired it at least in part from searching London scriveners' registers of contracts made between the English sellers and their alien customers. The two registers which remain among the Exchequer records provide a further 177 instances of credit allowed to alien merchants.[33] A total of 287 cases clearly invites analysis.

The 110 prosecutions of 1459/60 stretch back to offences committed in January 1454, and come forward to some committed in August 1459 itself; clearly merchants continued to give credit to their alien customers even though the Exchequer had started prosecutions the previous May. The dates of offences were fairly evenly spread out, with seven from 1454, twenty from 1455, twelve from 1456, thirty-two from 1457, twenty-four from 1458 and eleven from 1459; in four cases the date is unspecified. Ninety-three English merchants were prosecuted, sixty-nine from London and twenty-four country woolmen and clothiers. Most were charged with one offence only, although the debt registers in fact show them allowing too much credit to others at the same time; thirteen Londoners and three countrymen were charged with two offences, two Londoners and one countryman with three offences, Stephen Forster, the London alderman and fishmonger, was charged with four, and John Forthey, a dyer from Cirencester, with five.[34] Those prosecuted seem to be the sort of cross-section of merchants one might expect given the pattern of England's trade, with no evidence of any political bias against a particular London faction among them, although some individuals may have been treated more favourably than others. The offenders prosecuted ranged

from the ranks of the aldermen, sheriffs, mayors, members of Common
Council, and masters and wardens of the great companies, to the more
modest members of some of the lesser guilds.[35] The proportion of those in
the upper ranks seems high (25 per cent were aldermen or just about to
enter that group, and a further 10 per cent were notable as masters and
wardens of their companies). But this is less likely to have been a
deliberate political decision than an economic one, since they were the
richer group from whom the Crown expected to extract more money. But
the decision may not even have been as deliberate as that implies: these
men were simply those most likely to be dealing in overseas trade, to have
the resources to allow long-term credit, and thus to be principal offenders.
It is possible that the Crown pursued countrymen more deliberately, since
these make up 26 per cent of those prosecuted, whereas in the debt
registers examined below they make only 13 per cent of the contracts with
aliens. The country woolmen certainly allowed some of the longest terms
of credit to their Italian customers, but prosecutions did not depend
entirely on the size or length of the credit allowed. Sums ranged from £8 to
£800: at one extreme, John Chamber, mercer, was prosecuted for selling
ten kerseys worth £8 to Antonio Baroso on 26 July 1455 for payment in
eleven months; at the other, John Elmes, senior, of Henley on Thames
was prosecuted for selling 120 sacks of wool worth ten marks each, making
altogether £800, to Antonio Centurioni on 12 May 1457, to be repaid in
three instalments at the next three feasts of the Nativity of St John the
Baptist (24 June). On the other hand, Matthew Philip, alderman and
goldsmith, who lent £251 14s. 6d. to four Venetians for a term of fourteen
months was not prosecuted at all: perhaps some personal favour was
involved here.[36] Time ranged from three months (which was in fact not
illegal) to the five years and two months which William Athelam of
Westbury in Wiltshire allowed Gerard de Wert and Matthew Nunzigh-
mark in February 1459 for the payment in five instalments of £99 for
twenty-six cloths.[37] Most of the commodities on which credit was allowed
were England's usual exports of wool, cloth, tin, and pewter. The debtors
cited included Dutch, Spanish, Gascon, and German merchants, but in
92 of the 110 cases (84 per cent) they were Italians, perhaps to be
expected as these traded on the longer routes which demanded longer
terms for credit. The same names occur over and again, and the balance of
nationalities within the group probably accurately reflects the Italian
presence in England: thirty-three cases involved sales to seventeen
Genoese; twenty-two cases involved eleven Venetians; twenty-two cases
involved six Florentines; eight involved three Lucchese; and the other
seven cases involved six Italians not yet identified by city. The cases show
a concentration of business contracts drawn up in one or two places, as
would be expected: most of the contracts with countrymen were made at

Westminster, most Londoners selling to Italians did so in the parishes of St Mary Wolnoth, and St Edmund, with a few contracts made in St Stephen Walbrook, St Mary le Bow, St Botolph, Billingsgate, and St Swithin. Sales to Germans and Dutchmen took place in All Hallows Dowgate, St James Vintry, and St Augustine Cheapside.

The cases ended in a variety of ways. Mainly they underline the difficulties of the Crown in enforcing relatively minor trade legislation, and in making money from it, but although the Crown did not extract much from the merchants, the cases certainly were irritants for several merchants who were committed to the Flete and for others who had to appear or send attorneys to the Exchequer court. One who might have felt particularly aggrieved was the innocent William Partrych of Chipping Norton, accused on 12 November 1459 of selling twenty-one-and-a-half sacks and twenty-two cloves of wool for 220 marks to Giovanni da Ponte of Venice for payment in two instalments, the second on 24 June 1460, just seven-and-a-half months after the deal was struck. Three writs to the sheriffs of Middlesex and Oxford failed to find him but on the fourth he was found and arrested in Oxfordshire, and sent up to the Flete. He was able to prove that at the time he sold the wool, da Ponte had already taken out denization papers and so did not fall within the scope of the statute.[38]

In all, forty-three cases seem to have been resolved by the time of Henry VI's deposition. Partrych was the only one to deny the offence and win the case; seventeen cases ended because, although they denied the offences, the accused none the less bought pardons to avoid further trouble; five ended with the offenders paying fines to avoid the expense of a jury to prove their innocence; one was actually found guilty and paid for a pardon. Nineteen other cases ended because the accused already had letters of general pardon broad enough to cover this offence. Henry therefore received money from only 17 individuals who were involved in 23 of the 110 offences. The amounts paid were not always recorded in the Fines section of the Memoranda Rolls, but it is clear that the four paying fines to avoid juries paid £35, and five of the thirteen paying for pardons paid £93 6s. 9d. altogether. Thus from about half of those who paid anything in his reign, Henry received only £128 6s. 8d., a useful sum in the dire circumstances of 1459 but possibly hardly worth the trouble and expense of the 110 prosecutions.

A further forty-three cases, especially those against most of the countrymen, were progressing very slowly at the time of Henry's deposition, with frequent non-appearances and adjournments. Some of these cases then remained moribund for years under Edward IV: the case against Ralph Josslyn, for instance, was not pushed actively again until 1474.[39] Other cases came to an end more quickly with the presentation at various dates during Edward's reign of general pardons dated 4 November 1461, which he had granted as an amnesty at his first parliament. Clearly Edward IV had received money for these pardons, but they were not issued specifically for these credit cases, so the cases themselves cannot be said to have brought money to the Exchequer. The other twenty-four cases have no recorded ending in the Memoranda Rolls. Some dragged with adjournments through to dates between 1461 and 1466 and then disappeared, a few were specifically revived in 1468/9 but also came to no recorded end. Presumably the offender similarly produced letters of pardon and the cases were dropped.

For the prosecution the Crown's attorney needed very precise information on the loans, and this seems to have come, at least in part, from what must have been a series of London debt registers. Only two of these, those kept by William Styfford and John Thorpe, remain in the Public Record Office, probably because the scriveners for some reason did not claim them back.[40] The exact standing of the registers is not clear: Professor Postan called Thorpe's book a scrivener's day book, while Dr Jenks recently suggested that these were more formal registers of the mayor's court.[42] Whatever their precise status, they clearly provided most but not all of the information the Exchequer used, and some of the recorded debts are exactly those prosecuted.

The register of William Styfford is a continuous roll of parchment and that of John Thorpe a paper ledger of six folios, but the form used is common to both. The borrower, identified by name, occupation, and nationality, acknowledged the sum of money due to the lender, similarly identified by name, occupation, and nationality or, if English, by town. The registers do not only record sales by Englishmen to aliens, but also those between Englishmen, and between aliens (especially between Italians). The date of the contract (by the month in Styfford's book but by the day as well in Thorpe's) and the date of repayment, or repayments if by instalments, were also given. Neither names the goods bought and neither names the place of the transaction, yet both of these are named in the prosecutions in the Memoranda Rolls; the debt registers were clearly not the only information available to the king's attorney, but they may well have provided the initial information. Certainly they have been used and annotated by an Exchequer official, although the significance of the marginalia is not entirely clear. The three main marginal marks are a small black dot; an 's' probably indicating *soluta* or *solutum est*; and *fiat*, possibly indicating an intention to prosecute. There are 18 marginal dots in Styfford's book and 37 in Thorpe's, making 55 contracts marked up, but only 44 denote cases of credit beyond six months; 11 are of less than six months and therefore legal. Moreover only 14 of these 55 contracts were eventually prosecuted and there were at least a further 77 contracts which were for over six months but were not marked up. However 43 of the 55 marked contracts did involve individuals who were prosecuted, even if not for the exact cases recorded in these two registers. There were 20 cases marked as *soluta* or *solutum est* in Styfford's book and 13 in Thorpe's. Of these 33 contracts, 23 were prosecuted and payments were made by the accused for pardons or fines, and 10 were not prosecuted, but the offenders may have made payments out of court. *Fiat* marked 13 contracts in Styfford's book and 3 in Thorpe's, of these 9 were prosecuted and a further 5 contracts involved individuals who were prosecuted for other offences. Only 2 were not found in the Memoranda Rolls at all.

The marginalia, although they do not tally exactly with the cases as finally prosecuted, probably indicate an intention to prosecute, which was later changed in some cases either because of payment or influence. The books were certainly carefully scrutinized but the Crown did not sue all those whom it could have done. Indeed it took up only a minority of the actual offences. In Styfford's book, which recorded eighty-seven debts in the nine months from May 1457 to January 1458, sixty-three debts were for over six months. Forty-four of these were allowed by Englishmen to aliens so were illegal under the statutes of 8 and 9 Henry VI, yet only eight cases were pursued – a take-up rate of 18 per cent. A similar pattern appears in Thorpe's book. Thirty-five of the 104 contracts were for more than six months. Thirty-three (possibly thirty-four) were allowed by Englishmen who could therefore have been sued, but only six were pursued – again a take-up rate of only 18 per cent. It is true, however, that prosecutions hit a higher percentage of the offending creditors than this suggests, since some who made several contracts for more than six months were prosecuted for only one; others were prosecuted for offences not recorded in these two registers, but which were probably in other registers called into the Exchequer at the same time. In Styfford's book nineteen of the thirty-six cases not pursued, none the less involved men prosecuted at this time for offences against the statutes of 8 and 9 Henry VI. For instance, John Forthey of Cirencester, prosecuted for five offences committed between April 1458 and February 1459 involving sales of wool worth £1,480 1s. 2d., was not prosecuted for the offence which was recorded in Styfford's register, a sale worth £247 made in June 1467 to Giacomo Salvati, Giovanni de' Bardi, and Niccolo de Rabata, repayable over two and a half years. Similarly Henry Brice, the London fuller, prosecuted for two offences committed in 1454 and 1458, was not brought to court for two offences in Styfford's register, a sale of £190 2s. 8d. of goods to Marco and Humfredo Giustiniani, and one of £50 7s. 10d. to Raffaello Doria and Galioto Centurioni, both with repayment dates in excess of a year, nor for one in Thorpe's register involving a sale of £30 to William Ketweigh, repayable in just under two years.[43] With these cases taken into account some 61 per cent of known offending individuals were actually brought before the Exchequer. A similar proportion occurs in Thorpe's register.

In one way the registers diverge markedly. William Styfford's register records mainly sales to Italian merchants: 86 per cent of the sales are to Italians alone, a further 8 per cent to partnerships of Italians and Englishmen, and the final 6 per cent include sales to Dutchmen and Spaniards. John Thorpe's register records predominantly sales to Germans: 72 per cent are to Germans alone, 9 per cent to partnerships of German and English merchants, and the remaining 19 per cent include sales to Englishmen, Spaniards, Brabanters, Zeelanders, and Italians. The difference in the buyers recorded in the registers produces different patterns in the sellers and the terms of the sales. In both registers the sellers are mainly Englishmen (90 per cent in Thorpe's, 70 per cent in Styfford's, which also records a number of sales between Italians), but Thorpe's register shows that the Londoners who dealt with the Germans were mainly mercers, tailors, and pewterers, while Styfford's shows that those who dealt with the Italians were mainly drapers. The length of credit varied too, with generally shorter terms allowed the Germans than the Italians, who traded to more distant markets.

Although the two registers and the 110 prosecutions of 1459/60 are different types of sources and must be a far from complete record of the credit at the time, together they do provide interesting detail about how international credit was working at the time – about debtors and creditors, commodities, amounts and length of credit, and terms of repayment – and some general comment can be made.

Credit was allowed to all nationalities. This evidence shows that the takers were predominantly Italians and Germans, which is probably correct, reflecting the largest and busiest alien groups in London in the 1450s; but Dutchmen, Brabanters, Zeelanders, Spaniards, Gascons, and men from Navarre were also allowed credit. The prosecutions in the Exchequer and the two debt registers show some seventy-eight members of the Italian community in England receiving credit in the late 1450s. Thirty were Genoese, twenty-six were Venetians, eleven were Florentines, five Lucchese, and for six the home town is uncertain. The prosecutions indicate that the Florentines and Venetians were the biggest buyers of wool, taking 72 per cent between them, but the Genoese were the main buyers of cloth. The creditors not unexpectedly included many well-known figures of the time: members of the Doria, Cattanei, Centurioni, Lomellini, Nigroni, Salvago, and Spinola families of Genoa were frequently allowed extended credit, as were Francesco Guinigi of Lucca, and Homobono Gritti, Humfredo and Marco Giustiniani, Antonio Morosini, Giovanni da Ponte, and Niccolo da Veghia, all of Venice. Although the number of Florentines was relatively small, some dealt frequently: Antonio Lutiano was cited six times in the prosecutions and Lodowico Strozzi four times; but Giovanni Lomellini of Genoa was also cited five times.

The English creditors included both countrymen and Londoners. The countrymen were predominantly Gloucestershire men, especially in dealings with Germans. Of the twenty-four countrymen prosecuted in 1459/60, twelve were from Gloucestershire, five of them dealing with Germans in cloth and wool, while seven dealt in wool with Italians; eight Oxford men sold wool to Italians; three Wiltshire and Somerset men sold cloth to Italians and Germans; and a Berkshire man sold wool to Italians. In Styfford's register the countrymen dealing with Italians are fairly evenly spread over Gloucestershire, Oxfordshire, and Wiltshire together with one from Somerset, but in Thorpe's register the German trade is heavily in the hands of Gloucestershire men, with twelve of the thirteen country contracts involving them. The Londoners naturally included many from the upper social and economic strata, men such as Geoffrey Boleyn, Geoffrey Feldyng, Ralph Josselyn, Thomas Oulgreve, John Walshawe, Hugh Wyche, and John Young, and others who were aldermen, sheriffs, mayors, masters and wardens of their companies, and members of Common Council. These were the men who regularly dealt heavily in overseas trade, and who had sufficient capital and turnover to bear long-term credit transactions, but credit was not confined to them, for lesser men offered credit too, some preferring at this stage in their careers to act with partners, as did the draper Richard Payn, who sold cloth to Percivale Grillo and Giovanni Lomellini jointly with other members of his company.[44] The Londoners belonged to a wide range of companies. Among those prosecuted were skinners, fishmongers, a goldsmith, a girdler, a brasier, and a haberdasher, as well as merchants, and a member of the king's household; on the debt registers there also appear shermen, ironmongers, beer-brewers, a vintner, and a clerk. However, many belonged to the Drapers', Mercers', and Grocers' Companies. Of the sixty-nine Londoners prosecuted, almost all for dealings with Italians, twenty-four were drapers, ten were mercers, and nine were grocers. This pattern is reflected in Styfford's book, which deals mainly with the Italian trade and where 45 per cent of the contracts recorded invoved drapers, and 11 per cent each grocers and mercers. It is markedly different from the pattern in Thorpe's book, which deals with more German trade, where 38 per cent of the debts registered were for mercers, 19 per cent each for tailors and pewterers, and only 2 per cent involved drapers. This shows the expected interest of the drapers in the Mediterranean trade, where they could easily sell cloth, and of the mercers, tailors, and pewterers in the German and Low Country trade, where they could acquire the linen and other mercery they wanted for sale and where pewter made a useful alternative to cloth when the Low Countries showed themselves hostile to English cloth.

The debt registers unfortunately do not record the commodities sold, but this information was acquired elsewhere and given in the prosecutions. The bulk of the transactions, unsurprisingly, touched wool and cloth. Forty-one cases involved credit sales of wool for £8,643, 41 per cent of sales being to Florentines and 31 per cent to Venetians; fifty-three cases involved sales of cloth for £5181, 47 per cent being taken by Genoese merchants. Seven further cases involved tin worth over £504, and eight cases involved the resale of Mediterranean goods – cotton, alum, oil, pepper – to Genoese and Venetian merchants who perhaps found they had run out of supplies to satisfy customers. The cases provide detail on the market prices of wool and cloth, but not always on the quality. Wool was sold from about £3 14s. 0d. to £12 the sack, but most was sold for between £5 6s. 8d. and the eleven marks (£7 6s. 8d.) which Cotswold wool generally cost. Although in the late 1450s wool prices were at their lowest ever, these prices are above those found by Dr Lloyd and reflect a continued Italian willingness to pay reasonable prices for good wool, although they most probably also include interest payable on the loan.[45] Much cloth was coloured broadcloth of 24 yards length which fetched prices ranging from £2 12s. 0d. to £16, but most fetched between £3 and £5 each. Kerseys and straits were cheaper, kerseys ranging from 15s. to 18s. each (the equivalent of £2 5s. to £2 14s. a broadcloth at the customs computation of three kerseys to the broadcloth), and straits fetched between 6s. 10d. and 9s. each (the equivalent of £1 7s. 4d. to £1 16s. a broadcloth, at the computation of four to the broadcloth).

The amount of credit allowed varied enormously: prosecutions were for allowing credit of £8 and of £800, credit in Styfford's book ranged from £5 to £800, but sums in Thorpe's for the German trade were lower, from £1 2s. to £201 10s. However, even in the Italian trade most debts were for under £200: in Styfford's register 53 per cent of debts were under £50, 21 per cent between £51 and £100, and 18 per cent between £101 and £200, and among the prosecutions where the Crown might have been expected to pursue the cases involving the largest sums, still 22 per cent were under £50, 25 per cent between £51 and £100, and 33 per cent between £101 and £200. The time allowed for repayment similarly varied widely, although usually under two years. Even among the cases prosecuted, 22 per cent had been for credit between six months and a year, and 38 per cent between a year and eighteen months, although 18 per cent had been for between two and three years and 15 per cent for over three years. In Styfford's register 86 per cent of the debts had been for under eighteen months, and indeed 26 per cent had been legitimate at under six months, while in Thorpe's register, which dealt with the nearer German markets,

97 per cent had been for under eighteen months, and no less than 65 per cent had been, in fact, for less than six months.

The amount of credit allowed and received by some individuals was substantial. The country woolmen and clothiers seem to have allowed the greatest amount of credit to aliens. William Athelam of Westbury in Wiltshire allowed two Germans an exceptional five years and two months to repay £99 for cloth,[46] and Italians were regularly allowed eighteen months to two years to repay large sums. John Briddock of Northleach, on 19 September 1457, sold wool worth £205 6s. 8d. to Bartolomeo Shyatis (degli Sciatti?) for £54 down and two instalments over one year and eleven months, and more wool worth £293 6s. 8d. to Shyatis and Manfredo Gentile for no immediate payment but three instalments over one year and nine months.[47] He thus had at least £444 13s. 4d. outstanding for the autumn months of 1457. John Forthey of Cirencester through his various transactions was owed at least £935 between July and Christmas 1458; this rose to £1,066 between February and Easter 1459, and dropped to £889 between Easter and the following Christmas as some instalments fell due.[48] John Townsend of Lechlade in two transactions alone in March 1457 sold wool worth £800 to Antonio de Camela, and £1,078 to Eduardo Cattaneo and Raffaello Doria for only £356 down.[49] He was thus prepared and able to allow £1,522 credit until the following February, when one instalment fell due, and still £1,161 to August 1458, when another instalment was due. The debt of Cattaneo and Doria was not due to be cleared until February 1459 and that of Camela not until August 1460. The Italians' credit was clearly generally good at this point, despite the bullion shortage and the looming crisis for the Genoese of compensation for the Sturmy affair. A few men, such as John Worksop of London in four transactions in January 1458, preferred the security of having English woolpackers or drapers act as guarantors by taking joint liability with Italians, and John Elmes of Henley on Thames did the same for the very large sum of £840 which he allowed to Genoese merchants in May 1457, but most English merchants continued to trust the credit worthiness of their Italian clients. Trade was regular and the merchants were well-known dealers. Antonio Lutiano of Florence was referred to in six cases in the Memoranda Rolls for debts of £1,050 16s. 8d. between 1456 and 1459, and for eight-and-a-half months in 1459 four of these overlapped, leaving him liable for £896; similarly Humfredo Giustiniani of Venice owed £661 for wool at one time.[50] Since we have incomplete records the total sums they owed were doubtless much larger. The picture is already well known, but it is interesting to see it continuing in a period of tight money.

Despite the money shortages, there is little evidence at this level of a return to direct barter. An exchange of goods would need to be precisely specified for amounts and price. This would be done through indentures separate from the registration of the debt, but one might expect a note in the register of such a conditional debt. However, only one such condition was recorded in Styfford's register, when Thomas Wattes sold goods worth £147 16s. to Francesco Dyas in return for oil. Moreover, out of the 110 cases prosecuted at the Exchequer, where more detail about the debts is produced, only seven mention repayment in kind. One is the same deal between Wattes and Dyas recorded in Styfford's register, and the other six concern two fishmongers who jointly sold 28 cwt. of pewter vessels in March 1458 to a Dutchman for 28 cwt. of corverfish to be delivered in June; John Young who sold wool worth £135 13s. 4d. to Lutiano in return for thirty-six butts of malmsey to be delivered at Christmas in fifteen months' time; John Jourdan, tailor, and Henry Brice, fuller, who both separately sold cloth to Giovanni Lomellini for oil; and two further cases in which defences were made that the sales had been for immediate payment, one in woad and the other in silk.[51] All the other debts were simply expressed in money terms, usually noting that the debt was in silver, and often with a statement that the repayment was expected in silver. This common form is shown in the accusation against Henry Waver, draper, that he had sold to Giovanni de' Bardi twenty-three sacks of wool, valued at £108, for £108 of silver payable at the following 10 October and not promptly.[52] It is, however, likely that many of these debts simply expressed in money terms might in the end have been repaid either in money, or in easily transferable money substitutes which needed no further specification than the sum of money itself. The precise form of the repayment could be arranged later. Repayments from Italians in particular, with their mastery of financial techniques, could easily be by letters of exchange, as the *Libelle of Englyshe Polycye* had complained in 1436, but equally some repayments from Italians might well have been in silver, since Venice was one of the few centres in Europe in the late 1450s still to have incoming silver supplies from Serbian and Bosnian mines.[53] Occasionally the debt registers mention, where it was already agreed, payment by bill of exchange or by transfer of bills. Both William Fyncheham and Thomas Porter arranged to be repaid by letters of exchange in Antwerp. Thomas Dounton was to receive money owed him by two Germans from the mercer, Thomas Fyler, doubtless receiving from the Germans a bill in which Fyler promised to pay them for goods he had bought from them. This is made explicit in the case of Richard Payn, who sold goods to William Ketweigh, who in return formally transferred seven obligations from him by six London skinners and a tailor. Presumably Ketweigh imported furs and used his own debtors to pay his creditor.[54]

Dealings with the Italians as shown in the Memoranda Rolls and Styfford's book do not suggest marked seasonal rhythms of buying or repayment to fit galley or convoy sailings. Repayments in particular were steady throughout the year at various dates in most months, although there is some concentration round the traditional quarter days of the Nativity of St John the Baptist, Michaelmas, Christmas, and Easter. On the other hand Dr Jenks has established that the credit allowed to Germans and their repayments does reflect to some extent a credit chain in the Low Countries which is partly dependent on the rhythm of the fairs. He found that the majority of debts were incurred at times which allowed export to the main fairs, and some repayments were stipulated for the fairs. William Fyncham, for instance, was owed £40 by two Germans, payable at the following Pentecost, unless they paid him by letter of exchange at the next Antwerp fair. Repayment dates in general were not so clearly tied to the fairs, as many of these too were at traditional Church festivals.[55] What does seem clear is that individual creditors, whether lending to Germans or Italians, made sure that they had a fairly steady stream of repayments through the year, to avoid the personal embarrassment of lack of cash.

The debt registers also offer a few other details. They show women allowing credit to aliens on a small scale: Alice Gladman was associated with her husband William in allowing £16 to the German, William Ketweigh, repayable in eleven-and-three-quarter months; Elene Sterre, a widow of Cirencester, allowed £10 16s. 8d. to Henry Stefart over one year and two months, and two London widows allowed similar sized credit to Germans for less than six months.[56] They show Italians in London allowing credit to others, as in September 1457, when Homobono Gritti of Venice allowed credit of a year on nine separate transactions, seven to Genoese, one to a Florentine, and one to a Spaniard.[57] They also show allowance of credit to Italians to pay off their customs duties: two Genoese at Southampton were allowed four months to pay £12 in 1458, but six Genoese were allowed twenty months to pay £98 6s. 8d. at Chichester in 1457.[58] Not all debts recorded were for the simple purchase of goods. The insistence of John Gaussem, a former merchant of Bordeaux who emigrated to London after 1453, that three merchants of Spain, Navarre, and Bayonne should repay him abroad eight days after the safe arrival of the *Mary* of Navarre, which the Navarrese merchant owned, two round sums of £12 and £5, one in gold, one in sterling, or double the sums later in London, may indicate straight loans to them for trade or for victualling the ship, loans which Gaussem needed repaid promptly abroad for his own trade; it may also indicate an element of insurance in the transaction.[59]

What conclusions might be drawn from these two sets of documents? Overall they show that in the period of the bullion shortage of the late 1450s credit was allowed for large and small sums, over long and short periods, by and to rich merchants and lesser men. All this is already well known, but there is enough information here to put these details into a working perspective of regular trade in the late 1450s. The amounts allowed varied widely but the majority, even those allowed to Italians, were well under £200. The time for repayment also varied considerably, but many repayments from merchants from the nearer eastern markets actually did fall within the legal limit of six months. The contracts for credit on that route also reflect the seasonal rhythms of the Low Country fairs. Repayments from Italians, especially of debts to the country wool and cloth suppliers, were understandably allowed longer to fit the rhythms of voyages to Italy and back, but many of these too were expected to be paid within eighteen months. Even in a time of tight money there is only limited reference to payment in kind. There is also relatively little mention of letters of exchange and transfer of bills, but it is arguable that these were normally more likely to be produced, as available, at the time repayment was due, rather than be foreseen and specified at the time of the original sale one or two years before. The prosecutions and the debt registers make clear that credit was a regular feature of many individuals' trade, repeated over and over again, often with the same clients. Whatever had been the fears of the protesters in 1429/30, whatever the author of the *Libelle* said about the deceit of the Italians, whatever the strictures of the statutes of 8 and 9 Henry VI, English merchants continued to allow credit to aliens.

Yet, clearly, those who framed the statutes were right to distrust credit. Things could go wrong, as lawsuits regularly show. Quite aside from the spectacular defection of Francisco Dyas in 1458, others were also in trouble. Antonio Lutiano of Florence was seen by many as a good credit risk, and probably repaid much as it fell due, but he overreached himself at about this time. As the Crown prosecution against John Forthey of Cirencester continued into the first year of the reign of Edward IV (1461/2), there is a note that Lutiano was then in prison because he had failed to pay £253 3s. 0d., two instalments of the £379 14s. 6d. debt he had contracted with Forthey; he also owed £30 to Henry Benet. At Michaelmas 1463 he was either again or still in prison with outstanding debts of £3,381 to three fellow Italians.[60] John Forthey of Cirencester also had to sue Simone Nori of Florence for £130 10s. 0d. outstanding from a debt of £180 10s. 0d. contracted with Forthey's namesake, the woolman, and due in 1460.[61] Also, as shown above, some Englishmen looked for English guarantors for sale to Italians. Possibly the late 1450s were indeed proving to be more difficult years with more defaults due to cash-flow problems but this remains difficult to prove. English lenders tried to ensure a steady stream of repayments which they could then use to pay their own suppliers, and no doubt foreign merchants did the same. Italians could also use their own exchange system to cover difficult periods, but undoubtedly they found themselves from time to time in difficulties if ships were delayed, or goods were slow to move. On the other hand it is clear that despite hard times, credit continued to be offered as necessary. Even at the height of the anti-alien movement and hostility to Italians, their regular suppliers continued to allow them credit for the goods they bought. Moreover, a little later, in the early 1460s, Englishmen such as Geoffrey Boleyn were willing to make straight loans to Genoese merchants to help them pay the compensation demanded over the Sturmy affair. The interest charged was high at about 14 per cent a year, no doubt reflecting the monetary shortage of the time, but it was made available when the Genoese wanted it.[62] No doubt many of the Londoners, especially the drapers, saw their fortunes as tied up with regular and smooth Italian trade, while the Staplers might still have seen the Italians as unwelcome competitors.

The exact scale of this credit within England's overseas trade, however, continues to elude us. Crude speculation is possible but the value of any conclusions would be highly suspect. None the less, one possibility follows. In the two years from May 1457 to May 1459, in the debt registers of Styfford and Thorpe alone, one of which in fact runs only for nine months, 191 debts were recorded for some £9,400. At least 181 of these were contracted by foreigners, or by a foreigner with an English partner, and most, if not all, were certainly for goods bought with a view to export. Prosecutions recorded on the Memoranda Rolls for credit offences include fifty-six actually committed within those same years (fourteen of them drawn from the above registers) involving £8,800 of credit. Unfortunately we do not know what proportion of the total transactions, or of the total offences, these sets of documents represent, but if the Crown take-up of 18 per cent of offences from these two registers was typical of other registers too, then possibly the fifty-six cases represent some 311 offences known to the Crown; if the sums involved in the fifty-six cases were representative than perhaps overall nearly £49,000 of illegal credit was allowed to aliens in the two years, or on average some £24,500 a year. These cases occurred when England's export trade in wool, cloth, and tin, her main export commodities, might have been worth some £115,000 to £120,000 a year,[63] so illegal credit alone might have been extended to a fifth of England's export trade. But what proportion were these offences of the total credit transactions? In Thorpe's register 65 per cent of recorded debts of aliens were for legitimate credit of less than six months, whereas in Styfford's the proportion was only 26 per cent, but in either case the total amount of credit allowed to alien exporters would have been considerably higher than the amount given above. To this must be added credit transactions between English exporters, many of whom might also have been part of a chain of credit. It would not be surprising (given also what historians know about credit throughout the wool trade) if well over half

England's exports were locked into a chain of credit, legal and illegal. Unfortunately, such suggestions remain pure speculation. Also unfortunately, from these documents we still have no means of estimating whether the amount of credit increased as money grew scarcer, or whether (as is more likely) it was declining as a period of tight money produced a period of credit limitation.[64] None the less, although they do not in the end enable us to push forward very far the debate on the scale and changes of credit in the economy, they do throw a concentrated light on the problem in a period which was probably the worst in the later Middle Ages for the extension of credit. They suggest very strongly indeed that even in a time of considerable commercial, financial, and monetary difficulties, and even if the scale was lower and interest rates higher, credit in international trade remained not only necessary but also widespread.

APPENDIX A

Analysis of 110 credit cases prosecuted at the Exchequer in 1459/60 (PRO E159/235, 236).

1 Amount of credit:

Sum	Percentage of cases in which allowed
Under £50	22
£51–100	25
£101–200	33
£201–300	11
£301–400	6
£401 and over	3

2 Length of credit:

Time	Percentage of cases in which allowed
6 months to 1 year	22
1 year to 18 months	38
18 months to 2 years	7
2 years to 3 years	18
3 years to 4 years	9
over 4 years	6

3 Commodities and values for which credit was allowed:

Commodity	Value	Percentage of cases in which involved	Percentage of total value
Wool	£8,643	37	54
Cloth	£5,181	48	32
Tin	over £504	6	3
Lead	£24	1	–
Misc.*	£1,644	7	10

*These are sales by Londoners of pepper, oil, cotton, and alum back to Italians.

4 Nationalities of debtors:

Nationality	Percentage of cases in which involved
Italian	84
German	8
Spanish/ Gascon	3.5
Dutch	1
Uncertain	3.5

5 Buyers of wool and cloth by nationality.

Nationality	Percentage of wool bought (by value)
Florentines	41
Venetians	31
Genoese	15
Lucchese	12
Germans	1

Nationality	Percentage of cloth bought (by value)
Genoese	47
Venetians	11
Florentines	9
Spaniards	8
Lucchese	5
Germans	5
Uncertain (most probably Italian)	15

APPENDIX B

Analysis of eighty-seven debts registered by William Styfford: May 1457–January 1459 (PRO E101/128/36).

1 Amount of credit:

Sum	Percentage of debts in which allowed
Uncertain	1
Under £50	53
£51–100	21
£101–200	18
£201–300	3.4
£301–400	0
Over £400	3.5

2 Length of credit:

Time	Percentage of debts in which allowed
Under 6 months (legal)	26.5
6 months to 1 year	41.5
1 year to 18 months	18.5
18 months to 2 years	8
2 to 3 years	4.5
3 to 4 years	1

3 Nationality of creditors:

Nationality	Percentage of debts in which involved
English	70
Italian	30

4 Nationality of debtors:

Nationality	Percentage of debts in which involved	Percentage of value of debts in which involved
Italian		
Venetian	32	29
Genoese	28	23
Florentine	14	14
Lucchese	7	7

Nationality of debtors:

Nationality	Percentage of debts in which involved	Percentage of value of debts in which involved
Flor/Lucc jointly	2	3.5
Italian unspecified	1	0.5
	84	77
Italian/English jointly		
Flor/Eng jointly	5	5
Gen/Eng jointly	2	12
Ven/Eng jointly	1	0.5
Lucc/Eng jointly	1	0.3
	9	18
Spanish	5	3
English	1	1
Dutch	1	1

APPENDIX C

Analysis of 104 debts registered by John Thorpe, May 1457–May 1459 (PRO E101/128/37).

1 Amount of credit:

Sum	Percentage of debts in which allowed
Uncertain	1
Under £50	84
£51–100	7.5
£101–200	6.5
£201–300	1

2 Length of credit:

Time	Percentage of debts in which allowed
Uncertain	1
Under 6 months (legal)	65
6 months to 1 year	24
1 year to 18 months	8
18 months to 2 years	1
2 to 5 years	0
Over 5 years	1

3 Nationality of creditors:

Nationality	Percentage of debts in which involved
English	90
German	10

4 Nationality of debtors

Nationality	Percentage of debts in which involved
German	70
German/ English jointly	9
English	10
Brabant	1
Brabant/ English jointly	1
Zeeland/ English jointly	1
Spanish/ Gascon	5
Spanish/ English jointly	1
Italian	2

APPENDIX D

Names of creditors prosecuted in the Exchequer (PRO E159/231–236, Recorda)

1   Countrymen

Gloucestershire:

Thomas Arnold of Cirencester, gentleman, 236 Mich. m. 51
John Briddock of Northleach, 231 Trin. m. 16, 234 Easter m. 22, 236 Mich. m. 31
Hugo Calcote of Calcote, chapman, 236 Mich. m. 41
Richard Doo of Lechlade, 235 Trin. mm. 9, 12
John Forthey of Cirencester, dyer, 235 Trin. mm. 40, 64, 66, 236 Mich. m. 58, Hill m. 7
Henry Gayrstange of Cirencester, 236 Mich. m. 74
John Hardyng of Tetbury, 236 Mich. m. 53
Simon Hardyng of Tetbury, 236 Mich. m. 53
John Lenard of Chipping Campden, 234 Hill, m. 17, 236 Trin m. 4
John Nycholl of Stow-on-the-Wold, 231 Trin. mm. 16–17.
John Stoby of Cirencester, clothman, 235 Trin. m. 21
John Tame of Fairford, 236 Mich. m. 32d

John Townesende of Lechlade, woolman, 233 Easter 23d, 234 Hill, m. 18

Henry Wakefield of Chipping Campden, gentleman, 236 Mich. m. 73

Oxfordshire:

John Austyn of Woodstock, woolman, 236 Mich. m. 43
Henry Bysshop of Burford, 234 Hill, m. 20, 235 Trin. m. 10
John Colles of Deddington, merchant, 236 Mich. m. 61
William Colles of Deddington, merchant, 236 Mich. m. 61
John Elmes senior of Henley on Thames, 236 Trin. m. 7
John Hochon of Chipping Norton, 236 Mich. m. 81
William Partrych of Chipping Norton, 236 Mich. m. 82
William Stodham of Burford (alias William Symon, woolman), 236 Mich. m. 84
John Stokes of Chipping Norton, 234 Hill, m. 27

Wiltshire:

William Athelam of Westbury, clothmaker, 235 Trin. m. 52d
John Wyke of Trowbridge, merchant, 236 Mich. m. 40

Berkshire:

William Hales of Abingdon, 235 Trin. m. 56

Somerset:

John Estmond de la Rode, clothman, 236 Mich. m. 55

2   Londoners.

Drapers:

Thomas Bernewey, 236 Mich. m. 18
Amoneus Bertet, 236 Mich. m. 36
William Bray, 236 Mich. 67
William Brogreve, 235 Trin. mm. 31, 51
John Brokford (alias John Wakeley) 236 Mich. m. 36d
John Claymond, 235 Trin. m. 44, Mich. m. 48
William Dellowe, 235 Trin. m. 34, 236 Mich. m. 45
John Derby, 235 Trin. mm. 33, 54
Richard Fordell, 235 Trin. m. 61
Thomas Heyward, 236 Mich. m. 35
Bartholomew James, 235 Trin. m. 47
Ralph Josselyn, 235 Trin. m. 20
John Pake, 235 Trin. m. 48

Richard Payn, 235 Trin. m. 61, 236 Mich m. 18
Thomas Rede, 236 Mich. m. 70
Richard Seman, 236 Mich. m. 35
Thomas Stalbroke, 236 Mich. m. 25
Robert Symson, 236 Mich. mm. 44, 57
William Waldyngfeld, 236 Mich. m. [86]
John Walshawe, 236 Mich. m. 60
Thomas Wattes, 235 Trin. m. 46
Henry Waver, 235 Trin. m. 16
John Worksop, 235 Trin. m. 67
John Wykes, 236 Mich. m. 59
Thomas Wynselow, 236 Mich. m. 19

Mercers:

Geoffrey Boleyn, 235 Trin. m. 42
John Chamber, 236 Mich. m. 33
Thomas Dounton, 236 Mich. m. 66
William Elyot, 236 Mich. m. 32
Geoffrey Feldyng, 235 Trin. mm. 15, 62
John Lambert, 236 Mich. m. 38
Thomas Muschamp, 236 Mich. m. 68
John Salmon, 236 Mich. m. 76
Ralph Verney, 235 Trin. m. 45
Hugo Wyche, 236 Mich. m. 30

Grocers:

Thomas Beleter, 236 Mich. m. 28
John Byllyngton, 236 Mich. m. 56
John Higdon, 236 Mich. m. 61d
John Kyng, 235 Trin. m. 41, 236 Mich. mm. 28d, 72
William Lemyng, 236 Mich. m. 71
John Payn senior (alias John Payn senior of Southampton, mer-
    chant), 236 Trin. m. 6
John Shelley, 236 Mich. mm. 42, 46
Henry Turney, 236 Mich. m. 65
John Yong, 235 Trin. m. 11

Merchants:

Robert Byllyngay (also hurer, capper, clothmaker), 236 Mich. mm.
29, 34
William Cache, 236 Mich. m. 39
Robert Colyns (also cofferer), 236 Mich. mm. 17, 20d, 37

William Dere, 236 Mich. m. 80
Robert Stok, 236 mich. m. 24

Tailors:

John Bolte, 235 Trin. m. 55, 235 Mich. m. 63
William Boylet, 236 Mich. m. 50
John Jurdan, 235 Trin. m. 43, 236 Mich. mm. 52 [85]
John Langwith, 235 Trin. mm. 49, 63

Fishmongers:

Stephen Forster, 236 Mich. mm. 21, 22, 22d, 23
Thomas Fowler, 236 Mich. m. 20
William Howlak, 236 Mich. m. 20

Pewterers:

Peter Bysshop, 236 Mich. m. 69
John Dogowe, 235 Trin. m. 60
John Parys, 236 Mich. m. 47

Skinners:

William Constantyn, 235 Trin. m. 30, 236 Mich. m. 54
John Forster, 235 Trin. m. 14, 236 Mich. m. 49
Thomas Oulgrave, 336 Mich. m. 26

Brasier:

Thomas Reseby, 236 Mich. m. 62

Fuller:

Henry Brice, 235 Trin. m. 58, 236 Mich. m. 27

Girdler:

Reginald Langdon, 236 Mich. m. 64

Goldsmith:

Germanus Lynce, 236 Trin. m. 5

Haberdasher:

William Bacon, 236 Hill, m. 23

Unstated:

John Lyon, 235 Trin. m. 50

King's Household:

William York senior, 236 Hill, m. 23

Notes

I would like to acknowledge the help of a grant from the British Academy while I was working in the Public Record Office and London Record Office for this paper.

1   M.M. Postan, 'Credit in medieval trade', *EcHR*, I (1928), reprinted in *Medieval Trade and Finance* (Cambridge, 1973).

2   J. Day, *The Medieval Market Economy* (Oxford, 1987); P. Spufford, 'Coinage and currency', in M.M. Postan and E. Miller (eds.), *The Cambridge Economic History of Europe*, II, *Trade and Industry in the Middle Ages*, (2nd edn., Cambridge, 1987); *idem*, *Money and its use in Medieval Europe* (Cambridge, 1988).

3   PRO E 159/235, 236; E101/128/36, 37.

4   Postan, 'Credit', *Trade and Finance*, p. 22; W.R. Childs, *Anglo-Castilian Trade in the Later Middle Ages* (Manchester, 1978), pp. 5l, 192; J.L. Bolton, *The Medieval English Economy, 1150–1500* (London, 1980), p. 303; S. Jenks, 'War das Hanse kreditfeindlich?', *Vierteljahrschrift für Sozial- und Wirtschaftsgeschichte*, 69 (1982), pp. 328–32; *idem*, 'Das Schreiberbuch des John Thorpe und der Hansische Handel in London 1457/59', *Hansische Geschichtsblätter*, 101 (1983), pp. 67–113.

5   A. Luders, et al. (eds.), *Statutes of the Realm*, I, (1810) pp. 53, 98; R.R. Sharpe (ed.), *Calendar of Letter Books preserved among the Archives of the Corporation of the City of London, Books A and B* (1899–1900); London Record Office, Recognizance Rolls I-X; T.H. Lloyd *The English Wool Trade in the Middle Ages* (Cambridge, 1977), pp. 288–306.

6   M.K. James, 'A London merchant of the fourteenth century', *EcHR*, 2nd series, VIII (1955–6); an edition of Maghfeld's account book is being prepared by Dr Jeremy Griffiths; Postan, 'Credit', *Trade and Finance*, p. 22; E. Power, 'The Wool Trade in the Fifteenth Century', in E. Power and M.M. Postan (eds.), *Studies in English Trade in the Fifteenth Century* (London, 1933) pp. 59–72; A. Hanham, *The Celys and their World* (Cambridge, 1985), pp. 398–405.

7   Day, 'Money and Credit in Medieval and Renaissance Italy', *Market Economy*, pp. 141–2.

8   Power, 'Wool Trade', p. 67; PRO E101/128/37, Jenks, 'Schreiberbuch', p. 99 (no. 54); Bolton, *Medieval English Economy*, pp. 304–5.

9   PRO C1/60/92.

10 Day, 'The great bullion famine of the fifteenth century', *Market Economy*, pp. 1–54; Spufford, *Money*, pp. 339–62; E.M. Carus-Wilson and O. Coleman, *England's Export Trade 1275–1549* (Oxford, 1963), pp. 55–64, 88–101, 122–3, 138–9.

11 *Statutes*, II, pp. 17, 76, 122, 138, 142, 203, 210, 219; J.H. Munro, *Wool, Cloth, and Gold* (Toronto, 1972), pp. 84–92; Lloyd, *Wool Trade*, pp. 257–69.

12 *Statutes*, II, p. 257.

13 Ibid., II, p. 264; *Rotuli Parliamentorum*, IV, 377a, 450a.

14 Sir G. Warner (ed.), *The Libelle of Englyshe Polycye* (Oxford, 1926), lines 396–455; G. Holmes, 'The "Libel of English Policy"', *EHR*, 299 (1961), pp. 201–2.

15 R.A. Griffiths, *The Reign of King Henry VI* (London, 1981), pp. 785–90.

16 Jenks, 'Schreiberbuch', pp. 68–9.

17 Spufford, *Money*, pp. 356–62; Day, 'Crises and Trends in the Late Middle Ages', *Market Economy*, pp. 213–17.

18 Carus-Wilson and Coleman, *Export Trade*, p. 139; Bolton, *Medieval English Economy*, pp. 305–8, 311, 330–1.

19 A.A. Ruddock, *Italian Merchants and Shipping in Southampton 1270–1600* (Southampton, 1951), pp. 162–79; J. Heers, 'Les Genois en Angleterre: la crise de 1458–66', *Studi in onore di Armando Sapori*, I (Milan, 1957), pp. 809–15; Griffiths, *Henry VI*, pp. 790–5.

20 PRO E159/231 Recorda Trin. mm. 16, 17.

21 Ibid., 233 Recorda Easter m. 23d.

22 Ibid., 234 Commissiones m. 2, Recorda Hill. mm. 17, 18, 20, 27, Recorda Easter m. 22.

23 PRO C76/136 m. 14.

24 PRO C1/22/119.

25 Southampton City Record Office (hereafter SCRO), Southampton Port Book 1455-6, Liber Alien, f. 42v; PRO E101/128/36; CCR 1454-61, p. 311.

26 PRO C76/139 mm. 23, 12.

27 SCRO, Southampton Port Book 1455-6, Liber Alien, f. 42v.

28 PRO E101/128/36 (June and September); E28/86, 88; E159/235 Recorda Mich. m. 54, Trin. mm. 26d, 33, 46, 54; 236 Recorda Mich. m. 37.

29 PRO E159/235 Recorda Mich. m. 54, Hill. m. 11.

30 PRO E28/86,88.

31 The number of cases in the rolls (which each run from Michaelmas to Trinity term) is as follows:

E154/231	(1454–5)	2
232	(1455–6)	0
233	(1456–7)	1
234	(1457–8)	5
235	(1458–9)	35
236	(1459–60)	75
237	(1460–1)	0
247	(1470–1)	1

There seem to have been perhaps eight other cases relating to credit for which men were summoned to the Exchequer or for which they appointed attorneys (E159/235 Brevia retornabilia, E159/236 Attornati, Trinity), but which do not appear in the adjacent Recorda sections. These include John Crosby, who appointed attorneys in a case involving Antonio Lutiano, and who bought a pardon in 1459 (CPR 1452–61, p. 485). Probably the cases were dropped very early on payment to the Exchequer.

32 PRO E159/235 Recorda Trin. mm. 10, 31.

33 PRO E101/128/136 (book of William Styfford: eighty-seven debts registered); E101/128/37 (book of John Thorpe: 104 debts registered). Dr Jenks, in his recent edition of Thorpe's book, counted 103 debts, but I think his No. 7 is more likely to be two separate debts.

34 PRO E159/236 Recorda Mich. mm. 21–23 (Forster); 235 Recorda Trin. mm. 40, 64, 66; 236 Recorda Mich. m. 58, Hill m. 7 (Forthey).

35 I am indebted to Dr Caroline Barron for a discussion on the Londoners, and for help with identifications. For further comment on those prosecuted see below pp. 81–2.

36 PRO E159/235 Recorda Mich. m. 33 (Chamber), Trin. m. 7 (Elmes); E101/128/36, July 1457 (Philip).

37 PRO E159/236 Recorda Mich. m. 20 (three months); 235 Recorda Trin. m. 52d: E101/128/37: Jenks, 'Schreiberbuch', p. 103 (no. 86) (five years).

38 PRO E159/236 Recorda Mich. m. 82.

39 PRO E159/235 Recorda Trin. m. 20.

40 PRO E101/128/36, 37. Styfford had been admitted to the scriveners' company in 1440 and Thorpe in 1447; F.W. Steer (ed.), Scriveners' Company Common Paper, 1357–1628 (London Record Society, 4, 1968), pp. 21–2. Dr Jenks appears to have missed Thorpe's entry to the company, 'Schreiberbuch', p. 92.

41 Jenks, 'Schreiberbuch' as in note 4 above.

42 Postan, 'Credit', *Trade and Finance*, p. 22; Jenks, 'War des Hanse kreditfeindlich?' pp. 328–32; *idem*, 'Schreiberbuch', pp. 71–2.

43 PRO E159/235 Recorda Trin. mm. 40, 64, 66; 236 Recorda Mich. m. 58, Hill, m. 7; E101/128/36 June (Forthey). E159/235 Recorda Trin. m. 58; 236 Recorda Mich. m. 27; E101/128/36 May and October; E101/128/37: Jenks, 'Schreiberbuch', p. 102 (No. 70) (Brice).

44 See note 35 above; PRO E159/235 Recorda Trin. m. 61; 236 Recorda Mich. m. 18.

45 T.H. Lloyd, *The Movement of Wool Prices in Medieval England*, (*EcHR* Supplements, 6, 1973), pp. 43, 49, 50–1, 64.

46 PRO E159/235 Recorda Trin. m. 52d.

47 PRO E159/234 Recorda Easter m. 22; 236 Recorda Mich. m. 31.

48 PRO E159/235 Recorda Trin. mm. 40, 64, 66; 236 Recorda Mich. m. 58, Hill, m. 7.

49 PRO E159/233 Recorda Easter m. 23d; 234 Recorda Hill, m. 18.

50 PRO E101/128/36 (Worksop and Elmes); E159/235 Recorda Trin. mm. 9, 11, 12, 40, 48; 236 Recorda Mich. mm. 36d, 72 (Lutiano); 235 Recorda Trin. mm. 15, 62, 66; 236 Recorda Hill, m. 7 (Giustiniani).

51 PRO E101/128/36; E159/235 Recorda Trin. mm. 11, 15, 43, 46, 58; 236 Recorda Mich. mm. 20, 25.

52 PRO E159/235 Recorda Trin. m. 16.

53 Spufford, *Money*, pp. 357, 359.

54 PRO E101/128/37; Jenks, 'Schreiberbuch', pp. 95–6, 99 (Nos. 25, 29, 53, 54).

55 Ibid., pp. 77–82.

56 PRO E101/128/37; Jenks, 'Schreiberbuch', pp. 102–4 (Nos. 74, 83, 85, 92).

57 PRO E101/128/36 (September).

58 Ibid., (July and December).

59 PRO E101/128/37; Jenks 'Schreiberbuch', p. 100 (Nos. 60, 61). For Ganszem there, read Gauszem.

60 PRO E159/235 Recorda Trin m. 9.

61 P.E. Jones (ed.), *Calendar of the Plea and Memoranda Rolls preserved among the Archives of the Corporation of the City of London at the Guildhall AD 1458–1482* (Cambridge, 1961), p. 14.

62 Heers, 'Genois en Angleterre', pp. 815–24.

63 Figures for wool and cloth exports are taken from Carus-Wilson and Coleman, *Export Trade*, pp. 63, 99–100. I have adopted the prices suggested by J.L. Bolton of £5 a sack for denizen wool, of £7 for alien wool, of £1 15s. for denizen and Hansard cloths, and of £2 for Italian cloths; *Medieval English Economy*, pp. 292–3, 306. Estimates of tin values are taken from J. Hatcher, *English Tin Production and Trade before 1550* (Oxford, 1973), pp. 170–5. The estimate of the overall value of exports for the decade 1452–61 given by Bolton, op. cit., p. 307, Table 9.3, might suggest a lower annual export value than I have given, thus increasing the importance of credit.

64 Spufford, *Money*, pp. 347–8; Dr Pamela Nightingale's current work on the credit transactions of the London grocers in the late fourteenth and early fifteenth centuries so far confirms the picture of tighter credit as the bullion shortage was prolonged.

5

'That Kindliness Should be Cherished More, and Discord Driven Out': the Settlement of Commercial Disputes by Arbitration in Later Medieval England[1]

Carole Rawcliffe
History of Parliament

Historians have only recently come to recognize the true importance of arbitration, not simply as an alternative to the established legal system, but also as a valuable complement or adjunct to it. So far, studies have concentrated upon the use of private treaties by the gentry and nobility, probably because rather more is known about their activities, and on account of the valuable insight which such research can provide into the complex network of relationships within county communities or baronial retinues.[2] Yet, in point of fact, arbitrament was even more widely employed, more sophisticated in its application and probably more effectively enforced in the commercial sector than it was elsewhere in society. The reasons for this are not hard to find. The same considerations of economy, flexibility and speed which led a country gentleman to prefer arbitration to litigation were, in many cases, even more urgent for a merchant or master craftsman. While law term succeeded law term, and cases dragged on from year to year, perishable cargoes could be lost, influential customers disappointed, and, worst of all, large sums of capital, badly needed for other ventures, tied up without any real hope of recovery. Municipal authorities, such as those at Ipswich, who derived a substantial part of their profits from visiting merchants, recognized the need to provide 'men of other lond, or . . . other of fer cuntrees passand, or . . . maryneres aryvyng up to the foreseid toun with her goodys and her merchaundyses there to sellyn, or straunge men passaunt in tyme of feyre or market' with a fast and effective means of obtaining redress in local courts, although such regulations as were passed proved notoriously hard to enforce.[3]

Even the court of the mayor and aldermen of London, which tried commercial cases according to the law merchant, and boasted a body of judges who had themselves achieved wealth and position through trade, could prove dilatory. In October 1362, for example, a suit between a member of the Westminster Staple and a Lombard merchant for a debt of £475 encountered delays because of the non-appearance of the jury, which, in keeping with the requirements of mercantile law, had to comprise an equal number of Lombards and Englishmen.[4] Eventually, after several adjournments, the parties submitted to the arbitration of five Genoese merchants, who promptly delivered their award.[5] Pressure of business must help to explain why the mayor so frequently referred cases to mediators almost as a matter of course; although it is no less apparent that, as in the law courts at Westminster, litigation was commonly seen as a preliminary stage in the arbitration process: the means as it were, of getting an opponent into the ring ready for the serious business of fighting one's case before a panel of arbitrators.[6]

There were, furthermore, occasions when a judge had no real alternative but to recommend a private settlement simply because the evidence in question could only be understood or properly evaluated by a small group of experts from outside the legal profession. A large proportion of commercial litigation comprised actions of debt, detinue and account. The recognizances, bills of exchange and accounts produced in court, particularly in disputes between merchants operating on the international market, could be extremely complicated, not least because of language problems and different systems of reckoning. The obvious answer was to call in a small group of specialists, whose award could be used as the basis of a final judgement. A classic instance of the methods adopted by the common law courts in the face of such difficulties is to be found in a law suit of 1291 between one Gettus Honesti of Lucca, and his erstwhile receiver, Pelegrin of Chartres, from whom he claimed a sum of 50,000 marks, withheld over a period of twelve years. The suit was initially heard before the treasurer and barons of the Exchequer, who consulted first with four auditors and then with a jury of Italian merchants, summoned because the barons, on their own admission, neither understood 'the idiom' of the accounts presented to them, nor had much knowledge of 'the laws and customs used between merchants'. After further delays, occasioned by Pelegrin's stubborn refusal to comply with the court, the treasurer and barons conferred with the king's justices and appointed a second panel of auditors to examine the evidence. The latter's report 'that certain difficult and complicated reasonings are propounded before them in this case, which, on account of their difficulty remain undecided and undiscussed so that they are not able to arrive at the conclusion of a true award by a clear and sufficient process', led the judges to appoint three arbitrators from the Italian merchant community (one chosen by each of the two parties and the third agreed upon by both) to join with the auditors in making an award. The evidence must have been very hard to interpret, because the arbitrators demanded an extension of time in which to reach an agreement. In the end they charged Pelegrin with debts totalling £275; and it was as a result of his inability to pay this sum that the treasurer and barons confined him to prison.[7]

Disputes over the relative competence of a craftsman or the quality of his merchandise also lent themselves readily to specialist arbitration. Who better to determine the outcome of litigation over the sale and delivery of ten casks of Gascon wine than a group of arbitrators drawn from the Vintners' Company, or to assess the claims of rival parties in a quarrel concerning the purchase of woollen cloth than the two wardens of the Drapers' Company and four of its leading members?[8] In one or two cases, however, a suspicion of partiality attaches itself to those officials of small guilds, whose primary concern as arbitrators was to preserve the reputation of their colleagues. An award made by a distinguished group of physicians and surgeons in London, in 1424, following a suit brought against a surgeon and two barber surgeons in the mayor's court for compounding the damage to a wounded thumb, not only exonerated the defendants completely but also imposed permanent silence upon the plaintiff, lest he be tempted to slander them further. (The arbitrators' incidental pronouncement that, since the wound had been inflicted while 'the moon [was] consumed in a bloody sign, to wit Aquarius, under a very malevolent constellation', there was no real hope for the patient anyway, can only have added insult to existing injury.)[9] Professional bias quite probably worked the other way in a similar dispute submitted, in 1383, to several members of the Mystery of Bottle-makers. They were called upon to settle a law suit in the sheriffs' court of London between William, Lord Windsor, and a local tradesman who, he claimed, had supplied him with defective goods, causing him to lose 180 gallons of wine while on the king's service in France. The arbitrators found for Windsor, and awarded him costs and damages of £28, although the defendant later accused them of conspiring 'to drive him out of the liberty of the city because he exercised the same trade as themselves'. At all events, his attempt to contest the award failed, and he was dispatched forthwith to Newgate for refusing to settle his debts.[10]

The need for technical knowledge on the part of mediators was nowhere greater than in disputes involving maritime law, particularly where the competence of a captain and crew – not only at sea but also with regard to the loading, freighting and unloading of cargoes – was concerned. The court of admiralty had frequent recourse to arbitration, either by the admirals and their deputies, or, as was more often the case, by 'aimables compositeurs' recognized for their nautical skills. At a time when any sea voyage, however short, represented a real risk, and the loss of merchandise through wreck, piracy or war was all too common, quarrels between shipowners and merchants were a regular feature of commercial life. The rules set out for the guidance of masters and the managing owners of ships made clear provision for appeals to 'the judgement of skilled and experienced men, who are well and accurately versed in the art of the sea', as well as for evaluation by such experts as coopers, timber merchants or shipwrights where claims for damages or salvage occurred.[11] 'In all matters the mediation and the equity and the arbitration of Prudhommes is a good thing' ran one ordinance, which urged disputants always to seek for compromise, if only because 'no one knows nor can know nor is certain when his own loss and his own peril may come on'.[12] Not surprisingly, some merchants covered themselves by arranging in advance for independent assessors to be approached in the event of any loss or damage to goods in transit, and actually agreed in their contracts of sale for arbitrators to act should any misunderstanding arise over the terms of reparation.[13]

Besides giving disputants the opportunity to argue their case before experts in their own field, arbitration offered other distinct advantages to anyone involved in trade or commerce. Unless the local authorities undertook collectively to determine a quarrel (as often happened in towns and cities throughout England), the parties were free to choose their own arbitrators, generally opting for members of the same guild, or merchants with related interests, whose standing in the community lent further weight to their findings. As we have seen, foreigners engaged in litigation with the native English were entitled by the law merchant to claim trial before a jury 'of the half tounge'; and when resorting to private treaty they could likewise, if they wished, choose arbitrators of their own nationality.[14] They did not always make use of this privilege, however, apparently having sufficient confidence in the probity of English arbitrators, or at least feeling that an award made by the latter might be more easily enforced.[15] Quarrels between merchants from different parts of the country were similarly placed before mediators from both areas, as in an early sixteenth-century case over the seizure of a consignment of lead from a London dealer trading in York, which was settled by the recorders of the two cities.[16]

Arbitrators could, moreover, be instructed to operate within precise terms of reference, which might or might not omit certain aspects of a quarrel if the parties so required. Usually their brief was fairly wide-ranging,[17] but sometimes the agenda would be restricted to a few specific points at issue, leaving others to be settled elsewhere. In 1446, for instance, a London joiner had an arbitration annulled on the ground that the mediator had agreed, under oath, to limit his award to a pre-arranged list of grievances, but had, in fact, taken additional factors into account as well.[18] It was, on the other hand, perfectly permissible for arbitrators to interrogate a far larger number of witnesses or undertake a more extensive and painstaking search of evidence than might prove feasible within the narrower procedural confines of the established legal system. While investigating an action of account brought in 1410 by a London brewer against one of his agents, the arbitrators discovered through a minute scrutiny of his ledgers that one folio containing a list of costs and expenses sustained by the defendant had been cunningly removed so as to strengthen the plaintiff's case. Because of this attempted fraud they found against the brewer, who was, moreover, ordered to provide a general release of all further legal actions.[19] Again, in 1430, it was as a result of a long series of interviews with 'many ancient and trustworthy men' and the diligent searching out of 'other kinds of proof' that a panel of mediators was able to rule out of court the 'bare and unsupported' claims of a Lincoln merchant to be owed £74 by the widow of a London apothecary.[20] Although they themselves may have been very knowledgeable, arbitrators still considered it appropriate to call on other experts for advice when necessary. This is obviously why a shearman was asked for his professional opinion in a case of 1470, one aspect of which involved a dispute over the cutting of woollen cloth; and why the wardens of the Goldsmiths' Company were assisted by the celebrated Parisian craftsman, Raymond de Wachter, when required to determine exactly how much it would cost in time, labour and materials to execute a medallion depicting the martyrdom of the 11,000 virgins for Humphrey, Duke of Gloucester.[21] Conversely, the arbitrators who met in 1388 to settle a quarrel over the sale and freighting of a quantity of Rochelle wine were quite happy to produce an award with regard to the value of the merchandise, but refused to assign liability for the cost of transporting it, 'without the aid of merchants cognisant of the facts'.[22] The scrupulousness shown by mediators in verifying and assessing evidence suggests that in most instances a serious attempt was made to proceed fairly, according to strict rules. When acting as referees between foreign merchants, for example, the mayor and aldermen of London went to some trouble to obtain authenticated proof of transactions conducted overseas, even going so far as to demand the production of sworn testimonials under the appropriate seals of the monarchs or civic authorities to whom the disputants owed their allegiance.[23]

Speed, besides thoroughness, constituted one of the most attractive features of the arbitration process. Except in particularly difficult cases where due allowance was made for the problems posed by distance, poor communications or the complexity of the evidence,[24] private settlements could be effected very quickly in the mercantile community, where such a well-organized and efficient system of referral either through the courts or at a personal level lay readily to hand. Few awards were completed at the breakneck speed of one, which was pronounced in the Church of St John

Zacchary, London, on 17 July 1389, less than a day after being sent to arbitration by the mayor. One of the four mediators had to leave the city on urgent business, and it says much for the conscientious attitude which he and his colleagues maintained towards their responsibilities that they were prepared to act so promptly.[25] Even so, a very precise time limit was customarily imposed upon arbitrators, who were expected to produce their awards within a matter of days or weeks rather than months. Trade and craft guilds, in particular, were able to mobilize their forces very quickly, since the wardens customarily sat as a type of informal tribunal and could be summoned at short notice. The Barber Surgeons of London allowed only six days for the reconciliation of disputants by the company authorities, after which the parties concerned were free 'to take the benefice of the common lawe wythin the Citee', but their associates and sometime rivals, the Surgeons, set aside a more typical period of five weeks for the masters of their fellowship to attempt mediation.[26]

In the event of arbitrators failing to agree, or encountering some other problem, an umpire, who was often a high-ranking civic official, would be called in. Thus, in April 1461, two London merchants offered securities of £200 each to accept the award of four of their fellows provided that it was given by Whitsuntide, and agreed that should none have been made by then they would be ruled by the mayor and aldermen instead.[27] An interesting dispute between the Mayor of York, Sir William Todd, and one of his aldermen, who had reputedly slandered him with 'misreportes and unfitting language', came before two arbitrators on 10 September 1487. They had nineteen days in which to reconcile the parties, but failed to do so; and no doubt because of the potential threat which the quarrel posed to civic order, the Archbishop of York was invited to act as umpire. His award was delivered on 21 October, less than six weeks after the mediation process had begun, so the hope, expressed at the outset by the disputants, that 'further great expense' might be avoided was clearly justified.[28]

The rulers of all the major towns and cities of medieval England regarded arbitrament as both an important weapon for the enforcement of law and order and a means of fostering peace and prosperity. The idea that good government and the ready availability of facilities for the settlement of disputes went hand in hand is nowhere more clearly expressed than in an account of the duties of the Mayor of Bristol, set down in about 1479, but describing a long-established practice. Except on Saturdays and feast days, he and the sheriff were expected to be available at the counter

at viij at the clok at [sic] sitte untill xj, and atte ij afternone, sittyng untill v, for to hyre compleyntes and varyaunces betwene parties and parties, and to discerne and determyn the same after theire discre-

cion, and, by thaduyce of theire brethern there beyng with them, to
sett parties in rest and ease by theire advertysement, compromesse, or
otherwise; ynless then it so requyre that they must remit theym to the
lawe, as they can be aduysed by the Recorder . . . which Audience
kepyng by the Maire and Shiref in the saide Counter is the grettyst
preseruacion of peas and gode rule to be hadde within the toune and
shire of Bristowe that can be ymagened, for yf it wer anywhiles
discontynewid there wolde right sone growe grete inconvenyence
amongst thenhabitauntez of the same, which God forbede.[29]

The right of civic or municipal authorities to determine quarrels free of
outside interference was inseparably linked in the public mind with the
liberties and franchises accorded to urban communities by royal or
baronial charter, and as such was jealously guarded. The ever-present fear
that failure to uphold reasonable levels of order, or maintain acceptable
standards of justice for native and alien alike might lead to unwelcome
intervention by the Crown helps further to explain why urban officials
showed such alacrity in their resort to arbitration. An indenture of 1424,
drawn up between the mayor, sheriffs and aldermen of Norwich during a
period of acute civic unrest, imposed a fine of 20s. upon any official who
sued one of his fellows at common law before first approaching the mayor
for independent mediation. A further injunction, which forbade each of
the twenty-four aldermen from so much as *agreeing* to arbitrate on behalf of
persons then in dispute with one of their colleagues provided an additional
safeguard against the spread of factionalism, although exceptions were
made in the case of those connected by ties of kinship.[30] Members of the
governing body in Leicester faced even stiffer penalties for failing to
submit internal disputes to the mayor and masters of the dominant Corpus
Christi Guild, since disobedience meant expulsion from the fellowship
and this, effectively, spelt both social and economic ruin.[31]

Confrontations between rival guilds or other organized bodies of
tradesmen and merchants, always a potential source of disruption, had
likewise to be contained promptly before blows were exchanged. A long
and detailed award compiled in Coventry in 1424 in the hope of settling
internal problems within the Weavers' Company was, we are told in the
preamble, achieved at the earnest request of the mayor, who not only
attached his seal to the document but also had it copied into his 'paper
book', so that he and his successors could better enforce it.[32] The city of
York witnessed a number of similar quarrels during the fifteenth century.
Here, as elsewhere, popular religious festivities such as Corpus Christi day
processions or mystery plays were marked by some spectacular brawls,
when deeply felt ill will about restrictive practices or trade monopolies
found expression in fights for precedence and heated exchanges over the

organization, cost and staging of pageants.[33] The mayor usually managed to impose a degree of 'peace, luffe and amyte' upon the aggrieved parties;[34] but every now and then matters got out of hand. A crisis seemed imminent in April 1491, when Henry VII wrote sharply to the authorities, ordering them to settle without delay a dispute between the weavers and cordwainers 'for the beryng of torchez on the morwe after Corpus Christi day', which threatened 'the perversion and breche of our peas and inquietacon of our subgiets'. The cordwainers evidently stood less in awe of King Henry than did the mayor, for they persistently refused to accept the award, even when faced with a fine of £10 for contumacy. Having allowed the mayor two years in which to assert his authority, Henry VII finally decided to appoint the Abbot of St Mary's, York, and two of his councillors as arbitrators instead, and thus precipitated something of a local constitutional crisis. An urgent meeting was held on 8 May 1493 at the Church of the Austin Friars between the abbot and the rulers of the city, during which the latter made great play of their entitlement to determine internal disputes as they saw fit, claiming that any infringement of this right would constitute a breach of those liberties enshrined in their recently-confirmed royal charter. The abbot, who knew well enough from first hand experience how obdurate the citizenry could be in defending their real – or imagined – rights, protested that 'rather he should do or consent to any manner thyng that wer to the breche of the libertiez and fraunchisez, or unto prejudice of eny ordinauncez of this citie he wer lever to take a thousand pound of the tresory of his monastery and cast down the water of Ouse'. In the end, however, neither party dared risk offending the king, and it was agreed as a compromise that the abbot would act under the mayor's direction, doing nothing contrary to his wishes and delivering the award formally before him and the city council one month later.[35]

The same considerations which led the Mayor of York so tenaciously to defend his rights as an arbitrator exercised an equally powerful influence lower down the civic hierarchy. Almost all the leading mercantile or craft guilds of later medieval England expected their members to submit any grievances to settlement by the masters or wardens, and many imposed fines or other penalties upon those who resorted to litigation before exhausting all the possibilities of private treaty.[36] 'Yf ther be any controversies and debates among eny of the seid crafte . . .', ran the ordinances of the Guild of Tailors in Lynn, 'noon of them to sewe other in no manner wise but to come to the 2 hedesmen and to compleyne to hem yf nede be, and thei to do ther partes to drawe hem to acord. And yf thei may not, that than thei to make relacion to the meyre, every man doyng the contrary shal ye payne accordynge to the statute in the halle.'[37] An act of court of the Mercers' Company of London, made in 1457, introduced similar regulations 'for unite rest and peas to be had withyn the Felyshipp of the Mercery, worschip and profitt of the same', stipulating, moreover, that any actions pending in other courts between contesting parties should be completely withdrawn while an arbitration was in progress.[38] As befitted a guild whose members included some of the richest men in London, the financial penalties imposed for obduracy or disobedience could be very heavy. The brothers, Thomas and John Shelley, whose violent tempers enlivened company meetings throughout Edward IV's reign, were drawn into a number of bitter quarrels, both with each other and their respective trading partners. Their 'diuers and uncurtes langwage', as much as their 'full unmannerly' conduct towards the wardens, led to the imposition of fines in excess of £40; and at one stage John was further ordered to pay £26 13s. 4d. into the 'common box' for impugning the honesty of an agent who had done business for him in France.[39]

The great majority of awards pronounced by the wardens of the Goldsmith's Company during the fifteenth century concerned the slander and abuse of members by each other and their respective spouses. Both William Sayles and Henry Exning suffered because of 'the ungodly langage and unwomanly demenyng' of their wives, being bound over in heavy securities to control them better in future. As well as imposing money fines for 'wordes of grete reprof and disclaundre', the wardens frequently ordered disputants to provide a 'competent dyner' or a pipe of wine for all concerned. How far these bibulous affairs actually succeeded in their purpose is, of course, a matter of speculation, since tempers may well have risen while the wine flowed.[40] The Company of Grocers of London likewise maintained an efficient system for the reconciliation of their feuding members. Established in the original company rules of 1345, and further elaborated over the years, the arbitration machinery proved especially useful when it came to the presentation of annual accounts by the wardens, over which there seems to have been quite frequent disagreement.[41]

Not all guilds made specific provision in their regulations for the referral of difficult arbitrations to a higher authority, but in most cases the master or wardens could confidently rely upon support from above, a factor which greatly enhanced their own position as mediators.[42] In September 1411, for example, the wardens of the Cutlers' Company complained to the Mayor of London that one of their number had consistently refused to 'be ruled and corrected' by them. A short interview with the city fathers sufficed to make him see the error of his ways; and he humbly submitted himself to the judgement of his peers without more ado. Some years later the Guild of Tailors of Exeter resorted to similar tactics when faced with a recalcitrant offender, who was brought before the mayor and forced to make peace with his adversary.[43] Even more notable is the case of the goldsmith, John Tewkesbury, whom the Mayor of London sent to prison, in 1422, for failing to accept the terms of a settlement imposed by the wardens of his guild. An attempt by chief justice Hankford to question the mayor's authority met with a terse and effective rejoinder; and, far from reproving the mayor for his temerity, Hankford actually ordered the offender back to gaol, where he remained until ready to apologize before the entire company on bended knee.[44] Awards in disputes between members of the same guild were quite often entered in the records of the court of the Mayor and aldermen of London, as were details of the bonds offered by parties as an earnest of good faith.[45]

A significant proportion of these quarrels arose over the terms or conditions of apprenticeships, a matter in which the authorities could legitimately claim an official interest, over and above their involvement as arbitrators. Some of these awards illustrate graphically how the mediation process could be tailored to fit individual circumstances in a way that was clearly impossible at common law. An apprentice who had evidently proved negligent in keeping his accounts was not only ordered to render a precise statement of receipts and expenses, but also 'as a sign of obedience and respect . . . to contribute 40s. towards a horse and hold the stirrup when his master mounted'. Another young man was packed off to Middleburgh and Bruges with orders to produce written evidence that he had, indeed, aquitted his employer's creditors there; but a third, whose claims to have been unfairly treated found a receptive ear, was promised 60s. a year as well as food and drink for the rest of his term of service.[46]

Like a town or city in microcosm, every guild was torn by internal factions and disputes which had to be pacified quickly before they attracted the attention of outsiders. Royal or baronial intervention was certainly dreaded as much (if not more) by the companies of medieval London as it was by the civic authorities;[47] so both went to great lengths to be seen as capable agents of law enforcement. Some awards were quite demonstrably intended to curb potential trouble-makers, and involved prompt, even ruthless, action against those who appeared disruptive. A mercer named John Hammer protested in vain to the court of Chancery that the arbitrators who had ordered him to remove his household, servants and goods from the parish of St Mary Bow lest he further antagonize a neighbouring member of the same company had acted 'against reason and conscience'. They had, quite simply, employed the best available means of defusing the situation and avoiding further trouble.[48] In practice, of course, the machinery for the containment of discord could break down, as happened in 1468, when a long-standing feud between two particularly belligerent goldsmiths (who had the misfortune to live next to each other) escalated into a full-blooded vendetta, 'with outrageous, heinous and malicious language and also in assaults and making affrays'. Such was the level of violence that Edward IV instructed his redoubtable brother, Richard, Duke of Gloucester, to take the matter in hand. Fear that they might lose some of their hard-won liberties finally galvanized the Goldsmiths' Company into action; and strenuous efforts were made to discipline the offenders, who were bound over in sums of £100 each to obey an internal award, fined £12 for their previous misdeeds, and obliged to do penance before the entire company in abject contrition. The Goldsmiths had, however, to pay a price for their independence, since as well as giving a reward of 40s. to one of Gloucester's retainers for his help in 'remityng the mater hole to the wardeins and to the ffeleship', they also found it expedient to lay out 38s. on two dinners for the aldermen of London, who had clearly grown alarmed at this worrying turn of events.[49]

Discord within the mercantile community could on occasion pose a serious threat to the stability of the whole body politic, not least because of the intimate connexion between commercial prosperity and the buoyancy of the royal finances. On being informed, in 1431, of 'certeyn hevynesses and grevances hanging betwix certains persones of the companye of the [Calais] staple' and John Reynwell, the then mayor, the lords of King Henry VI's council hastened to appoint a panel of extremely distinguished and experienced arbitrators to settle the quarrel before the Staple, upon which the Crown relied heavily for credit, was ridden with discord. Reynwell's subsequent declaration that the mediators had 'so notably, so indifferently and so truly laboured theese materes, that all manere hevynesse et grevances been concluded to parfite reste and pees' cannot necessarily be taken at face value, since he was such a notoriously truculent and difficult character that his judges probably insisted upon a very public act of reconciliation, even if they had to write the speeches themselves.[50]

It was, however, one thing to pronounce an award and quite another to ensure that it was observed. A variety of means were employed to make disputants accept the terms imposed upon them, the most common being a request for securities, often in heavy sums, as a guarantee that the parties would comply with the arbitration. In mercantile cases bonds of £100 or £200 were by no means unusual, either given jointly by a group of mainpernors or else provided by the protagonists alone.[51] To lend weight to the undertaking, and also to provide an incontrovertible legal record should any subsequent misunderstanding occur, these pledges were sometimes taken by the Chancellor of England or one of his representatives, and duly entered upon the Close Rolls.[52] A few even contained a clause referring the original dispute to the Court of Chancery should no award have materialized within a specific period, obliging the protagonists to appear there personally when required if a compromise could not otherwise be reached.[53] The bonds themselves were retained either by the mediators or the officials of the court where the case had initially been heard until they were satisfied that all the necessary conditions had been met. Predictably, this practice itself gave rise to a good many dis-agreements, prompting allegations of fraud, deception or collusion over the withholding of securities;[54] but on the whole the system provided a useful means of constraint, not least because the bonds were enforceable at common law or in Chancery.

Painstaking attention was, moreover, paid to the observance of formal-ities designed to impress the solemnity of the occasion upon the par-ticipants, and remind them of the permanent and binding nature of the proceedings in which they had become involved. Many awards were actually pronounced in church before being copied into the appropriate civic or municipal records.[55] Churches were, of course, regularly used for the transaction of secular business, but a strong religious aspect entered independently into the arbitration process. In a quarrel of 1364 between a purser and a saddler over the services of an apprentice, for instance, both parties were 'sworn upon a book' by the Mayor of London to submit to six mediators who duly gave their award in the Church of St Thomas of Acres.[56] And in 1475 the Mayor and Chamberlain of Chester insisted that two men who had fallen out about 'a pak of ffrise of Irissh ware' should be 'condecendet, agreit and sworne upon a boke' that they would reach a compromise out of court. Part of the ensuing settlement actually specified that 'the seides parties [were] to take by the handes and to be gode frendes and fully agreit and accordett of and opon all the premysez', an act of public reconciliation frequently enjoined upon those who submitted to private treaty.[57]

Mediators, too, made a great display of reading, witnessing, sealing and verifying their awards, as well as ensuring that duplicates were produced at once, often in English rather than French or Latin, for all interested parties. The Abbot of St Mary's, York, was taking no chances when he delivered his arbitration in the celebrated dispute between the cordwainers and the weavers, for besides stipulating that it should be 'recorded in the book belonging to the chamber of the city and there remain so both crafts may have copies of it', he also obtained the written consent of two members of both guilds before a capacity audience.[58] The terms of an award made in a quarrel between John Bradman, a merchant of the Calais Staple, and the Mayor and community of Winchelsea, in April 1491, actually required that a full copy was to be entered in 'the brotherhood book' of the Cinque Ports before the end of June, presumably to avoid any further confusion in an already complicated case.[59] Meticulous care seems to have been taken in London with regard to controversies between foreigners. In 1380, for example, a special note was made in the records of the court of the mayor and aldermen to the effect that, in a dispute involving rival merchants from Pistoia and Florence, each of the Genoese arbitrators 'added a certificate of his own hand to vouch the authenticity of the award, together with their marks and impression of their signets'. In an earlier case which concerned two traders from Lucca, the mediators, who were of mixed nationality, got William Bridport, the public notary of the diocese of Sarum, to attest their award for greater security.[60] It was a brave – or foolish – man who came into direct confrontation with an arbitrator, or at least presumed to question his probity. Roger Dawson, a London tailor, ended up in the pillory for his 'disclaunderowes and sedicious langage' in asserting that one of the mediators in his quarrel with a Venetian had 'falsely and disseyvably begeled hym'.[61]

The hierarchical and authoritarian structure of urban society in later medieval England in itself tended to support the arbitration process, pressurizing disputants to accept private treaty, and buttressing the authority of referees. It is, even so, important to remember that not all the awards set down in painstaking detail in the surviving records were successful, and that a significant proportion merely exacerbated existing quarrels. Sometimes, the arbitrators simply failed to agree and abandoned their attempts at reconciliation;[62] but there were many occasions when the protagonists themselves were either intransigent or dishonest. Merchants with a grievance in this respect often had recourse to the court of Chancery, whose equitable jurisdiction shared many similarities with the law merchant, a body of international rules based on natural law. A large number of commercial disputes were determined here rather than in the common law courts, where procedure was often too slow, cumbersome and circumscribed to deal with the needs of the mercantile community.[63] Indeed, the Chancellor himself occasionally agreed to act as an arbitrator or umpire in such cases, notably where one or more of the parties was foreign. In 1433, for instance, John Stafford, Bishop of Bath and Wells, undertook to impose a settlement upon two Flemish merchants who were at odds over the ownership of a cargo of wine and salt captured at sea by English pirates; and some years later Cardinal Kemp intervened personally, first to determine the claims of rival Genoese factors to an unspecified consignment of goods, and then to end a quarrel involving the Florentine and Venetian communities in London. Another of Kemp's attempts at mediation concerned a petition for damages submitted by a group of Scottish merchants whose vessel had been impounded at Harwich, and whose position raised a number of sensitive diplomatic issues which he was able to tackle directly by virtue of his office.[64] The Chancellor could also bring considerable indirect influence to bear on disputants by persuading them to abandon litigation in favour of private treaty. In October 1446, for example, Stafford (who had by then become Primate) selected the arbitrators in a complicated Chancery case between a merchant from

Epinal in France and William Bowes of York in the hope that they would 'chaunge the seide contraversies and discordes in to tranquillite and goode accorde'. Despite the difficulties posed by the evidence, the award was actually produced in two days, no doubt because the archbishop was impatient to reach a settlement out of court.[65]

It followed logically that complaints about the implementation of awards should also be heard in Chancery, albeit on a more formal basis. The most common reason by far for the failure of arbitrations was the decision by one of the parties either to resume or commence litigation against his adversary, earlier assurances to the contrary notwithstanding. Disputants were almost always required to abandon whatever lawsuits they might have against each other while mediation was in progress, but the temptation to keep both irons in the fire could not always be resisted. The experience of John Spring, a successful wool merchant from Lavenham in Suffolk, is fairly typical, in that during the early 1470s he was sued for debt, trespass and malicious damage in the local court at Colchester, while himself seeking redress against his opponents at the Exchequer. Eventually, both parties agreed to drop their respective actions and seek arbitration, but Spring alone kept his side of the bargain, and still had to stand trial.[66] Merchants with overseas interests were in an even worse position, because their frequent absences abroad made them more vulnerable to sharp practice. They could, on the other hand, disappear quickly once an award had been given, following the example of Franceys Bonesyan, a Venetian merchant who left for home as soon as a panel of arbitrators found him liable for insurance cover of £300 on a cargo of goods lost at sea.[67] Allegations of bias or duplicity on the part of the arbitrators themselves were comparatively rare; and it must have required considerable courage to charge the Mayor and aldermen of London with overt favouritism, or to claim that the Mayor of Norwich was a party to fraud. One Northampton merchant even went so far as to accuse an arbitrator of tampering with vital evidence by pulling the seals off two recognizances, but on the whole those who were dissatisfied with their treatment adopted a less confrontational approach.[68] The two mercers who objected to a settlement imposed upon them by their own company in London, and were peremptorily ordered to accept the award first and then 'as petitcioners to requyre the Charetie of the felishipp', were certainly more representative.[69]

Even though the arbitration process could break down, and might well give rise to the litigation it was supposed to prevent, we can be reasonably sure that in the majority of cases it provided an important means – or at least the best means to hand – of maintaining law and order and reconciling adversaries. This was notably the case in the mercantile community, where, as we have seen, it answered a particular need and was thus actively encouraged and supported by all manner of municipal and guild authorities. The element of compromise, designed, in the words of one seventeenth-century jurist, to provide 'something benefficiall in apparance at least' to each of the parties was, moreover, irresistibly attractive in an age when the legal system, far from attempting to achieve a *modus vivendi* between suitors, offered either all or, more usually, nothing to those who went to court.[70] Although never slow to apportion blame or mete out suitable penalties, arbitrators did their best to satisfy disputants by following principles of natural justice. One award, made in 1451 in the course of a quarrel between the Bishop of St David's and a Bristol dyer over the ownership of a vessel called the *Mary de Montrigo*, provides a telling instance of this desire for rapprochement and fair play. The bishop was required to quitclaim the ship and its cargo to his opponent for a year and a day, but he, in turn, was promised 200 marks as compensation, payable in regular instalments under sureties of £400. Neither party could reasonably claim to have suffered by the terms of the settlement, and both had emerged with some positive gains.[71]

In the final analysis, however, any assessment of the lasting value and importance of arbitration in late medieval society must remain impressionistic, since insufficient evidence has survived to enable us to quantify our findings statistically, or, indeed, to discover how permanent the majority of awards actually were. It may be argued that the constant recourse to private treaty by merchants and tradespeople was more a cynical attempt to manipulate the law for personal advantage than proof of commitment to the idea of compromise in itself, but whatever their motives, the hard-headed businessmen of fifteenth-century England would never have devoted so much time and energy to a practice which did not yield tangible results.

Notes

1   This paper was originally read in March 1988 at Mr J.L. Bolton's seminar on Late Medieval English History at the Institute of Historical Research, London; and I would like to thank him and the members of the seminar, particularly Dr Caroline Barron, Dr P.A. Brand and Dr L. Wooder, for their many useful comments and suggestions. I am also indebted to Dr Linda Clark and Mr R.P. Martin for discussing the final version with me.

2   As, for example, E. Powell, 'Arbitration and the Law in the Later Middle Ages' (*TRHS*, 5th series XXXIII, 1983), pp. 49–67; I. Rowney, 'Arbitration in Gentry Disputes of the Later Middle Ages', *History*, LXVII (1982), pp. 367–76; and C. Rawcliffe, 'The Great Lord as Peacekeeper: Arbitration by English Noblemen and their Councils in the Later Middle Ages', in J.A. Guy and H.G. Beale (eds.), *Law and Social Change in British History*, (Royal Historical Society Studies in History, XL (1984), pp. 34–54).

3   T. Twiss (ed.), *The Black Book of the Admiralty*, 4 vols. (Rolls Series, 1871–6), II, pp. 115–17.

4   This principle was clearly established in the regulations of 1353 and 1354 (27 Ed. III, Statute II, c. 8 and 28 Ed. III, c. 13) with regard to the jurisdiction and privileges of the Staple courts, which were governed by the law merchant (*Statutes of the Realm*, I, pp. 336, 348). An entertaining account of trials before mixed juries in London is to be found in C.A. Sneyd (ed.), *A Relation of the Island of England about the Year 1500* (Camden Society, XXXVII, 1847), pp. 32–3, where the author, an Italian, confuses jurors with arbitrators.

5   A.H. Thomas (ed.), *C[alendar of] P[lea and] M[emoranda] R[olls of the] C[ity of] L[ondon], 1323–1482* 6 vols. (Cambridge, 1926–61), *1323–64*, pp. 258–9.

6   A substantial proportion of commercial disputes were first heard in court before proceeding to arbitration. In London, the majority of these were referred to mediators by the court of the mayor and aldermen (as, for example, ibid., pp. 258–9; *1364–81*, pp. 75–6, 201–2; *1381–1412*, pp. 140–2, 162–3; *1413–37*, p. 10); but others came initially from the sheriffs' court (ibid., *1323–64*, p. 278; *1381–1412*, pp. 121–2, 230–2, 302; *1413–37*, pp. 256–8; CCR *1429–35*, p. 154; PRO C1/66/264). It was, indeed, sometimes alleged that the mayor used physical coercion to force disputants to accept private treaty (C1/43/214), an accusation also levelled at the Mayor of Northampton (C1/43/127).

7   H. Hall (ed.), *Select Cases Concerning the Law Merchant* (Selden Society, XLVI, 1929), pp. lxiii–iv, 53–62, 148–50; CPMRCL, *1381–1412*, pp. x–xi.

8   CPMRCL, *1381–1412*, pp. 162–3; *1413–37*, p. 9. Similarly, a dispute between a dyer and a tailor, in 1417, was examined by a fuller and a tailor (ibid., *1413–37*, pp. 62–3).

9   Ibid., *1413–37*, pp. 174–5. For a rather less partial award by a group of barber surgeons with regard to an alleged case of 'trespas del mayheme' see M. Sellers (ed.), *York Memorandum Book*, II, (Surtees Society, CXXV, 1914), p. 17. Another arbitration, made in 1433, specified that the mediator himself would supervise a course of treatment to ensure that it was given a fair trial. W.P. Baildon, 'Notes on the Religious and Secular Houses of Yorkshire' (*Yorkshire Archaeological Society*, Record Series, XVII, 1895), p. 78.

10   CPMRCL, *1381–1412*, pp. 77–8.

11   *The Black Book of the Admiralty*, I, p. 275; III, pp. 116–17, 266–7, 286–7, 292–5, 303, 405, 632–3, 642–5; R.G. Marsden (ed.), *Select Pleas in the Court of Admiralty* (Selden Society, VI, 1894), pp. lxix, 90–1.

12   *The Black Book of the Admiralty*, III, pp. 618–19.

13   Datini Archive, Prato, 777/312993, 664/407474. I am grateful to Miss Helen Bradley for providing me with transcripts of these documents.

14   For awards involving Italian arbitrators see CPMRCL, *1323–64*, pp. 258–9; *1364–81*, pp. 75–6, 86, 158, 278–80; *1381–1412*, pp. 75, 82–3; *1458–82*, p. 13.

15   As, for instance, A.H. Thomas (ed.), *Calendar of the Early Mayors' Court Rolls, 1298–1307* (Cambridge, 1924), pp. 43–4; CPMRCL, *1381–1412*, pp. 162–3; *1413–37*, pp. 1, 70–1, 80–1.

16   York City Archives, YC/FZ (formerly G27).

17   As in the above-mentioned dispute between Gettus Honesti and Pelegrin of Chartres, where both men agreed to accept every aspect of an award 'concerning all manner of chattels and gain, receipts, disbursements, charges, discharges and all other matters, articles and contracts whatsoever, as well foreign as domestic, had and derived as well from parts beyond the sea as those on this side, touching the aforesaid account . . .' (*Select Cases Concerning the Law Merchant*, pp. 59–60).

18   CPMRCL, *1437–57*, p. 91. Not surprisingly, disputants sometimes tried to avoid complying with an unfavourable award by claiming that the arbitrators had exceeded their brief. In London, the mayor would refer such cases to a jury, ibid., *1381–1412*, pp. 244–5.

19 Ibid., *1381–1412*, p. 302.

20 Ibid., *1413–37*, p. 242.

21 Ibid., *1458–82*, p. 68; T.F. Reddaway (ed.), *The Early History of the Goldsmiths' Company 1327–1509* (London, 1975), pp. 107–8, 126, 157; Goldsmiths' Company Records, Goldsmiths' Hall, London, Book A, 1332–1442, f. 182.

22 CPMRCL, *1381–1412*, pp. 136.

23 Ibid., *1413–37*, pp. 233–4.

24 A case concerning the alleged liability of an apprentice for a debt of £90 contracted at Middleburgh on 9 December 1386, reached the court of the Mayor of London on 28 January following, but was not finally settled by arbitration until late May 1388. This was partly because the umpire, who was governor of the Middleburgh Staple, spent a long time searching for evidence there (ibid., *1381–1412*, pp. 140–2).

25 Ibid., pp. 162–3. In November 1413 the mayor and aldermen produced an award in a fairly complicated case involving a debt of £60 incurred overseas in just two days (ibid., *1413–37*, p. 10); and two Genoese arbitrators settled a quarrel in the Italian community in November 1380 in the space of three days (ibid., *1364–81*, pp. 278–80). But these examples are exceptional, mediators being commonly allowed rather longer (CCR, *1435–41*, p. 480; *1447–54*, pp. 202, 264, 440).

26 S. Young (ed.), *The Annals of the Barber Surgeons of London*, (London, 1890), p. 45; R.T. Beck, *The Cutting Edge, Early History of the Surgeons of London* (London, 1974), pp. 132–3. The Company of Mercers, too, was well organized in this respect. On 28 February 1480 two mercers bound themselves in £300 to abide by the arbitration of six aldermen and two mercers of London as long as it was given by 15 March. The award was read out in the company's hall on 12 March, that is in just a fortnight. L. Lyell (ed.), *Acts of Court of the Mercers' Company, 1453–1527* (Cambridge, 1936), pp. 43–4.

27 CPMRCL, *1458–82*, p. 17. See also ibid., *1437–57*, p. 26; CCR *1409–13*, pp. 85, 408–9; *1413–19*, p. 106; *1435–41*, p. 480; *1461–68*, pp. 246–7. Occasionally in mercantile cases the umpire might be a judge, ibid., *1429–35*, p. 347; *1447–54*, p. 173.

28 *York Memorandum Book*, II, pp. 288–9.

29 L. Toulmin Smith (ed.), *English Guilds* (EETS, XL, 1892), p. 426.

30 W. Hudson and J.C. Tingey (eds.), *The Records of the City of Norwich*, 2 vols. (Norwich, 1906), I, pp. 110–11.

31 M. Bateson (ed.), *The Records of the Borough of Leicester*, 3 vols. (Cambridge, 1899–1905), II, p. 299.

32 M.D. Harris (ed.), *The Coventry Leet Book*, (EETS, CXXXIV–V, 1908), pp. 91–6.

33 As occurred at Chester during the reign of Edward IV, Chester City Record Office, M/B/5k, f. 26.

34 A. Raine (ed.), *York Civic Records*, II, (Yorkshire Archeological Society, Record Series, CIII, 1941), pp. 161–2, 183–4; *York Memorandum Book*, II, pp. 125–8, 242–5, 247–9; J. Percy (ed.), *York Memorandum Book*, III, (Surtees Society, CLXXXVI, 1973), pp. 196–7.

35 *York Civic Records*, II, pp. 70–1, 90, 93, 97–100.

36 The Surgeons of London imposed a fine of 20s. upon members who infringed this rule (Beck, *The Cutting Edge*, pp. 132–3), and the Barber Surgeons one of 13s. 4d. (Young, *Annals of the Barber Surgeons*, pp. 31, 33, 45). It is worth noting that parish guilds and fraternities, which fall outside the scope of this paper, placed equal, if not greater, stress upon the need 'to make an ende and unyte and love betwyne partyes'. See H.F. Westlake, *The Parish Gilds of Medieval England* (London, 1919), pp. 71–3.

37 D.M. Owen (ed.), *The Making of King's Lynn* (Records of Social and Economic History, IX, Oxford, 1984), pp. 267–8. The rules of the Tailors of Lincoln were even stricter, threatening any recalcitrant member who would not accept the award of his brethren with expulsion unless he changed his mind within three days and paid a stone of wax to the guild (*English Guilds*, p. 183). The Weavers of Hull, on the other hand, had to

contribute directly into the municipal coffers if they objected to an arbitration (J. Malet Lambert, *Two Thousand Years of Gild Life* (Kingston upon Hull, 1891), p. 206).

38 *Acts of Court of the Mercers' Company, 1453–1527*, pp. 43–4.

39 Ibid., pp. 43–4, 60–1, 81, 85–6.

40 Goldsmiths' Company Records, Book A, 1332–1442, ff. 43v, 173; 1444–1516, ff. 37, 39, 41, 47, 118, 119, 122.

41 J.A. Kingdon (ed.), *Early Records of the Company of Grocers of the City of London*, 2 vols. (London, 1886), I, pp. 10, 20, 121; II, pp. 224, 291, 294, 367, 398; CPMRCL, *1458–82*, p. 1. For disputes over municipal accounts and their settlement by arbitration at Kingston upon Hull, see *Victoria County History, Yorkshire East Riding*, I, pp. 32–3.

42 Thus, whereas the regulations for the trade of alien weavers in London established that anyone who would 'not submit to be adjudged before the wardens' should be arrested forthwith and brought before the mayor (H.T. Riley (ed.), *Memorials of London and London Life in the XIIIth, XIVth and XVth Centuries* (London, 1868), p. 307), the Company of Drapers of London left parties who could not 'make an end' after a diligent effort by the wardens to their own devices (A.H. Johnson, *The History of the Worshipful Company of the Drapers of London*, 5 vols. (Oxford, 1914–22), I, p. 270). In point of fact, however, drapers whose quarrels remained unresolved had still to accept the 'denomonacion and assignement' of arbitrators chosen by the mayor (CPMRCL, *1413–37*, p. 237).

43 CPMRCL, *1381–1412*, p. 307; *English Guilds*, pp. 322–3.

44 This event is misdated by W.S. Prideaux in his *Memorials of the Goldsmiths' Company*, 2 vols. (London, 1896–7), I, p. 18. It occurred in 1422–3 not 1419; see Goldsmiths' Company Records, Book A, 1332–1442, ff. 132–3.

45 CPMRCL, *1437–57*, pp. 7–8, 66, 70–1, 74, 75.

46 Ibid., *1323–64*, p. 268; *1381–1412*, pp. 127–8, 146. For other cases involving apprentices see PRO, C1/64/324, 72/73. Apprentices sometimes received a surprisingly sympathetic hearing. In 1481, for instance, the master and wardens of the Tailors' Company of Exeter ruled that a young man who had been badly beaten by his employer should have 5s. 'for leechcraft', 15s. in damages and 3s. 4d. to pay for a month's supply of food (*English Guilds*, pp. 322–3).

47 Although occasionally noblemen were invited to arbitrate in mercantile disputes (as, for example, Rawcliffe, 'Arbitration by English Noblemen', pp. 43–4; and E. Gillett, *A History of Grimsby* (Oxford, 1970), p. 58), care was always taken to ensure that their presence did not constitute a threat to civic liberties.

48 PRO C1/43/214.

49 Reddaway, *Early History of the Goldsmiths' Company*, pp. 151–4; Goldsmiths' Company Records, Book A, 1444–1516, f. 170. Similar concern on King Edward's part over deteriorating relations between English and Italian merchants in Southampton, for which the rabidly xenophobic mayor, John Payne, was largely to blame, probably explains why, in 1464, Payne was at last forced to accept the award of a group of London merchants, with the keeper of the rolls of Chancery as umpire. He had been removed from office by the king in the previous year: A.A. Ruddock, *Italian Merchants and Shipping in Southampton, 1270–1700* (Southampton, 1951), pp. 170–3.

50 N.H. Nicholas (ed.), *Proceedings and Ordinances of the Privy Council*, 7 vols. (Record Commission, 1843–7), IV, pp. 85–6. It was not unknown for arbitrators to insist that the parties to an award should recite a speech by way of public apology (Rawcliffe, 'Arbitration by English Noblemen', p. 42).

51 As, for example, PRO C1/43/216, 45/344, 59/50; CCR 1461–68, pp. 252–3; CPMRCL, *1381–1412*, pp. 207–8; *1413–37*, pp. 70–1; *1458–82*, pp. 13, 17, 31, 65.

52 As, for instance, CCR 1409–13, pp. 57, 61, 85, 202, 310, 330, 408–9, 425; *1413–19*, pp. 106, 117; *1429–35*, pp. 66, 109, 194, 347; *1435–41*, p. 408; *1441–47*, p. 370; *1447–54*, pp. 173, 202, 253, 264, 325, 440; *1461–68*, pp. 208–9, 246–7, 252–3, 390.

53 Ibid., *1409–13*, p. 324; *1413–19*, p. 187; *1429–35*, p. 222; *1441–47*, pp. 319–20.

54 Most plaintiffs alleged that their securities had either been unjustly kept back from them after the due performance of an award, or, even worse, that their opponents had actually taken them to law on the strength of bonds which had already been honoured: ibid., *CPMRCL, 1381–1412*, p. 239; *1437–57*, pp. 36–7; PRO C1/43/216, 45/318, 59/50, 64/82, 918, 324, 343, 66/106, 67/183, 72/73.

55 *CPMRCL, 1381–1412*, pp. 77–8; *1413–37*, pp. 174–5, 256–8; *1437–57*, pp. 36–7.

56 Ibid., *1323–64*, p. 278. In 1375, the vintner, Thomas Gisors, and his agent, William Misseburgh, who were at odds over an action of account, swore an oath to give every possible assistance to the arbitrators mediating between them (ibid., *1364–81*, pp. 201–2).

57 Chester City Record Office, M/B/5k, f. 215v. Note, too, an award of 1457, in which two mercers 'were made to take yche other by the honde and to be frendes' (*Acts of Court of the Mercers' Company, 1453–1527*, pp. 46–7).

58 *York Civic Records*, II, p. 100. See also *CPMRCL, 1413–37*, p. 166, where four arbitrators came personally to the court of the Mayor and aldermen of London in August 1423 to acknowledge an award made by them in the previous June; and ibid., p. 237, for a sworn statement by the mercer, Robert Large, to 'alle cristen peple' that he had just settled a dispute between two of his fellows at the 'denominacion and assignment' of the mayor.

59 F. Hull (ed.), *A Calendar of the White and Black Books of the Cinque Ports* (Kent Archaeological Society, XIX, 1966), pp. 109–10.

60 *CPMRCL, 1364–81*, pp. 75–86, 278–80. An award of 1431 (also delivered in the church of St. Thomas of Acres) was sealed first by the umpire and arbitrators, and then, 'for better evidence' with the mayoral seal of London (ibid., *1413–37*, pp. 256–8).

61 Ibid., *1458–82*, p. 68.

62 As, for instance, ibid., *1323–64*, p. 278; *Select Cases Concerning the Law Merchant*, pp. lx-lxi, 34–9.

63 *Select Cases Concerning the Law Merchant*, pp. xiii-xiv.

64 *CCR, 1429–35*, p. 259; *1447–54*, pp. 183, 276, 477. See also: ibid., *1405–9*, p. 470; *1409–13*, p. 400; *1461–68*, pp. 208–9.

65 Ibid., *1441–47*, pp. 444–5.

66 PRO C1/48/135. See also C1/46/320, 60/106, 64/541, 740, 829, 918, 66/264, 67/183, 69/176.

67 C1/46/279, 320.

68 C1/43/124, 126–8, 214–17, 73/91.

69 Acts of Court of the Mercers' Company, 1453–1527, p. 146.

70 W. West, *The Second Part of Symboleography* (London, 1627), f. 167v.

71 *CCR, 1447–54*, p. 275.

6

Scriveners and Notaries as Legal Intermediaries in Later Medieval England

Nigel Ramsay
British Library

The aim of this paper is to draw attention to both the range of skills increasingly deployed by the late medieval scriveners and notaries and the fluidity of the distinction between them and the other men, notably attorneys, whose professional skills lay in the preparation or use of legal documents. The scribe's significance or status varies according to the extent to which he is the originator of his text and depending on whether he can uphold its legal validity by his own actions. A mere copyist will never count for much, no matter how beautifully he can pen a character, but it is different if he can compose his text, and still more if the courts will automatically accept as valid what he has claimed as his authentic work. Notaries public (whether appointed by papal or imperial authority) were in the latter position, so far as the Church's courts were concerned; in the course of the fifteenth century, however, they increasingly chose to operate more like scriveners, acting for laymen in a wide range of commercial transactions. Scriveners themselves in the same period came to act at times more like attorneys, advising on the substance of the law as well as preparing documents that satisfied its form.

The fields with which the paper is concerned have hardly been investigated by modern scholars. It remains unclear how the scriveners and notaries learnt their skills – whether as apprentices (as was probably the case for most scriveners) or in writing-offices – and it is hard even to estimate what was understood by the term 'clerk' in this period, as it lost its former catch-all position. How many scriveners and notaries were there, in London and in the rest of England? Notaries are the more clearly distinguishable group, since they had to be formally appointed to office, but much of their world remains shadowy. C.R. Cheney, whose study of *Notaries Public in England* is the only detailed modern treatment of any of the professional writers, but who limited himself to the thirteenth and fourteenth centuries, found evidence of just one examination of notarial competence, in 1402: this was of notaries already practising in the diocese of London, of whom there were no fewer than sixty-one.[1]

Similarly, the expansion of writing activities in the fourteenth and fifteenth centuries has yet to receive much discussion, let alone any treatment to match that given to previous centuries by M.T. Clanchy's *From Memory to Written Record: England 1066–1307*.[2] From the numbers of thirteenth-century charters that survive, it could be guessed that clerks who could write them were numerous, but it is easier to learn details about the book trade, especially in the university towns of Oxford and Cambridge. Yet the book trade's professionals were mostly highly specialized individuals: one reads of parchmenters, limners, stationers and samplerers (*exemplarii* – men who specialized in copying academic texts), but only occasionally of plain writers – scribes or scriveners.[3] The scribes of charters relating to properties in Oxford do not seem to have been members of the book trade.[4] And yet, just as Oxford seems to have been at the source of the book trade's expansion, it seems likely that many writers trained there. Suggestive, for instance, is the ownership of a tenement in the suburbs of Canterbury in 1293 by William le Scriveyn of Oxford and Helewyse his wife.[5] Furthermore, the training of young men or boys in 'business skills', such as the keeping of accounts and assisting in the holding of manorial courts as well as instruction in the French language is known to have taken place at Oxford in the fourteenth century, since there survive formularies with close Oxford associations.[6] H.G. Richardson even traced such teaching back to the mid-thirteenth century.[7] Employers like Elizabeth de Burgh, the Lady de Clare (d. 1363), might sometimes send their clerks to Oxford for a few weeks' or months' schooling – instruction which was in no way intended to be seen as akin to university training, for all that it was very likely imparted by the university's grammar masters.[8]

The term 'scrivener' was rarely used in the late thirteenth or early fourteenth centuries, the craft's practitioners being disguised from us as clerks. In small towns they perhaps acted as the town clerk as well as being common clerks, they had very probably taken the first steps towards ordination to hold orders (i.e. receiving the first tonsure or being ordained to the minor order of acolyte), they were able to plead benefit of clergy if indicted, and they were sometimes married. They *were* clerks, and yet the term must have been felt to be stretched beyond its natural usage.

The poll-tax records show the writers in this transitional state, metamorphosing from clerk to scrivener. In York the 1381 returns include eighteen clerks, of whom thirteen were married, and three scriveners (one of whom was married).[9] Those three scriveners may have been text-hand (or book) writers primarily, for the late fourteenth-century ordinances of the York scriveners are headed as ordinances of *escriveners de Tixt*.[10] Ordinary scriveners may thus still be disguised as clerks.

The spread of scriveners in the late fourteenth century and early fifteenth century cannot easily be quantified: the evidence is sketchy. But corroborative hints come from such matters as the investigations into lollardy at this time, where it is striking both how many scriveners were involved and how small were the towns that some of them worked in.[11] The copying of bills, such as a scrivener of Braybrooke (Northampton-shire) was accused of, would of course have been second nature to them.

That there would have had to be an expansion in the number of writers in the mid- to late fourteenth century and subsequently can be inferred from the changes in legally binding practices that were then taking place; pre-eminent among these were the making of wills (as distinct from testaments) and enfeoffments to uses, and the readiness of the king's Chancellor to accept bills (or petitions) that sought his intervention, sometimes in areas where the common law could not provide a remedy.

Will-making was particularly productive of increased documentation – it led to the making of several separate instruments, the will (with its directions to feoffees) and the testament, and also of a deed of con-veyance of the estate to the feoffees as well as the later deeds of release from each of the feoffees. The Chancellor's readiness to hear or at any rate to receive petitions was of importance as opening up a fresh and probably cheaper channel for litigation; more particularly, it led to increased writing because Chancery litigation was so largely dependent on written submissions. That is hardly surprising of course; quite apart from the Chancellor's disinclination to rely on oral plaints (suggested as having been, as a general rule, unacceptable from c. 1440,[12] and perhaps rare long before that), there was the Chancery clerks' general attachment to form and, one may even say, obsession with copying. As R.F. Hunnisett has put it, 'without the evidence of the [surviving] rolls and files it would be incredible that the Chancery made two [copies of such ephemeral documents as coroners' and verderers' writs], or three if one counts the original'.[13] Hunnisett took the multiplication of records of various aspects of Chancery business as presenting 'a picture of an institution whose lesser members wasted innumerable hours unthinkingly and unnecessarily copying and recopying documents of minor impor-tance'.[14] The lay counterpart to this was also a resort to copying – for instance, in legal actions it became common for one party to seek copies of the writs obtained by the other side, perhaps on the off chance of a fault in the form or on the face of the writ. One result was that the cost of litigation outside the Chancellor's equitable jurisdiction was of course increased by the need to pay for the enrolment of writs. The Chancery clerks did not transcribe for free.

Outside litigation there were other developments, such as the increased practice of tenure by lease and the common resort of entering into bonds –

written, sealed bonds (or specialty) – for really quite minor contractual agreements.[15]

Let me now turn to the men who directed, drafted or drew out the documentation engendered by all these and other changes. Consider first the Chancery, Privy Seal and Exchequer, the government departments most generally involved in the legal and other written processes we are dealing with. The end of the household of the Chancery and, in the later fourteenth century and earlier fifteenth century, the ending even of the general keeping of households of clerks by the principal officials in the Chancery are changes that may be associated with the laicization of the Chancery and the increasing independence of action of the lesser officials. For most of the fourteenth century it was not uncommon for major landowners to retain the services of prominent officials at the Chancery and other departments, paying fairly large sums to these men. For instance, John of Gaunt in c. 1383 retained the services as 'gentz de conseil deinz la courte nostre tres redoute seignur le roy' of an Exchequer clerk for 60s. per annum, and he paid ten marks per annum to his attorney in Chancery and £10 per annum (later reduced to ten marks) to his attorney in the Exchequer, these attorneys being officials of those departments; by contrast he only paid 40s. per annum to each of four serjeants-at-law.[16] Landowners paid such sums partly because they could leave it to the officials to do what work was needed (doubtless using the clerks in their household); but by around 1400 it was not really practicable to operate in this way because so many, admittedly minor, transactions were required, and it was really only feasible to pay on a piecemeal basis. Each Chancery and other government clerk measured his time, or his own clerk's time – or both – more carefully. In 1406 ordinances stated that the Chancery officers and other court clerks were not to take excessive reward for their labours.[17] Quite apart from the laicization of these officials, and their transformation into 'gentlemen',[18] they increasingly became drawn into commercial and legal life. The very expansion of the Chancellor's equitable jurisdiction in the late fourteenth century was accelerated by the extent to which his officials used their privilege as his officers to sue in his court, while they are also early found acting as the pledges for the prosecutions brought before him by other people.[19] As pledges, they were of course acting in a role more commonly filled by common lawyers. In a sample of nearly four hundred Chancery pledges described as being 'of London, gentleman' of the late fifteenth century, approximately 10 per cent were found by J.H. Baker to be legal officials of some kind, mostly of the Chancery – that is, about 5 per cent of all the pledges.[20] And that is a full hundred years after the start of the process of opening up the Chancery; the proportion would have been higher, earlier.

I think it probable that the Chancery clerks would have been drawn into ordinary commercial and legal business even if they had retained their celibate status – for instance, Thomas Haseley before the mid-fifteenth century at different or the same times was clerk of the Crown in Chancery, had at least one Chancery clerk, William Godying, dwelling with him, and was a JP for Middlesex, a deputy coroner of London and a twice-married man.[21] Since royal charters had to pass through the fee-collecting office of the Chancery, it was only natural that people seeking charters should turn to the Chancery clerks for assistance in that sort of matter. For instance, when the monks of St Albans wanted a new charter of liberties in 1440 they paid 20s. to a master in Chancery for the first draft (*pro prima conceptione*), and 6s. 8d. to a Chancery clerk for writing it out; it was then sent to William Paston, the justice for correction; and eventually it was recopied by another clerk.[22]

Until the late fifteenth century the masters in Chancery were not men with university degrees, and it is probable that, like their clerks, they may have had some training of a so-called 'business' kind, but that otherwise they learned their skills on the job.[23] The first master who had not risen through the ranks was Richard Wetton, DCL, who was appointed in 1448.[24]

The Privy Seal and Signet offices had clerks of perhaps greater literary ability, and these were turned to for the writing of letters – both letters that passed under those seals, of course, and private letters. For instance in 1442/3 New College, Oxford, made payments to William Crosby, clerk of the king's secretary, for writing a letter sent to Lady Bardolf; to Thomas Este, for writing a letter and for correcting a Chancery bill (or petition); to John Blackney, clerk of the king's secretary, for writing a letter for the Privy Seal; and John Frank, both for writing a letter under the Privy Seal to the king's Chancellor, and for correcting a Privy Seal.[25] The fifteenth century was of course the heyday for florid, stylized letters, heavily reliant on models no doubt,[26] and the Privy Seal clerks profited accordingly.

A similar sort of story could be told of the Exchequer clerks – becoming citizens of London, writing all kinds of transcripts, acting as attorneys in the Exchequer, and getting involved in a range of commercial transactions.

Nor has that exhausted the range of types of writers who were officials – clerks of (or at) the Guildhall, in London and elsewhere, were often turned to for miscellaneous pieces of work; thus the corporation of Rochester in c. 1460 employed John Ryponden of the Guildhall in London 'to make us a boke out of French into Latin, and out of Latin in English for the enquiry of all manner of things that belong to the justice of peace'.[27] The former London town clerk John Carpenter sought to help the Guildhall clerks by his bequest in 1442 'of all my little books . . . of the modes of entering and engrossing of acts and records as well according to the common law of the realm as the custom of the city of London' to Robert Blount (a lawyer) for life, and after Blount's death to revert to the chamber of the Guildhall, for the instruction (*informatio*) of the clerks there. [28]

Finally I come to the men most commonly called scriveners *eo nomine*. The greatest concentration of them was in London, and it is with this group that I shall principally be concerned. The craft of writers of court hand, by which we can understand scriveners, is first mentioned in 1357, when they, along with the writers of text hand, the limners and the barbers were exempted from service on sheriffs' inquests;[29] sixteen years later, in 1373, they had their own ordinances approved and enrolled by the mayor and aldermen and so can be said to have become a guild or company.[30] These ordinances refer to the problems resulting from all sorts of people, including chaplains, 'who are ignorant of London's customs, franchises and usages, and yet call themselves scriveners and also undertake to make wills, charters and all other things' concerning the craft of scrivenery. Henceforth, none were to keep scrivener's shop [*de tenir shope*] in London or its suburbs unless free of the city and also made free of the scriveners' craft by men of it; applicants for freedom were to be examined for fitness; and every scrivener was to put his name to the deeds he made, so that it would be known who had made them.

The reference to scriveners' keeping of shop is significant: it may be that only men who were free of the company did keep shop henceforth, and it is not uncommon to find references to people 'going to a scrivener's in Lombard Street' or the like.[31] On the other hand, one may note a large number of scriveners, some called writers of court letter, who were practising in London and yet were not free of the company; they are easy to detect since the company kept a register, its Common Paper, in which all admissions from 1391 are recorded.[32] Some of these evading scriveners are doubtless men who had acquired considerable expertise in, say, one of the government departments – for instance the two elderly scriveners who at the close of the fifteenth century gave evidence as to the burial place of Henry VI: one of these men had been clerk to Thomas Hunt, clerk of the king's works (1472–85), and the other had had John Brown, the under-treasurer (1455, 1456–c.1457), as master.[33] A few so-called scriveners were no doubt incompetent, if not worse; like the man who in 1391 was sent to the pillory for his ignorance, he having held shop after being a mere hireling with a scrivener for two years and never apprenticed. But the activities of fraudsters probably strengthened the Scriveners' Company, by highlighting its own standards.[34]

The members of the Scriveners' Company were by and large obviously competent, and were turned to for their skills by clients from other parts of England as well as from within London; they gained enough experience for them to be turned to in lieu of lawyers, at times, and they sometimes became highly prosperous. Two that may be singled out are William Kingsmill and Robert Bale. Kingsmill was admitted free by 1402, and is found acting in a range of transactions in London until 1419; he was also under-marshal of the King's Bench, until dismissed.[35] In about 1420 he moved to Oxford. He produced a conveyancing manual – largely derivative of the fairly recent *cartuaria* of the Oxford grammar-master, Thomas Sampson – and also a manual of commercial French.[36] The latter includes a declaration by a twelve-year-old boy that in three months at Kingsmill's hostel he has learned to read and write, cast accounts and speak French, and so he is now reading for a London apprenticeship. This manual may therefore have been written for use in London. Did Kingsmill turn to the teaching of conveyancing because the bottom was falling out of the French-language market? But why was Oxford seen as the place to teach conveyancing? From what I have been saying, the move should have been *from* Oxford *to* London at this date.

Robert Bale was admitted as a scrivener in London in 1440, but is best known for keeping a chronicle during the 1440s and 1450s; his editor, Flenley, commented on his interests being strongly legal and 'constitutional', as in his relation of a session of *oyer et terminer* at the Guildhall (1456) which is only later followed by the explanation that this was held because of an anti-Lombard riot, or in his account of a riot between the 'men of court' (lawyers) and the Londoners of Fleet Street.[37] The other contents of the manuscript that contains his chronicle doubtless reflect his professional and social interests – notes about pawning, the probate of testaments and the leasing of tenements in London, a list of sums taxable to the wards of London, the freeman's oath, and the text of the City's charter of November 1384, together with a list of churches of the City and its suburbs, the measurements of St Paul's Cathedral, the foundation of Barking Abbey and a dictionary of saints.[38]

Notaries are all too easily seen as quite distinct from scriveners, but this division was increasingly eroded in the late fourteenth century and during the fifteenth century. That is not to deny that there were some men, termed notaries, who spent their entire lives in diocesan registries or ecclesiastical courts, acting as little more than high-grade copyists. Depositions by the clerks of the Bishop of London's registry in 1495 present a clear picture of this world: four of these clerks were notaries (three by apostolic authority and one, surprisingly, by imperial authority), while the fifth is described as '*literatus*', and one of the notaries had been a clerk in the registry for forty years and another for nearly that time.[39] Such men presumably had no wish or need to broaden their horizons, and this paper is not concerned with them.

Notaries and notarial practice came to England from Italy in ecclesiastical baggage, so to speak, in the mid-thirteenth century, and there were

English notaries public by the 1280s.[40] As has been seen, in 1402 there were at least sixty-one practising in the diocese of London alone.[41] Most fourteenth-century notaries in England, whether admitted by papal or imperial authority, were clerks, and papal commissions generally provided for notaries to be unmarried clerks in minor orders.[42] However, in the course of the fifteenth century one finds an increasing number of mentions of married notaries, while the Scriveners' Common Paper shows that there was a steady trickle of scriveners who were also notaries – beginning with the first two wardens of the Company in 1391 and becoming something more like a stream from the 1470s.[43] Besides, the Common Paper would only record men who were already notaries when admitted free of the scriveners, and obviously some scriveners only became notaries at a later date.[44] John Kendale, pardoned in 1474 as 'late of Westminster, notary, alias scrivener, alias late of York, clerk', who has recently been discussed in print by Anne Sutton, is a clear example of this sort of doubling up of notarial and scrivening activities.[45]

Much less commonly documented but very suggestive is the doubling up of scrivener and attorney; this I have so far found only in London and Norwich – for instance, William Fanside, who was admitted free of the scriveners in 1426 and who described himself in his will, in 1437, as citizen and attorney of London.[46]

The legal activities of scriveners and notaries are not easily traced. On the Continent it was the general practice for notaries to keep books in which they copied the instruments that they had authenticated with their mark; no such notarial books survive in England, so far as I am aware, although they undoubtedly once existed.[47] There are also sufficient references to indicate that it was standard practice for scriveners to keep copies or memoranda, in book form, of the deeds, charters and bonds that they had copied;[48] the pity is that only a very few such books survive – one of a Bury St Edmunds scrivener, of the 1460s,[49] and two others of London practitioners – John Thorpe, 1457–9, and William Styfford, 1457–8.[50]

Scriveners' activities are therefore best investigated in the accounts of the companies or guilds of London. These show that practice varied considerably from company to company, but that in general the companies found it inescapable to engage scriveners to write their deeds and contracts for them, and that the companies frequently found it helpful to get the scriveners to give advice and to draft and write out other things for them. Most companies made use of a variety of men, often paying two or three different ones in one year.

The Pewterers, for instance, in 1477/8 paid 12d. to Clifford, scrivener, 'to search for our evidences of the tenement in the Jury', and, in the following year, paid 20d. to John Green of the Mayor's Court for a copy of Whitehead's complaint; 3s. to Herry Wodecok (a prominent scrivener) for a note and for writing up an answer to the same complaint; 3s. 4d., for counsel, to Mr Vavasour, serjeant-at-law, with a reward for his clerk; 2s. paid in the Mayor's Court for a copy of Whitehead's replication; and 4s. to Richard Grene, scrivener, for drawing and writing the rejoinder to the same replication.[51] Wodecok, incidentally, was also a notary and a few years later became Secondary of the Poultry Compter.[52] Or in 1487/8 they paid 13s. 4d. to John Paies, scrivener, for drawing and writing of two supplications to the king and the Lord Chancellor – a sum which compares with the 20d. that they paid to Mr More (the future judge, Sir John More) for surveying a deed of release, or 3s. 4d. to Richard Magson, scrivener, for 'overseeing our writings, and writing and engrossing this account'.[53] The Mercers, by contrast, rarely employed scriveners, preferring to rely on their own liverymen for greater secrecy, or else to engage lawyers, while the equally wealthy Goldsmiths also tended to engage lawyers even for work that other companies would generally give to scriveners. When they acquired a property in 1468/9, they paid 6s. 8s. for 'the search of the deeds remaining in Clifford scrivener books' and then another 6s. 8d. to two lawyers 'for the oversight of the deeds and making of the notes thereof'.[54] But the Mercers and Goldsmiths were most unusual in this avoidance of scriveners.

The same Clifford was regularly engaged by the Carpenters in the late 1470s and subsequently, being paid several times for counsel, as well as for writing.[55]

The Merchant Taylors, another of the wealthier companies, made much use of lawyers, especially of those active in the City's own law courts, but none the less paid scriveners to be of counsel for making instruments (1407/8) as well as for ordinary writing purposes (1418/19).[56] In 1430/1 they first engaged William Brampton to write some documents, and in 1440/1 he and his wife joined the vast ranks of confrères of the company; he was not however favoured with any monopoly of company business, still having to share it with others.[57]

The London evidence could easily be multiplied many times over, either from other London sources, or from other cities and towns. If anything, this would sometimes show scriveners to have been even more successful in the provinces. In Norwich one can point to such a family of scriveners as the Attemeres in the late fifteenth century; there, too, scriveners are found doubling as attorney and as notary, as well as merchant.[58] The grounds of the scriveners' success were national in their applicability, and so their success was also on a national level. It would be wrong to present them as substitute lawyers in a general way, for their legal skills were obviously limited. They excelled as copyists and as form followers, and yet, paradoxically, it was where the law was at its most informal that they were able to make inroads into it. The rise of the practice of enfeoffment to uses, and thus of the last will, left the testament as a mere disposal of personalty, and so as an instrument that could safely be entrusted to a scrivener to draft and write out; from that business might follow the further engagement as executor, with the duty of having the testament proved. In a similar way, the lack of requirements of form for Chancery petitioners and defendants, or in town courts, provided easy business for a scrivener of competence. And in the scriveners' constant drawing up of bonds there presumably lay the seeds of their future business as money-scriveners, although there are certainly no direct signs of that in the fifteenth century.[59]

The scriveners were intermediaries between the ordinary public and the law – it is not suggested that they acted like solicitors as intermediaries between the public and other lawyers. The material that has been drawn on in this paper may be objected to as being drawn from the accounts of relatively well-to-do City institutions, and not from the accounts, if one could find them, of ordinary people, but ordinary people will surely have been even readier than institutions to engage scriveners rather than costlier lawyers. Indeed, the three scriveners' memoranda books that still survive contain almost exclusively the summaries of documents prepared for private individuals, while the accounts of fifteenth-century churchwardens show that their relatively poor institutions also made widespread use of scriveners.[6]

The scriveners may have thrived on the law's informality for their inroads into it, but, more importantly, in a more general way it is suggested that they made people familiar with the need to follow set forms, that they helped make people order their lives in accordance with a set of principles which readily resorted to legal machinery when matters did not turn out satisfactorily, and that they thus contributed to the expansion of the law's role in people's lives. The handling of litigation remained the attorneys' preserve, but the scriveners, and to a lesser extent the notaries, made people more aware of the legal significance of the contracts and dispositions of property that were written for them. And at the same time the scriveners and notaries created a new field of activity for themselves.

Notes

1 C.R. Cheney, *Notaries Public in England in the Thirteenth and Fourteenth Centuries* (Oxford, 1972), pp. 93–4.
2 (London, 1979).
3 For the book trade in thirteenth-century Oxford, see G. Pollard, 'The University and the Book Trade in Mediaeval Oxford', *Miscellanea Mediaevalia, Beiträge zum Berufsbewusstein des Mittelalterlichen Menschen*, III (1964), pp. 336–44, and idem. 'William de Brailles',

Bodleian Library Record, V (1954–6), pp. 202–9, and for Cambridge see M.B. Hackett, *The Original Statutes of Cambridge University: The Text and its History* (Cambridge, 1970), pp. 228–9. For England as a whole, see most recently M.A. Michael, 'Oxford, Cambridge and London: towards a theory for "grouping" gothic manuscripts', *Burlington Magazine,* CXXX (1988), pp. 107–15, and the cautionary words of N.J. Morgan, *Early Gothic Manuscripts,* [I], *1190–1250, A Survey of Manuscripts Illuminated in the British Isles,* IV (London, 1982), pp. 14–15, and in ibid., [III], *1250–1285, A Survey* . . . V (London, 1988), pp. 12–13.

4   Charter-writers figure in G. Pollard, 'The Medieval Town Clerks of Oxford', *Oxoniensia,* XXXI (1966), pp. 43–76; note also H.E. Salter's preface to his edition of *A Cartulary of the Hospital of St. John the Baptist,* I (Oxford Historical Society (old series) LXVI, 1914), pp. vi–ix, with the suggestion that in thirteenth-century Oxford there were at times up to eight charter-writers.

5   J.H. Harvey, *English Medieval Architects. A Biographical Dictionary down to 1550,* (2nd edn., Gloucester, 1984), p. 45.

6   H.E. Salter, W.A. Pantin and H.G. Richardson (eds.), *Formularies which bear on the History of Oxford,* c. *1204–1420,* 2 vols. (Oxford History Society, new series, IV–V, 1942), II, pp. 281–6, 331–45.

7   H.G. Richardson, 'Business Training in Medieval Oxford', *American History Review,* XLVI (1940/1), pp. 259–80; see also *idem,* 'An Oxford Teacher of the Fifteenth Century', *Bulletin of the John Rylands Library,* XXIII (1939), pp. 436–57, and reprinted separately with corrections.

8   C.A. Musgrave, 'Household Administration in the 14th century, with special reference to the household of Elizabeth de Burgh, Lady of Clare' (M.A. thesis, University of London, 1923), p. 14.

9   J. N. Bartlett, *The Lay Poll Tax Returns for the City of York in 1381,* reprinted from *Transactions of the East Riding Antiquarian Society,* XXX (1953).

10   These ordinances were printed by Robert Davies in *A Memoir of the York Press, with Notices of Authors, Printers and Stationers* . . . (London, 1868), pp. 1n–(2)n.

11   Anne Hudson, 'Some Aspects of Lollard Book Production', *Studies in Church History,* IX (1972), pp. 147–57, at 155; reprinted in her *Lollards and their Books* (London and Ronceverte, W. Virginia, 1985), pp. 181–91.

12   N. Pronay, 'The Chancellor, the Chancery, and the Council at the End of the Fifteenth Century', in H. Hearder and H.R. Loyn (eds.), *British Government and Administration. Studies presented to S.B. Chrimes* (Cardiff, 1974), pp. 87–103, at 89 n.2.

13   R.F. Hunnisett, 'English Chancery Records: Rolls and Files', *Journal of the Society of Archivists,* 4 (1973–4), pp. 158–68, at 164.

14   Ibid., pp. 167–8. From 1444 the signet office was instructed to keep copies of its warrants to the Privy Seal (B.P. Wolffe, *Henry VI* (London, 1981), p. 114).

15   Still useful as an introduction to the rise of the bond is M.M. Postan, 'Private Financial Instruments in Medieval England', reprinted from *Vierteljahrschrift für Sozial- und Wirtschaftsgeschichte,* XXIII (1930), pp. 26–75, in his *Medieval Trade and Finance* (Cambridge, 1973), pp. 28–64, esp. at 32–3.

For leases see, e.g., J.N. Hare, 'The Demesne Lessees of Fifteenth-Century Wiltshire', *AgHR,* 29 (1981), pp. 1–15.

16   E.C. Lodge and R. Somerville (eds.), *John of Gaunt's Register, 1379–1383,* II (Camden Society 3rd Series, LVII, 1937), p. 412, no. 1245; for ten marks p.a. paid to Richard Bank as his attorney in the exchequer, see PRO DL 28/3/2, f. 13.

See further N.L. Ramsay, 'Retained Legal Counsel, c. 1275–c. 1475', *TRHS,* 5th ser., XXXV (1985), pp. 95–112.

17   *Rotuli Parliamentorum,* III, p. 588. The broader question of Chancery clerks in private bureaucracies is discussed by C.W. Smith, 'A Conflict of Interest? Chancery Clerks in

Private Service', in J.T. Rosenthal and C.F. Richmond (eds.), *People, Politics and Community in the Later Middle Ages* (Gloucester and New York, 1987), pp. 176–91.

18 For which see R.L. Storey, 'Gentleman-bureaucrats', in C.H. Clough (ed.), *Profession, Vocation, and Culture in Later Medieval England. Essays dedicated to the memory of A.R. Myers*, (Liverpool, 1982), pp. 90–129.

19 This can be seen by examination of the early bundles of Early Chancery Proceedings – the bills in PRO C1.

20 J.H. Baker, 'Lawyers Practising in Chancery, 1474–1486', *Journal of Legal History*, IV (1983), pp. 54–76.

21 There is a biography of Haseley by A.F. Pollard, *Bulletin of the Institute of Historical Research*, XVI (1938/9), pp. 72–80; his wives are referred to in his testament, dated 23 May 1449, Lambeth Palace Library, Reg. Archbishop Stafford, f. 174. For Godyng's dwelling with him in 1428 see the testament of John Wodecok, dated 22 April 1428, PRO PROB 11/3 (P.C.C. 9 Luffenam), f. 69v.

22 H.T. Riley (ed.), John Amundesham, *Annales Monasterii S. Albani*, 2 vols. (Rolls Series, 28 (1870/1), II, pp. 294–5.

23 Some specific claims for 'business school' training are advanced by N. Pronay, 'The Chancellor, the Chancery, and the Council', (see note 12); although the evidence for these claims is not provided, the hypothesis seems very plausible.

24 Ibid., p. 91; A.B. Emden, *Biographical Register of the University of Oxford to A.D. 1500 [BRUO]*, 3 vols. (Oxford, 1957–9), III, pp. 2027–8. Wetton was Principal of the Civil Law School at Oxford from Sept, 1446.

25 Oxford, New College Archives, no. 7407, bursars' account roll for 1442/3.

26 Cf. E.F. Jacob, 'Verborum Florida Venustas', reprinted in his *Essays in the Conciliar Epoch*, (3rd edn., Manchester, 1963), pp. 185–206.

27 Extracts from the Rochester town accounts, printed in F. Grose et al.(eds.), *The Antiquarian Repertory*, (2nd edn., 1808), III p. 148.

28 Testament of John Carpenter, dated 8 March, 20 Henry VI, printed by Thomas Brewer, *Memoir . . . of John Carpenter*, (2nd edn., London, 1856), pp. 131–44, at 141.

29 F.W. Steer (ed.), *Scriveners' Company Common Paper, 1357–1628*, (London Record Society, IV, 1968), p. 1.

30 Ibid., p. 2.

31 An early mention of a scrivener in Lombard Street comes in a reference to a forgery copied by 'Doncastre, escryueyn' in 1380 (I.S. Leadam and J.F. Baldwin (eds.), *Select cases before the King's Council* (Selden Society, XXXV, 1918), p. 73).

32 The text of the Common Paper (London, Guildhall Library, MS 5370) was edited by Steer, *Scriveners' Common Paper*.

33 The depositions of these scriveners, John Dawson and John Bothe, were printed by A.P. Stanley, *Historical Memorials of Westminster Abbey* (London, 1868), pp. 510–11.

34 For the offender of 1391, Thomas Pantier, see Steer, *Common Paper*, p. 3. I have argued for the significance of this and other cases in leading to the establishment and laying down of rules by the Scriveners' Company, in 'Forgery and the Rise of the London Scriveners' Company', in M. Harris and R. Myers (eds.), *Fakes and Frauds: Varieties of Deception in Print and Manuscript* (Winchester, 1989), pp. 99–108.

35 Biographical materials about Kingsmill are brought together in Emden, *BRUO*, II, pp. 1074–5. For knowledge of his King's Bench post, I am indebted to Dr Edward Powell.

36 Richardson, in 'An Oxford Teacher' (see note 7, p. 455; offprint, p. 22), noted his adaptation of the *cartuaria* of Sampson, who lived until c. 1409 (Emden, *BRUO*, III, pp. 1636–7). For Kingsmill's French teaching see M.D. Legge, 'William of Kingsmill – A Fifteenth-Century Teacher of French in Oxford', in *Studies in French Language and Mediaeval Literature presented to Professor Mildred K. Pope* (Manchester, 1939), pp. 241–6, and references there cited.

37 Bale's chronicle was discussed by Ralph Flenley in the introduction to his edition of *Six*

Town Chroniclers of England (Oxford, 1911), pp. 66–74 and printed at pp. 114–53; his life was examined by C.L. Kingsford, 'Robert Bale, the London Chronicler', *EHR*, 31 (1916), pp. 126–8, and in his *English Historical Literature in the Fifteenth Century* (Oxford, 1913), pp. 95–6.

38   Trinity College Dublin, MS 509 (E.5.9); I take my account of its contents partly from M.L. Colker's draft catalogue description. The manuscript was once bound with MS 604, which contains the conclusion of Bale's Chronicle.

39   C. Jenkins, 'Cardinal Morton's Register', in R.W. Seton-Watson (ed.), *Tudor Studies presented . . . to Albert Frederick Pollard* (London, 1924), pp. 26–74, at 30–1.

40   Cheney, *Notaries Public*, Chapters 1, 2 and 3.

41   Cf. ibid., pp. 93–4.

42   Cf. ibid., pp. 79–81.

43   Steer, *Common Paper*, pp. 20–4, shows (in the editorial apparatus) just a few instances of this doubling, from the presence of notarial marks in the Common Paper; extrinsic evidence alone shows the doubling to have been far more common.

44   William Lettres, for example, admitted free of the scriveners in 1462 (Steer, *Common Paper p. 22*), in 1470 witnessed a grant of property in County Dublin as scriptor and notary public by imperial authority: J.G. Smyly, *Hermathena*, LXX (1947), p. 16. Other instances could easily be multiplied.

45   Anne F. Sutton, 'John Kendale, A Search for Richard III's Secretary', in James Petre (ed.), *Richard III: Crown and People* (Richard III Society, London, 1985), pp. 224–38. I am grateful to the author for this reference.

46   For Faside's admission, see Steer, *Common Paper*, p. 21; his testament is in Guildhall Library, MS 9171/3, f. 483v. In September 1436 he was appointed an executor of Peter Anketell, citizen and writer of court letters of London: *ibid.*, 9171/3, f. 469v.

47   See, for example, D.L. Douie (ed.), *The Register of John Pecham . . .*, 2 vols. (Canterbury and York Society, 1968/9), I, p. 118, and II, p. viii, for the register kept by John de Beccles, notary public, 1281; R.C. Finucane, 'The Registers of Archbishop John Pecham and his Notary, John of Beccles: some Unnoticed Evidence', *Journal of Ecclesiastical History*, xxxviii (1987), pp. 406–36, and especially p. 408, n. 5.

48   For references to scriveners' books see Postan, 'Private Financial Instruments', cited above at note 15, and cf. note 57 below.

49   Discussed by A.E.B. Owen, 'A Scrivener's Notebook from Bury St. Edmunds', *Archives*, XIV (1979/80), pp. 16–22.

50   Thorpe's register has been discussed and printed by Stuart Jenks, 'Das Schreiberbuch des John Thorpe und der hansische Handel in London 1457/59', *Hansische Geschichtsblätter*, 101 (1983), pp. 67–113. Both Thorpe's and Styfford's registers are discussed in detail by W.R. Childs, above, pp. 78–86. Styfford was also a notary (*Calendar of State Papers, Venetian*, I, p. 78), but the register is the memoranda-book of a scrivener, rather than the copy-book of a notary.

51   Accounts of the Pewterers' Company, Guildhall Library, London, MS 7086/1, ff. 67v., 70.

52   He is mentioned as a notary in 1476 (P.E. Jones (ed.), *Calendar of Plea and Memoranda Rolls . . . of the City of London . . . 1458–1482* (Cambridge, 1961), p. 101). He was Secondary of the Poultry Compter, *c.* 1486–1520, (B.R. Masters, 'City Officers, II. The Secondary', *Guildhall Miscellany*, II (1960–8), pp. 425–33 at 429). He had been admitted free of the scriveners in 1471 (Steer, *Common Paper*, p. 23). For his work for the Drapers' Company see A.H. Johnson, *The History of the Worshipful Company of the Drapers of London*, I (Oxford, 1914), pp. 153, 180.

53   Guildhall MS 7086/1, f. 93r.–v.

54   Accounts of the Goldsmiths' Company, Goldsmiths' Hall, London, Minute Book A, p. 127.
          In the same year they also paid the London lawyer Robert Blount 'for making and

writing of the same bill [i.e., one to the Chancellor] thrice'; this had been drafted by two other lawyers.

55 Bower Marsh (ed.), *Records of the Worshipful Company of Carpenters*, II, *Warden's Account Book 1438–1516* (Oxford, 1914), p. 52 (for counsel 1476/7), p. 55 (writing and counsel, 1477/8), p. 57 (counsel, 1478/9), p. 59 (writing, 1479/80), p. 61 (labour, 1480/1), pp. 64, 65 (writing, 1482/3).

56 Accounts of the Merchant Taylors' Company (consulted on microfilm at the Guildhall Library, London): MS A4 (First Book of Accounts), ff. 42 (1407/8), 111v. (1418/19).

57 Ibid., ff. 217v. (1430/1), 330v. (1440/1).

58 Henry Attemere, scrivener, was sheriff of Norwich in 1509. Robert Burgh, scrivener and merchant, was MP for Norwich in 1497 and 1508 (J.C. Wedgwood and A.D. Holt, *History of Parliament. Biographies of Members of the Commons House, 1439–1509* (London, 1936), p. 135). The doubling of scriveners as attorney and notary is found in the records of admissions to the city's freedom; e.g., Edward Sylke, scrivener and notary, 1 Richard III. W. Rye (ed.), J. L'Estrange, *Calendar of the Freemen of Norwich, 1317–1603* (London, 1888), p. 134.

59 It is worth noting that each of the six notaries and scriveners who is recorded in the *Calendar of State Papers Venetian*, I–III, *1201–1526*, as having registered a protest of a bill of exchange drawn in Venice, lived in Lombard Street. And was it just for social reasons that William Styfford paid five marks to become a liveryman of the Goldsmiths' Company (T.F. Reddaway and L.E.M. Walker, *The Early History of the Goldsmiths' Company, 1327–1509* (London, 1975), pp. 144, 146, 150)?

60 E.g., H. Littlehales (ed.), *The Medieval Records of a London City Church, St. Mary at Hill, 1420–1559* (EETS old ser.), 125, 128 (1904–5), pp. 83 (8d. to [Thomas] Masse, scrivener, for overseeing certain leasehold indentures, 1477–9), 187 (3s. 4d. to the scrivener in Lombard Street for writing of two deeds and the bede roll and other things for the church, 1492–3), 272 (17½d. to the scrivener for making of indentures after an arbitration between the parish and an individual, 1510–11).

7

Small Groups: Identity and Solidarity in the Late Middle Ages

Miri Rubin
University of Oxford

The preceeding papers, addressing agrarian investment and management, urban finance, enterprise and professions, have concentrated my mind on the urban/rural dichotomy, on the ways in which we apply this opposition as an organizing as well as an explanatory device when observing medieval society. The polarity touches not only on function, distinguishing between the sector which produced foodstuff and raw materials, where most people lived on the land, and the sector which consumed those products and worked those raw materials into manufactured goods to be exchanged. It touches on a far deeper distinction enveloped in the usage: rural life is often presented as possessing an essence which is familiar, close-knit, intimate, supportive and which rests on a bed of shared experience and moral understandings, shared goals and collectively orientated behaviour. Conversely, town life is perceived as a series of attempts to recapture, recreate, invent and compensate for the lack and loss of these essential communal and familial qualities. The village as a community is a strong concept, be it for conservative phantasizing about an ordered organic society, or for Marxists imputing a cohesion borne from class consciousness and common struggle. For both groups, as for others, community conjures a moral economy based on close interaction and clear attitudes between small and great, through deference, patronage, or struggle. Thus community operates as a measure of well-being, of proximity or distance from an ideal state of social relations. In its presence – robustness and cohesion; in its absence – as in towns, atrophy and instability.

In an illuminating article which appeared in 1984 entitled '"Modernization" and the corporate village communities in England: some sceptical reflections', Richard Smith provides a critical survey of the applications of the concept of community by historians of medieval and early modern England.[1] He traces the development of the use in the context of changing political, ideological and historiographical paradigms from the mid-nineteenth century, when many of the conventions of our discipline were created. *Gemeinschaft* is a concept developed by Friedrich Tönnies and later Max Weber,[2] as part of their critical engagement with the social face of industrial society, one in which contractual relations between atomized and alienated actors had come to replace a cohesive close-knit and organic community.[3] With the flowering of liberal democratic ideas, historians of law and society, like Maitland, posited the power of medieval towns and villages in the protection which they afforded to private property and the dignity of personal freedom which followed.[4] These two models of community shared an agreement about the superior nature of social relations in the pre-industrial world, and the use of community rose or declined in dialectical rhythm with current understandings of the relative benefits of individualism or communalism as the basis for political and social life. The term's attraction changed over time, and experienced a lull in its use in the mid-twentieth century when notions of modernization and development monopolized utopian energy. But in the last twenty years, following the disenchantment with the application of class theory to pre-industrial society, and with the inspirations of 'people's history' and 'history from below', we find community flourishing, arising again as the panacea of social analysis. It is an ideal for explanation and modelling and one which is rarely deployed without a concomitant sense of our fundamental difference from the past.

The veritable explosion of studies incorporating community in their titles is a phenomenon in its own right. Where would we be without recent contributions like *Autonomy and Community* by Marjorie McIntosh and its tale of 400 years in the manor of Havering,[5] or Michael Bennett's study of mobility and social obligation in Cheshire and Lancashire in *Community, Class and Careerism*.[6] Community is invoked in a study of relations between centre and periphery such as J.R. Lander's *Government and Community*,[7] in a study of feudal taxation in the twelfth century in T.K. Keefe's *Feudal Assessments and the Political Community*,[8] as in Rosenthal and Richmond's *People, Politics and Community in the Later Middle Ages*, within which one finds an article on the aristocratic household as a religious community.[9] Indeed, I am no small offender, with my use of community to sweeten the taste of a very disappointing show of charitability among Cambridge burgesses in *Charity and Community in Medieval Cambridge*.[10] Most important and comprehensive in the application of the concept is Susan Reynolds' *Kingdoms and Communities*.[11] While admitting that community is a fashionable word nowadays (almost any category of people is sometimes called a community), the book proceeds to a very useful discussion of medieval uses of the word community, and the underlying ideas in which such uses were grounded. This spectrum of uses of community has been taken to medievalists' hearts with a touching naïvety. Where social theories and their obvious ideological implications, Marxist, feminist, structuralist, psychoanalytic, have been treated with the greatest suspicion in the field of medieval studies, community has been adopted without a blink, as if it were a term so natural, so obvious, a metaphor so apt, that its use should require no reflection. I wish to suggest that community, like all coins for social and political explanation is and has always been discursively constructed and is always laden with aspirations and contests over interpretive power. Community is neither obvious nor natural, its boundaries are loose, and people in the present, as in the past, will use the term to describe and to construct worlds, to persuade, to include and to exclude. That our subjects lived, worked and played in groups, that they trusted, depended on each other, mutually helped, is beyond doubt – but they did so in a knowing and deliberating way, choosing communities when possible, or negotiating their places within groups when less freedom of choice was available. The fraternity, the borough, the village, the neighbourhood are as interesting for the tensions which were negotiated within as for the shared aims, means and culture which bound them. Using the term community at all these levels obscures rather than reveals.

But favoured as it is for its power to capture the alterity of the medieval past this usage exacts a heavy price. A static notion, it obscures difference and conflict: as it seemingly highlights the peculiar medievalness of the Middle Ages, it whitewashes shades of tension, distance, difference. In J.C. Calhoun's words: 'community . . . became for many authors a static category, referring, rather loosely, to a geographically or administratively bordered population, not to a set or variety of social relations'.[12] If community can describe at once the realm, the village, the town, the neighbourhood, the fraternity, the parish, even the household, then surely it is not much of a category at all. Through its widespread and loving application it has lost its cutting edge as a tool expressive of the diversity of experience, the complexity of context, the workings of power and ideology, the manipulation of language, all of which are the stuff of life and history anywhere and at any time. And fifteenth-century historians are the last to need reminding of such complexity: they too deserve a better tool.

Some realizations of this problem are cautiously arising, but there are few suggestions as to the way forward. In her forthcoming and fascinating book on the gentry of late medieval Warwickshire Christine Carpenter has identified and analysed social and political networks and this has led her to make the following comment about the 1420s and 1430s: 'The fact that the only real unity of this . . . county . . . came from the powerful affinity of Richard Beauchamp, Earl of Warwick, should give us pause in contemplating the notion of the county community'.[13] Gervase Rosser, too, in a sensitive study of the urban guild and parish, expresses some discomfort with the term community, but clings to it and hastens to reassure us that: 'to recognise the reality of change in medieval society is not . . . to neglect the possibility of community in its context'.[14] Perhaps the most brilliant solution to the historiographical problem has been offered by John Bossy in a highly inspired conformulation: admittedly, medieval society is complex, potentially full of tension and highly heterogenous, but sacramental religion provided ritual occasions which performed the social miracle.[15] Sacraments like baptism and marriage created horizontal as well as vertical coalitions, and the mass, the arch-sacrament, performed the dramatic coup of dissolving difference into unity, discord into harmony, through the ritual adhesion to a supernatural symbol.[16] Following Turner's anthropology of ritual, Bossy claims that through sacraments conflict and diversity of identity and orientation were periodically dissolved into a primary pre-historical and pre-political, undifferentiated *comunitas*, the clean slate of an as yet undeveloped social persona.[17] This inability to detach ourselves from community both reveals and feeds a certain escapism, which has always been one of the dominant subtexts of medieval studies.[18]

In this paper I shall work with the premise that identities are never lost, that they are negotiated and manipulated, that they evolve. I shall deconstruct for you the discrete charm of community, and in search of a more knowing and incisive grid of social explanation shall attempt a critique of two areas of social action which have been seen as the mainstay of medieval community, its toughest glue. I shall look at two activities to which powers of cohesion have been attached: at voluntary associations such as fraternities and at religious rituals such as Corpus Christi processions. I shall also suggest the notion of identity as a flexible working tool and claim that religious action services identity, because in Clifford Geertz's words: 'groups . . . adopt religious symbols to deal with their own problems through . . . difference and individual variation'.

The people we study and the societies which they formed were highly complex not only in their strategies for material survival but in their cultural and symbolic worlds. These experiences can be captured only partially through oppositions such as popular/elite, local/national, religious/secular, family/community, male/female. Identity is more complex and changeable, and its constituent parts are managed in a sophisticated manner: so sophisticated that some historians have thrown up their hands at seemingly inconsistent, contradictory and irrational behaviour. Any use of the notion of identity must provide space for gender, class, ethnic affiliation, region, learning, occupational identity, and working with their clusters we can begin to identify identity, and the ways in which its parts are interrelated. Rather than deploying a single hierarchy of interests and motives in the analysis of social behaviour, let us use an arsenal of analytically and politically significant categories, juggling them as each of us does our multiple selves in our own lives. The relation within this pack possesses dynamic, not static, features, which are amenable to analysis only in context and at their borderlines, here strong and interesting manifestations occur, like conflict or defence of identities. This is, to my mind, our only locus for historical inquiry, since as historians we choose to be constrained to the examination of what is in some sense testable and contestable. So we are bound to know more about confusion, conflict, about mistaken, forsaken, lost, perverted and manipulated identities. And this is as it ought to be, since such eruptions are *essential* to identity itself, not only to our historical penetration of it; since it is through conflict and threat and danger, through doubt and confusion that identities are understood, formulated and sharpened.

Religion was the framework of explanation and orientation in the world, it was the idiom applied in all venues of interaction, be they social, scientific, mercantile, political, charitable, and was itself an area for stronger or weaker identification and choice of personas of piety, virtue, merit, sanctity, authority or charisma. It seems therefore both intuitively and theoretically appealing to search for some insight into identity and its formation within the sphere of choices in religious action. Although the religious idiom attempts to obscure difference between its adherents under the mantle of charity and brotherhood, identity will unfailingly raise questions, even within that pious idiom, questions about the self and others, about the relation between personal goals and means, and those of larger groups such as family, neighbourhood and town. Like community, the religious idiom often obscures more than it reveals, and is biased towards the myth of consensus and to static interpretations. In face of this, when interpreting religious action and ritual, we must attempt to maintain identity as a set of individual and collective magnitudes. Identity lies at the basis of all cooperation inasmuch as its notions of the self, of aims, underpin trust, which is the necessary condition of all collective action. The historical examination of trails of trust, and equally of distrust, can lead us to an understanding of the identities which produced them and this is especially true in voluntarily joined bodies and activities. Whereas one is not free to choose one's family or one's village, one can choose with greater freedom one's friends, to some extent business colleagues, and partners in religious practice. Religious fraternities thus suggest themselves as an attractive area for the exploration of these questions.

Fraternities serviced identity in ways which combined the individual and the collective, binding them through elaborate presentations of their interdependence. Identities are predicated by the past, dominated by it, inasmuch as without memory of past sensations, we can make no sense of our lives. It is in the mesh of the past, the fluid presence, the promising and forbidding future that all sections of our identity are constituted. Collective identities probably operate similarly, and if this is true, then it is useful to test the ways in which a fraternity might possess such a mesh, such an historically constructed identity. Fraternities definitely had memories, and they could occasionally be made acutely aware of their past, and to articulate it ever more coherently, by the pressure of external intervention. Such an intervention was the royal inquiry into religious fraternities launched by the Cambridge Parliament of 1388.[19] The writ of Richard II required returns describing the circumstances of their foundation, the form of their government, their feasts and meetings, their income and their properties, to be sent into Chancery by Ladyday 1389. There must have been over a thousand returns from all over England, of which 504 survive and those are primarily from London, the eastern counties, and a number of provincial towns. They vary in detail and precision about their past, and probably in the honesty of their reports, but are the most comprehensive source reflecting the norms of voluntary fraternal life. This external intervention involved thousands of officials in the formulation of foundation tales. Throughout, there is attention to the dignity and person of the founding fathers, to their laudable aims, and to the adherence of current group custom to them. The myth of the Corpus Christi guild of Lynn was the following one:

> In the great pestilence which at Lynn was in 1349, in which the greater part of the people of the town died, three men, seeing that the venerated sacrament of the Body of Christ was being carried through the parts of the town with only a single candle of poor wax buring in front of it . . . thought this so improper that they ordained certain lights for it when carried by night or by day in the visitation of the sick, and designed this devotion to last for the period of their lives. Others, seeing their devotion, offered to join them and some thirteen drew up the ordinances.[20]

Another interesting tale comes from the fraternity of St John the Baptist in Spalding, which was said to have been founded in 1383:

> John de Rughton painted a beautiful image in honour of St John in 1358, and for some time he and other devout people found a light for it. In 1383 John Torarld took thought as to providing a chaplain to celebrate to the praise of the saint, and it was agreed to combine to provide one.[21]

So fraternities definitely had histories, and these were posited not only in their foundation myths, but in the artefacts which surrounded them. They were serviced by plate, books, relics, pictures, eating utensils, hangings, and costly liturgical vessels, many of which were granted in bequests made by past members for future ones. In cases where a series of inventories has survived, like those of Bridgewater, or of St Peter Mancroft in Norwich, one can trace the descriptions of a chalice or a painted window over time, and note that these were described not merely by their external attributes, but as being the gift of a particularly named individual, even a whole century after his or her death. Thus the fraternity of dead and living members was bound into a perennial state of debt, one which could only be repaid through continuous commemoration and intercession at fraternity altars, and by respecting obligations to the living kin of the dead. Liturgies for the dead not only bound the dead and the living, the past and present fraternity, into the future, but also symbolically articulated the interdependence and trust which informed the fraternity's present existence. It is the weight of the shared debt, combined with the constant scrutiny of members' abilities to contribute substantially to the pooling of resources which gave the fraternity its strength, that kept the group alive. Inasmuch as these were open-ended gifts, between generations, and where direct exchange could not be effected, the group was bound into a state of perennial debt to former generations, fixed in a never-balanced gift-exchange.[22] And as gift-exchange keeps relations alive through the imperatives of reciprocity we can understand the values of such exchange in forming memories, duties and their concomitant identities within the group.

Let us look more closely at one fraternity which was typical of a whole sub-group of patrician groups which evolved in medieval towns. In the fourteenth and fifteenth centuries these elite fraternities often assumed the new devotion to Corpus Christi as their theme. We know quite a lot about the Leicester Corpus Christi guild, and in that sense it is untypical. It was founded in 1343 by four servants of the Earl of Leicester a number of prominent burgesses of mayoral rank and included all leading businessmen and a number of baronial servants.[23] It soon became a large property owner in Leicester with an annual income exceeding that of the borough. A large portion of its income was spent on the maintenance of a chapel in St Martin's Church where regular intercessory services were provided for the founders and for dead brethren. On the feast of Corpus Christi, the prime processional event of the year, the members processed in gowns, carrying torches, and a chosen few carried the host.[24] The procession ended at the guildhall and was followed by a feast to which each brother made a contribution.[25]

So far this group of leading townsmen can be taken as a conventional body for the promotion of elaborate and expensive religious practices: it supported a chaplain, enjoined presence at funerals, supplied lights and decorations and celebrated Corpus Christi as a group. But our interest in the fraternity grows when we discover the role which it played in town government. Not only did town council meetings frequently take place in the guild's hall from the early fifteenth century on; additionally, leading guild members, two of its masters, were *ex officio* members of the town council. It was to them that fines for trespass of the collegial obligations of town officials were paid, and it was they who sat as an arbitration court for the mayor's council, confusingly called the twelve 'brethren' in Leicester usage. As put by the words of the ordinance of 1471:

> And if it so fortune that envy of the seid breder have any resonable cause or mater to other, every of them that fyndeth hym greved [shall] showe his cause or greff to the Maire and masters of Corpus Christi gylde for the tyme being.[26]

What does this suggest? It seems that a group of powerful men, leading officials and property owners in late medieval Leicester congregated to form a society for the provision of religious and social services. It was the trust fostered through the working of government which nurtured the group, but this trust also gained from socialization and cooperation, experiences within the voluntary fraternity. I said earlier that such bodies are typical in late medieval England and, indeed, Lincoln, Coventry, Norwich, Beverley, Cambridge, as well as other towns, possessed such patrician Corpus Christi fraternities in the fourteenth and fifteenth centuries. The connection with the new devotion is an interesting one. The feast reached England in 1318 and its celebration centred upon an elaborate public ritual, a procession, at the centre of which was the most dramatic manifestation of supernatural power in medieval culture, the eucharist, Christ's own body and blood, exposed and presented amidst an array of sumptuous vessels and decorations.[27] The leading men of these towns were attracted to Corpus Christi's potential as an occasion for the articulation of hierarchy, from which their own status could benefit through the proximity to the eucharist, and they invested in it. That they were drawn to this feast of feasts is a typical response of elites which by nature attempt to root their claims for legitimation in universal symbols expressed through ritual. And the most universal of claims was, of course, the sacramental claim for mediation and efficicacy; thus Corpus Christi became a truly patrician devotion. Through its language of exclusivity and control, through the imperative of separation and limited access to its power, the eucharistic symbolic world offered an array of possibilities for the expression of patrician claims to lead the town by virtue of universal suitability. The Corpus Christi fraternity thus became the venue for the articulation of most particularistic and sectional interests through symbols which were highly universal, widely disseminated and strongly rooted at all levels of culture.

Elite fraternities further boosted their membership and extended useful connections through the admission of members who enjoyed similar status in other towns. They were willing to recruit among people who were similarly situated in their towns, and to extend trust, relief and cooperation on those occasions when the foreigner visited their own town. The fraternity of the Assumption in Lichfield included great merchants and officials from other towns. [28] That the link was more than nominal is made clear in testamentary bequests made by merchants for the benefit of guilds in other towns. Alliances were struck, and mutual obligations for hospitality and cooperation in business were thus nurtured. In Cambridge the merchant from King's Lynn would have been preferred by the Corpus Christi fraternity to a local tailor; this surely must make us think afresh about terms like local communal identity.

The idiom employed in these groups is the idiom of kinship, and kinship's imperative principle of amity was extended through the type of rituals and practices experienced in families, such as eating and drinking together, burial, prayer, inheritance and common ownership. Yet the relation between real kin and ritual kin was not a simple one. Fraternities drew from kinship symbolism yet existed in competition with the kin; by definition their functions impinged upon those understood to be the prerogative and duty of the kinship group. Fraternity membership not only syphoned off resources outside the family, it also partially replaced it as potential reallocator of resources at a number of stages in the life-cycle. Put simply, fraternities did quite a few things that families did too, at crisis points in life such as sickness, old age, bereavement. It interposed where family was at its weakest: as a body which in theory could live on forever it could compensate for failure of issue, as a body bound by trust and voluntary brotherhood – it offered an alternative to family relations dense with memories, vengeance, and feuds. [29] Thus, in some ways the company of strangers stretching into eternity not through biological but through social reproduction, could seem more reliable a partner. If well managed, a fraternity could live forever, while families rarely did. The fraternity also neutralized, through collegiality, aspects of personal animosity, tension and feud which might seriously undermine amity within a family. The tension between natural and artificial kin is expressed in the oath taken by members of the York 'guild' of wealthy burgesses in 1303 who promised mutual aid when necessary 'even against fathers, mothers, wives, children and all others who were not members of the guild'. [30] Notwithstanding the development of hereditary rights of sons of members, especially within craft fraternities, and of the inclusion of wives as partial members and among beneficiaries of fraternity relief, the principle of organization in fraternities, although drawing from kinship symbolism, differed from the principle of kinship. It attempted to achieve a degree of trust and cooperation symbolically linked with family, among strangers.

Some societies with powerful networks of ritual kinship even placed higher value on the chosen and non-prescribed relationship than on the predetermined blood relationship.[31] And this tension is not to be overlooked as Jacques Chiffoleau has done when ascribing to the breakdown of family ties in the post-Plague world a causal primacy in creating late medieval fraternities. He sees them as the product of an orphaned population, disorientated and in disarray, seeking ritualized forms of kinship to compensate for the loss.[32] The simple demographic determinant is a very weak explanation for decisions to expand networks of trust and cooperation beyond the family; this is an inverted recourse to the notion of dense kinship and community networks, and their loss. The relationship between one's identity as son, father, husband, journeyman or master craftsman, head of household, friend, is fundamentally at variance, and often dialectically opposing, so that the areas inhabited by these identities are not determined in random. The fact that even in the rural parish of Croscombe (Somerset) young men ('yonglings') and maidens formed their groups for worship and contributed as a group to the parish's needs;[33] or that in Ashburton (Devon) there were separate altars around which congregated minute bodies called 'lights' sustained by groups such as 'the maidens', 'the bachelors', 'the married wives';[34] the existence of 'young men's groups' in the parish of Bassingbourn (Cambridgeshire),[35] as well as the 'Bachelors' light' in Boxford (Suffolk);[36] all come to show that even in a state of rest, if identity is at all conceivable, it is constructed and articulated by identification and interaction in a variety of groups and through an array of affinities. Identity can never be constituted through a single or overarching affinity – whether gender, class, or age – but rather at the intersection and the changing dynamic negotiation of these and other positions in the world. Identities are neither serviced within an all-embracing family, nor in the bosom of a cohesive and cosy community.

Fraternities fitted in with shifting needs and offered an identity, and thus were bound to change when members sensed some misfit between their own and other members' identities, aims and capacities. Fraternities were quick in expressing these changes and in reacting through a number of possible shifts. This could be through ritualized distancing when some fraternity members were seen as unsuitable and were allocated roles of clear symbolic submission and inferiority, which made any assumption about their similarity to other members impossible. Some London fraternities developed livery for easy distinction between richer and poorer members; thus, around 1430 the Grocers of London distinguished between three types of membership: fifty-five in full livery, seventeen in hoods alone, and forty-two who assumed no livery whatsoever.[37] To take groups which displayed such sensitivity to status, economic standing and reputation, as products of charitable brotherly impulses, robs them of their real significance. Their interest lies primarily in reflecting changing understandings of social relations, and in charting of horizons of cooperation within the complex and unequal towns of the later Middle Ages. These voluntary bodies were not static, just as the identities that underpinned them never reached a state of rest.

If fraternities have been shown to reflect change, rather than as providing a communal mantle masking it, then ritual and its effect is another case which is often heralded as being therapeutic if not magical, and which must be rigorously re-examined. So our next exercise in re-reading will look at what has become the symbol of the social miracle, the Corpus Christi procession. Freed from the functionalist-structuralist reductions, ritual can perhaps emerge as a locus in which individual and group identities are confronted, as each individual body becomes the instrument pure and simple for the formulation of a map of social relations.

The pioneering attempt to grapple with the intricate system of civic ritual has been Charles Phythian-Adams' study of the ceremonial of late medieval Coventry.[38] There he identified a civic half and a religious half to the year, and attempted to show, through a description of Hock Tide, Corpus Christi, inauguration ceremonies, and the great Midsummer Fair, that the tensions arising from the competition in the economically declining city of Coventry in the late fifteenth century, were largely resolved through frequent ritual contact. The procession of Corpus Christi was particularly singled out for its integrative power. The utility of such an approach is in preliminary marking of the possible dependencies between types of social relations and ritual actions, but it does not provide a sufficient framework for the understanding of change. No one familiar with the life of late medieval towns, can escape the realization that the nature of social relations was volatile, conditional, constantly tested, competitive and captured in powerful moments of symbolic display. Looking at the feast of Corpus Christi, it seems that any explanation of the extraordinary transformation of an early fourteenth-century eucharistic feast into a major civic, artistic and social enterprise by the end of that century, must provide answers more complex than those suggested by the functionalists of ritual. That ritual has form, and that it is repeated is true – but it cannot simply follow that this symbolic form also effectively reproduces a social order. Its repetitive nature provides merely a shell or a stage for the considered confrontation of roles and values. I believe that the medieval processional ritual of Corpus Christi, cannot be seen as more than an occasion for heightened and self-conscious imparting of information; a delineation of battle positions – a tentative picture of the stances from which the next day's business will continue. The Corpus Christi procession unfurled with the hierarchy rising from front to back. It began with elements of heralding and the announcing of the arrival of the eucharist: children would strew flowers, acolytes process with bells and censers. Next marched groups of clerics and mendicants in hierarchical order, and in mixed lay/clerical processions the corporations of craftsmen and fraternities with banners and candles. Then came the procession's centre of gravity: the eucharist placed in a monstrance or a tabernacle carried on staves, in the manner of a relic, in open air or under a canopy.[39] The eucharist was always carried by a priest, but when canopies appeared they were almost invariably carried by secular dignitaries, almost as if they had been invented for the purpose. Around the eucharist processed the highest ranks: bishop and high clergy, knights, mayor and aldermen, and behind them a mixed group of non-citizens and women, those who were not involved in the procession nor bore its expenses as members of a corporation.

In many towns, for instance Coventry, high ranking officials bore the canopy.[40] The Corpus Christi fraternity, which was often a prestigious patrician fraternity, came to play an important role at the heart of the procession in York, Lincoln and Leicester.[41] That of Leicester processed at the centre near the eucharist already by mid-fourteenth century,[42] while the York fraternity was entrusted with the keeping and carrying of the eucharistic tabernacle from the beginning of the next century.[43] The hierarchical procession displaying the eucharist and divided into lay and clerical spheres, tracing a sacred itinerary among crowds, and passing through the streets of a medieval town, was taken up and turned into an occasion for some of the most costly, creative and meaning-laden activities of late medieval burgesses.

Both in its procession and in its plays, notwithstanding long traditions and hallowed customs, the Corpus Christi ritual related to here and now. How else can we explain not only the expense and the care with which the financing of the growing urban endeavour were met, but also the amount of litigation, energy, violence and effort which it could inspire? Such as the many disputes of York traders who were locked in litigation for decades over their relative places in the procession; or the dispute between the Fletchers and the Coopers of Chester, which was resolved in arbitration in 1475, with a decision that the Coopers should bear their lights yearly, three on one side of the pavement and three on the other, from St Mary's to the College of St John *before* the lights of the Fletchers and Bowers.[44] Or consider the procession's effect in defining citizenship, since only those who wielded political power through membership in a corporation could process, while others stood on the sidelines or followed in a crowd. Those outside the procession were not merely day-trippers from surrounding villages, but members of the urban community who were to a large extent unenfranchised. So·masters and apprentices were separated from each other and their journeymen, creating a political and social mapping more polarized than that experienced in daily life. Related tensions between such groups may have induced the occasional fights between masters and journeymen around the Corpus Christi celebrations, like that in Chester on Corpus Christi day 1399, when a crowd of masters approached their journeymen 'at plures alii magistri textores venerunt vi et armis cum Polaxes, baculis premitis baslardis et aliis diversis armaturis'.[45] The ritual procession was not a fossilized pious event, to be reproduced meticulously in accordance with some long-standing model from the past – it was urgent and topical. It starkly displayed that power which sections of the town had tentatively managed to wrest for themselves.

It is interesting to test this claim on what seems to be the most enduring feature of any procession – its itinerary. Itineraries are diverse in nature but can be categorized as those *linking* territories and those *demarcating* territories. The first type was by far the most common in England: the itinerary which sewed together with a processional thread the periphery to the centre, the parishes to the cathedral, the suburbs to the market-place. The Bishop of Lincoln ordered in 1419 that a Corpus Christi octave Sunday procession should lead from the suburb of Wickford 'in surburbiis dictae nostrae civitatis' to the cathedral.[46] Medieval Beverley had processional plays performed along stations on the High Street, the town's backbone, passing through North Bar, the Billing (north end of the market), Cross Bridge, Fishmarket, the edge of the minster precinct, and the suburb of the Back; note that the minster was neither the starting point nor the high point in any sense.[47] While in Durham the procession, which included all crafts with banners and torches followed by the parish clergy and led by the cathedral chapter, carried the tabernacle which rested in the central parish of St Nicholas to St Cuthbert's Cathedral, where chants and blessings ensued, before the whole procession returned it to the parish church for another twelvemonth.[48]

Some continental towns chose to process along anachronistic routes tracing historic lines of fortification, settlement and long-past political spheres. The trails traced in Marseilles on Corpus Christi day marked the lines of its eleventh-century walls. In mid-fourteenth century Aix-en-Provence the Corpus Christi procession reflected a trajectory uniting the comital and cathedral sections, including no parish or suburb founded after the early thirteenth century; in fact it delineated an urban topography of c. 1200.[49] The Neapolitan procession marked the seats of great families of the thirteenth century, long defunct by the fifteenth. These survivals point to the importance of symbolism in a group's collective experience; be they long-forgotten boundaries, or long-trespassed borders of influence, these lines represent the collectively remembered past, which is an important component in the construction of identity. But even more, such choices were a definite rejection of any updated picture of status and power, the adoption of which may have implied an unquestioning acceptance of an existing political order. The rituals related to these itineraries seem to feed and to be fed by some deeper and more permanent identity: an identity which supersedes the one constituted by a changing political scene, or by hierarchy, which is by nature arbitrary and tentative and which I believe to be *negotiated* rather than *reflected* in the order of the procession.

It is perhaps clear now that any explanation which denies the place of tension and change at the very heart of ritual, will fall short as an interpretive framework for these central events of medieval life. Particularly constraining are generalizing attempts, like those made by Mervyn James and recently for Germany by Charles Zika, to draw political meaning from the body imagery implied by the doctrinal message of Corpus Christi as the sacramental body of Christ.[50] That Corpus Christi's message was far from perceived as a simple orthodox symbol is amply demonstrated by the fact that the elite Corpus Christi fraternity of Leicester was, in the late fourteenth century, a hive of Lollard activity, which harboured Lollard preachers and disseminated heretical tracts.[51] To these members of the Corpus Christi fraternity, who occupied prime positions around the heart of the procession, the eucharist was no simple salvific body. It was, however, a forceful symbol of power, so they continued to march proudly by its side, while doubting its sacramental efficacy.

A further interpretation of the body imagery inherent in Corpus Christi has been put forward by Mervyn James, stressing the importance of the body as an integrative image, and its sacramental divine body as the most powerful representation.[52] The pronouncements of town officials and ordinances governing Corpus Christi celebrations often used a language which likened the patriciate to the head of a peaceful and healthy body-town, with its head, heart and limbs as its interdependent community of members. But to claim that, even if current, this picture possessed some integrative effective force, is quite another matter. The language of officialdom for formal and directed interpretations of the political system through the feast must be tested against real experience. Was Corpus Christi, the feast of the divine body which is also the body of Christian society, indeed *inherently* imbued with integrative social power? At Beverley the integrative feast was Cross Monday (Monday in

Rogationtide), when a procession with the relics of St John was watched by guild members from their respective castles, wooden booths which some of the more organized crafts were allowed to possess, while its Corpus Christi procession was smaller and less important.[53] Conversely, the Corpus Christi procession of Durham displayed the banner of St Cuthbert, the town's dearest relic from its foundation.[54] In both cases we see that the body imagery implied in Corpus Christi was only secondary to the contents of the local processional ritual. So where a more momentous event pre-existed, Corpus Christi was secondary; where a more powerful symbol in the town's history and identity existed, it became the focus of the processional. Additionally, inasmuch as the procession exposed the bare bones of the political structure, it surely suggested the possibility of overthrowing the ruling head, of dismembering the body altogether. When this did happen, and Corpus Christi was occasionally the time for mass movements of criticism and revolt, like the Peasants' Revolt of 1381,[55] it cannot be explained merely as studied violence which set off deeper stillness. Quite the contrary, these were not accidents, not occasions when the ritual went wrong – and thus fulfilled the portents of ritual liminality. Occasions which exposed the social structure and the balance of power in unambiguous linear terms, served to exacerbate perceptions of injustice and competition. Corpus Christi probably exaggerated the power of some and obscured a whole penumbra of social relations which cannot be captured in clear hierarchical terms, like friendship, neighbourly relations, or patronage, which may exist between the politically unequal. This mesh of relations was sacrificed in the production of a neatly unfolding processional line.

So processions are important events, but important as imparting political knowledge by sharpening political positions, not by obscuring the picture of power relations into an undifferentiated *communitas*. They are acute, inasmuch as they *inform*; but what that information will further spur men and women to do is unpredictable and indeterminable. As we have seen, the type of informing which the ritual induced could be at the level of *identity*, of placing the individual within the contexts of meaning and allegiance. And insofar as a collective aspect was present, it was expressed in the realm of display of identity; the identity of the town arising from its mythical past, the identity of an individual as a member of a craft. Identity was also displayed in such symbolic action as the use of children, who were often given a special place in Corpus Christi processions. Dressed up as angels, they heralded the event, they were dressed in liturgical vestments and placed at strategic points in the procession. Similarly evasive of clear political acceptance was the choice of participants such as the two almshouse bedesmen of Sherbourne who processed in the local Corpus Christi procession, or the boys of *Ave Maria* college in Paris who processed in the parochial Corpus Christi celebration,[56] or the boys of Florence who represented the neighbourhoods and accompanied the host on Corpus Christi.[57] The importance of such groups in the ritual can, perhaps, be seen, following Richard Trexler's interpretation for Florence, to reside in their very seemingly apolitical nature, one which allowed them to express qualities which lay beyond the rigidly corporate hierarchy of the procession; to express wishes for virtue, expiation and good fortune enfolded into their symbolic purity, wishes and aspirations which many members of any society hold in common.

So there are coexisting levels of integration in ritual action: at one level the public act fosters the ties that bind in any case, those that are rooted in shared experience and exigency. But it also operates at another level, that of articulation of the ever-changing balance of power between competing and adversarial interests and roles. In Robert Darnton's words, 'a procession must be read like a text', and I extend that all ritual must be read in this way.[58] But, like a text, its reception was and is determined by its reader's intent, interest and predisposition; by his or her willingness to believe, to take things on trust, to be sceptical, to be open or to be involved in reshaping a world view. That this is decided somewhat strategically and personally and not through ritual intoxication, expressed as *community*, is true both for past participants and for present observers.

At the basis of identity, and of its extension through cooperation and trust, lay the possibility of perfidy and betrayal, that if confronted with conflicting loyalties, today's friend could be tomorrow's traitor. Even the eucharist was betrayed by Lollard sympathizers of the Corpus Christi fraternity, who probably doubted transubstantiation, and definitely protected a notorious Lollard preacher, but who also recognized that processing as a group was of utmost importance. So were they mad? were they deeply dishonest? and does calling them a community illuminate their choices? This seems to be more our problem than theirs, since they obviously sensed what few of us do when looking at them, that rituals were occasions for exchanges of information about identity. They were processes which ought never and can never obscure the individual and group dilemmas of survival, the struggle for power and for space, which form the essence of life in any society. Because, if we seek piety, cohesion, doctrinal consistency, community, then we remain confused, but if we become sufficiently liberated to be able to appreciate the pragmatic and strategic action, the versatility in the use of a current religious language, the discerning nature of cooperation, only then do fraternities and processions and similar collective actions become interesting and revealing about the essence of social relations. The decision to join a fraternity, to invest in procession in one fashion or another, speak loudly about individual and collective assessments of politics and finance, of friendship and trust, are views which are never at a state of rest, nor captured in a set of rules and statutes. It is in the redrawing of frontiers, the creation of small groups, in negotiating between family, collectivity and state, be they large or small, centralized or decentralized, weak or strong; it is in change, in breaking off and joining associations, in fighting for a new place in the procession, that choice is revealed in a historically powerful way. It is only then that social relations can emerge as infinitely creative, pragmatic, subversive and manipulative, sometimes confused, at least as much as our own associations, friendships and alliances are.

Notes

1 R.M. Smith, '"Modernization" and the corporate medieval village community in England: some sceptical reflections', in A.R.H. Baker and D. Gregory (eds.), *Explorations in Historical Geography*, (Cambridge, 1984), pp. 140–79, 234–45.

2 F. Tönnies, *Community and Association*, trans. C.P. Loomis. (London, 1955); M. Weber, *Economy and Society: an Outline of Interpretive Sociology*, 2 vols. (Berkeley, 1978).

3 Smith, '"Modernization"', pp. 151–3.

4 Ibid., pp. 153–5.

5 M. McIntosh, *Autonomy and Community: the Royal Manor of Havering, 1200–1500* (Cambridge, 1986).

6 M.J. Bennett, *Community, Class, and Careerism: Cheshire and Lancashire Society in the Age of Sir Gawain and the Green Knight* (Cambridge, 1982).

7 J.R. Lander, *Government and Community: England 1450–1509* (London, 1980).

8 T.K. Keefe, *Feudal Assessments and the Political Community under Henry II and his Sons* (Berkeley, 1983). For another study of taxation which invokes the notion of community see J. C. Ward (ed.), *The Medieval Essex Community: the Lay Subsidy of 1327*. (Essex Historical Documents 1, Chelmsford, 1983).

9 J. Rosenthal and C. Richmond (eds.), *People, Politics and Community in the Later Middle Ages* (Gloucester, 1987): K. Mertes, 'The household as a religious community', ibid. pp. 123–39.

10 M. Rubin, *Charity and Community in Medieval Cambridge*, (Cambridge, 1987).

11 S. Reynolds, *Kingdoms and Communities in Western Europe, 900–1300*. (Oxford, 1984).

12 C.J. Calhoun, 'Community: towards a Variable Conceptualization for Comparative Research'. *Social History*, 5 (1980), pp. 105–29; at p. 106.

13 M.C. Carpenter, *Locality and Polity: Landed Society in Fifteenth-Century Warwickshire* (Cambridge, forthcoming).

14 G. Rosser, 'Communities of Parish and Guild in the Late Middle Ages', in S.J. Wright (ed.), *Parish, Church and People Local Studies in Lay Religion 1350–1750* (London, 1988), pp. 29–55; at p. 30.

15 J. Bossy, *Christianity in the West, 1300–1700*. (Oxford, 1985).

16 *Idem*, 'The Mass as a Social Institution, 1200–1700', *Past & Present*, 100 (1983), pp. 29–61.

17 V. Turner, *The Ritual Process; Structure and Anti-Structure* (London, 1969).

18 On approaches to the Middle Ages as reflected in trends in medieval studies see L. Patterson, 'Historical criticism and the development of Chaucer studies', in *Negotiating*

the Past: the Historical Understanding of Medieval Literature (Madison, 1987), pp. 3–39.

19 The returns are tabulated in F. Westlake, The Parish Gilds of Mediaeval England (London, 1919) pp. 138–238: on the background to the inquiry see C. Barron, 'The Parish Fraternities of Medieval London', in C. Barron and Harper-Bill (eds.), The Church in pre-Reformation Society: Essays in Honour of F.R.H. Du Boulay (Woodbridge, 1985), pp. 13–37.

20 PRO C47/42/279; Westlake, The Parish Gilds, p. 199.

21 PRO C47/40/166; Westlake, The Parish Gilds, p. 175.

22 On gift-exchange see the classic M. Mauss, The Gift: Forms of Exchange in Archaic Societies, trans. I. Cunnison (London, 1966). For a discussion see Rubin, Charity and Community, pp. 1–2.

23 PRO C47/38/71; Westlake, The Parish Gilds, p. 154.

24 See documents of the Corpus Christi gild in M. Bateson (ed.), The Records of the Borough of Leicester, II (Cambridge, 1901): rental for 1494/5, no. 244, pp. 346–50, account for 1493/4, no. 243, pp. 342–6, and rental in T. North, A Chronicle of the Church of St Martin in Leicester, (London, 1866), pp. 200–6, and compare with the borough's rental of 1453, The Records of the Borough of Leicester, II, no. 184, pp. 258–61.

25 PRO D47/38/71; Westlake, The Parish Gilds, p. 154.

26 Records of the Borough of Leicester, II, p. 299.

27 On the development of the feast of Corpus Christi see M. Rubin, Corpus Christi: the Eucharist in Late Medieval Culture (Cambridge, 1990), Chapter 4.

28 A.G. Rosser, 'The Town and Guild of Lichfield in the Late Middle Ages', Transactions of the South Staffordshire Archaeological and Historical Society 27 (1987), pp. 39–47; at p. 42.

29 Literature of religious guidance encouraged people to leave bequests for their soul during their lifetime, since wives and children could not be trusted to fulfil wishes after death; see, for example, Robert Mannyng of Brunne, F.J. Furnivall (ed.), Handling Synne (EETS, 119, 123 London, 1901–03), pp. 333–5, esp. p. 334, lines 10791–4.

30 G.O. Sayles, 'The dissolution of a Gild at York in 1306', EHR 55 (1940), pp. 83–98; at p. 88.

31 G. Herman, Ritualised Friendship and the Greek State (Cambridge, 1987).

32 J. Chiffoleau, La comotabilité de l'au-delà: les hommes, la mort et la réligion dans la région d'Avignon à la fin du moyen-âge (Rome, 1980), passim and esp. pp. 429–35.

33 E. Hobhouse (ed.), Church-Wardens' Accounts of Croscombe, Pilton, Patton, Tintinhill, Morebath and St Michael's, Bath, (Somerset Record Society, IV, 1890), see p. 12 for 1483/4, and p. 14 for 1485/6.

34 A. Hanham (ed.), Churchwardens' Accounts of Ashburton, 1479–1580, (Devon and Cornwall Record Society, new series, XV, 1970), pp. 15, 18, 43, 49.

35 Cambridge University Library Add. MS 2792.

36 P. Northeast (ed.), Boxford Churchwardens Accounts, 1530–1561, (Suffolk Record Society, XXIII, 1982): in 1535, p. 18.

37 G. Unwin, The Guilds and Companies of London (4th Edn., London, 1963), p. 190.

38 C. Phythian-Adams, 'Ceremony and the Citizen: the Communal Year at Coventry, 1350–1550', in P. Clark and P. Slack, (eds.), Crisis and Order in English Towns, 1500–1700 (London, 1972), pp. 57–85.

39 On the processions see Rubin, Corpus Christi, pp. 243–71.

40 C. Phythiam-Adams, Desolation of a City: Coventry and the Urban Crisis of the Late Middle Ages (Cambridge, 1979), p. 137.

41 See M. Rubin, 'Corpus Christi Fraternities and the Late Medieval Lay Piety', Studies in Church History, 23 (1986), pp. 97–107.

42 The Records of the Borough of Leicester, II, pp. 35–6.

43 A.F. Johnston, 'The Gild of Corpus Christi and the Procession of Corpus Christi in York', Mediaeval Studies, 38 (1976), pp. 372–84.

44   L.M. Clopper (ed.), *Records of Early English Drama: Chester*, (Manchester, 1979), pp. 15–16.

45   Ibid., p. 5.

46   D. Wilkins (ed.), *Concilia Magnae Britanniae et Hiberniae a.d. 446–1718*, III (London, 1737).

47   R. Horrox, 'Medieval Beverley', in K.J. Allison (ed.), *Victoria County History of the East Riding*, VI (Oxford, 1989), p. 47.

48   J.T. Fowler (ed.), *The Rites of Durham* (Surtees Society, CVII, 1902), pp. 95–6.

49   N. Coulet, 'Processions, éspace urbain, communauté civique' *Cahiers de Fan Feaux*, 17 (1982), pp. 381–98; especially pp. 388–9.

50   C. Zika, 'Hosts, Processions and Pilgrimages in Fifteenth-Century Germany', *Past & Present*, 118 (1988), pp. 25–64.

51   J. Crompton, 'Leicester Lollards', *Transactions of the Leicestershire Archaeological and History Society*, 44 (1968/9), pp. 11–44; especially pp. 29–30.

52   M. Douglas, *Natural Symbols: Explorations in Cosmology* (London, 1970); M. James, 'Ritual, drama and social body in the late medieval town', *Past & Present*, 98 (183), pp. 3–29.

53   Horrox, 'Medieval Beverley', pp. 45–6.

54   *The Rites of Durham*, p. 107.

55   R.B. Dobson (ed.), *The Peasants' Revolt of 1381* (London, 1970), pp. 155–81, 204–11.

56   A.L. Gabriel, *Student life in Ave Maria College, Mediaeval Paris: History and Chartulary of the College* (Notre Dame, Indiana, 1955), pp. 158–9.

57   R.C. Irexler, 'Ritual in Florence: adolescence and salvation in the Renaissance', in H. Oberman and C. Trinkaus (eds.), *The Pursuit of Holiness in Late Medieval Religion* (Leiden, 1974), pp. 200–64; especially pp. 222–3, 245–6.

58   R. Darnton, *The Great Cat Massacre and Other Episodes in French Cultural History* (New York, 1984), pp. 106–43.

Index

Capital, capitalism, ix, 1–3, 4, 5, 7, 9, 10, 20–1
Carpenter, John, of London, 122
Cattanei family, of Genoa, 80; Eduardo, 73, 83
Cely family, 69
Centurioni family, of Genoa, 73, 80; Antonio, 76; Galioto, 74; Leonello, 74
Chambre, John, 76
Charity, 5, 133, 136
Chartres, 100
Chester, 110, 143, 144
Chesterton (Cambs.), 56
Chichester, 72, 85
Chipping Barnet (Herts.), 54
Chipping Campden (Glos.), 73
Chipping Norton (Oxon.), 73, 77
Cirencester (Glos.), 75, 79, 83, 86
Clare, John, 38, 39
Clark: Cristina, 52; Isabel, 52; Thomas, 52; Walter, 52
Clere, Elizabeth, 38
Clerks, Chancery clerks, 119–32 *passim*
Clifford ——, of London, 125, 126
Cloth, xi, 16, 19, 20, 68, 70–1, 82, 86, 101, 103
Codicote (Herts.), 60
Colchester, 112
Cole, Robert, 33
Coleshill (War.), 18
Colyns, Robert, 74
Community, xii, 5, 8, 20, 99, 109, 111, 112, 132–48, *passim*
Cooke, Thomas, of London, 74
Corn (cereals, grains), 8, 11, 12, 17, 37
Corpus Christi, xii, 105–6, 135–47 *passim*
Cotswolds, 71, 72, 75, 82
Cotting, William, of Titchwell, 31, 32, 33
Cotton (Suff.), 31, 32
Courts: court records, xii, 43, 99, 127; chancery and exchequer, 44, 68–9, 72, 74, 77–8, 83–4, 100, 108–11, 121–7, 137; London, 69, 74, 99, 101, 103, 107–8, 110–11, 125; manorial, x, 44–5, 46, 50
Coventry, 11, 13, 105, 139, 142
Crafts, craftsmen, guilds, 7–8, 19, 80, 105–8, 110, 119, 123, 135, 141
Credit, credit and debt transactions, xi, 2, 33, 37, 68, 72–6, 78–81, 82–8, 100–1, 109, 112
Cressingham (Norf.), 26

Crictot Hall, Hevingham (Norf.), 46
Cromer (Norf.), 26, 34
Crosby, William, 122
Croscombe (Somerset), 141
Cubbell, family, of Coleshill & Estrop, 18, 20
Curson, Nicholas, 52

Dawson, Roger, of London, 111
Debts, *see* Credit
Demesne farming, 10, 13, 14, 15–17, 36–7
Derby, John, of London, 73, 74
Doria family, of Genoa, 80; Raffaello, 73, 79, 83
Dory: Matilda, 59, 60; John, of Botulesdale, 59, 60
Dounton, Thomas, 84
Dower, dowry, 27, 29, 44, 54, 55, 56, 59, 62
Drayton (Norf.), 31
Durham, 144, 146
Dyas, Francisco, of Spain, 73, 74, 84, 86

Earlham (Norf.), 34
East Beck[en]ham (Norf.), 26
East Tuddenham (Norf.), 26
Edward I, 69
Edward IV, 77–8, 107–8
Elmes, John, senior, of Henley on Thames, 76, 83
Enclosure, engrossing, ix, x, 9, 15, 16, 21
Entrepreneurs, enterprise, x, xiii, 15, 18, 27–8, 113, 138
Epinal, 112
Erl: Katherine, 50; Robert, 50; Thomas, of Martham, 50
Este, Thomas, 122
Estrop (Berks.), 18
Exeter, 107
Exning, Henry, of London, 107

Families, households, 5, 7, 8, 16, 27, 141
Fanside, William, of London, 125
Fastolf, Sir John, 28
Fastolf estate, 26, 31, 34, 35
Feldyng, Geoffrey, of London, 81
Feudal, feudalism, ix, xii, xiii, 3, 7, 9, 10
Fi[l]by (Norf.), 39
Flanders, 71; *see also* Merchants
Flegghall (Norf.), 26
Florence, 147; *see also* Merchants
Fordham (Cambs.), vicar of, 38